THE WAR
SIXTH YEAR

By the same author

THE WAR: FIRST YEAR
THE WAR: SECOND YEAR
THE WAR: THIRD YEAR
THE WAR: FOURTH YEAR
THE WAR: FIFTH YEAR

THE WAR

SIXTH YEAR

By

EDGAR McINNIS

ASSOCIATE PROFESSOR OF HISTORY
UNIVERSITY OF TORONTO

Toronto
OXFORD UNIVERSITY PRESS
1946

OXFORD UNIVERSITY PRESS
AMEN HOUSE, TORONTO

London, Edinburgh, Glasgow, New York
Melbourne, Capetown, Bombay, Calcutta
Madras

GEOFFREY CUMBERLEGE
PUBLISHER TO THE UNIVERSITY

The War: Sixth Year was originally published in four separate parts (as *The Oxford Periodical History of the War*), under the sponsorship of the Canadian Institute of International Affairs.

Printed in Canada

TO MY BROTHER AND SISTER

ACKNOWLEDGEMENTS

The help which I have received from official sources in the production of this series has been chiefly in the form of mimeographed material provided through the courtesy of various Information Services. My thanks for the aid and guidance thus made available are due to the Wartime Information Board in Ottawa, the Canadian branch of the United Kingdom Information Office, and the Office of War Information in Washington. I should like to express my particular appreciation to *The Round Table* for providing me with advance proofs of its quarterly summary entitled "Strategy of the War". In this final volume I am especially indebted to Lieutenant Commander R. D. Wall, secretary of the United Kingdom Information Office in Ottawa, for his kindness in providing me with much helpful material on the Burma operations which I should not otherwise have found easily available.

E. M.

CONTENTS

MAPS

THE WAR
SIXTH YEAR

I

OCTOBER TO DECEMBER 1944

VICTORY AND BEYOND

THE mood of the Allied world in the autumn of 1944 was one of hope deferred. The assurance of inevitable victory—a victory as complete and unqualified as the leaders and peoples had the will to make it—was overlaid by a renewed sense of implacable demands to be met before the final reward could be gained. The sweeping successes of the previous summer had seemed to herald the collapse of Germany before the end of the year. But the Germans had rallied at their own borders to check the Allied advances from east and west, and had imposed a stalemate in Italy by their tenacious defence of the Po valley. New campaigns of still greater magnitude would be needed to break this stubborn resistance and crush the Nazi régime. The prospect of the grim and protracted struggle which must still be waged in Europe placed a restraint on the elation that was roused by mounting successes in the Far East. Delay in crushing Germany, it was assumed, would also delay the victory over Japan; and Germany's ability to prolong the conflict in spite of successive disasters cast a sobering light on the prospects that must still be faced in Asia before the final triumph of Allied arms.

This situation imposed the need not only for unremitting efforts on the part of the Allied nations, but for even closer unity in action. Instead there appeared perturbing signs of misunderstanding and divergence. To a certain extent these reflected the strain and disappointment resulting from the delay in securing a final decision in Europe. But other and more profound factors were also involved. Beyond the last barriers on the road to victory, the problems of peace were looming more urgently than ever. Victory would be robbed of much of its meaning unless it was followed by a just and stable settlement; yet it seemed that the Allies were approaching this gigantic task with neither clear views nor agreed policies on the basic issues involved.

A number of these issues had been made sharply apparent by the aftermath of the Allied advance. The expulsion of the Germans from the occupied lands had not merely raised the immediate problem of restoring civil government. It had also released forces which would exercise a determining effect on the future of the liberated nations. The resistance movements which had kept alive the struggle against the conqueror were insistent on a leading part in the work of restoration. Yet these movements were themselves divided on the course to be pursued, and there were still deeper divisions within each nation as a whole. The forces of the left were more impatient than ever for a radical social reorganization accompanied by a drastic purge of collaborators. Opposed to them were still large groups of moderates and conservatives whose dread of social revolution had survived four years of Nazi occupation, and whose chief concern was the establishment of order and stability on the basis of the old social structure.

This clash of opposing principles created serious rifts in every liberated country. In France the government of General de Gaulle, by a series of compromises, achieved a precarious stability in spite of strong undercurrents of unrest. But Italy had fallen into a chronic state of disorganization and frustration; serious disorders were barely averted in Belgium; and in Greece the controversy flared briefly into civil war. The situation increased in gravity as the liberating Powers became directly involved. Allied military leaders in Belgium showed themselves ready to maintain order by the use of military force. British troops fought against Greek partisans in the streets of recently liberated Athens, to the accompaniment of shocked protests from the British public. In southeastern Europe, Russian control clamped down a silence only broken by faint sounds of unrest from Rumania. The unhappy controversy over Poland remained unresolved. Toward these events the United States, through the newly-appointed Secretary of State Stettinius, expressed an attitude of self-righteous aloofness which did little to diminish the growing irritation and confusion. To liberal opinion in the democracies it seemed that the Powers were following policies dictated by their own individual interests rather than by the needs and desires of the liberated peoples. The result was a widespread fear that the principles which the United Nations openly professed were being undermined by the deliberate pursuit of power politics on the part of their leading members.

One effect of these developments was to underline more heavily than ever the dominant position of the three leading Allied Powers and the extent to which both the attainment and consolidation of victory depended on their continued harmony. The realities of power would impose themselves in peace as well as in war. The defeat of the aggressors, the imposition upon them of the terms of peace, the maintenance of the post-war settlement, the creation and working of a genuine international organization, the establishment of the economic relations necessary for world recovery, all depended in the first instance on the actions of Britain and Russia and the United States. If they remained in agreement, no other combination would be strong enough to override them. If they drifted apart, not only would their rivalries hold potential dangers; they would also offer a chance for the revival of the defeated nations which would re-emerge as vital elements in the balance of power.

It was the latter prospect which made so alarming the apparent tendency toward spheres of influence on the part of the Big Three.

Russia was marking out a broad security zone covering eastern Europe and the Balkans in which she would be supreme. Britain was bent on restoring her hegemony in the Mediterranean, and appeared to be still pursuing the idea of a western European bloc in alliance with the British Commonwealth. The United States had its own sphere in the Americas, and under the indecisive official policy of the State Department could be discerned certain currents which tended to combine a retreat from participation in European affairs with expansion and consolidation in the Caribbean and the Pacific. To the anxious eyes of the rest of the world, such manoeuvres offered little encouragement to the hope for a just and durable peace and the creation of a true world community.

The attainment of such an end in fact involved not merely the continued unity of the Big Three. It also required the confidence and co-operation of the other United Nations. The lesser states might welcome leadership, but they were far from ready to accept dictation. Nationalism remained a paramount force in spite of the desire for world organization. Considerations of prestige strongly affected the policies of the secondary Powers, and could by no means be ignored. France, for example, was determined to regain her leading position in world affairs; and France was of vital importance in the structure of Europe, as China was in the Far East. Her desire to contribute to future solidarity was shown by her conclusion of a treaty of alliance with Russia and her refusal to join any western bloc which might draw her into rivalry with the Soviet Union. But her desire for full status among the leading states was also made evident, and she looked with no enthusiasm on any assumption by the Big Three of privileges which she did not share. Other states which could not rival France's claim for recognition as a Great Power were still sensitive to any derogation from the principle of sovereign equality. When the chief Powers after conferences at Dumbarton Oaks produced a skeleton draft for a future world organization, the hopeful nature of this step was considerably modified by the privileged position which they allotted to themselves on the Security Council, and still more by Russia's insistence that the Great Powers must be unanimous before military sanctions could be applied against an offender.

Against such a background the complex problems which were accumulating, and the unsatisfactory handling of the difficulties connected with Poland and Italy and Greece, provided a breeding ground for irritation and distrust. Each Power might be completely satisfied as to the purity of its intentions and the wisdom of its own actions, but this confidence was only too rarely shared by its associates. The basic divisions were political, yet their indirect effect on military co-operation might have serious consequences. New steps were urgently needed to restore harmony and confidence, and a new meeting of the three leading statesmen seemed the quickest and most effective way to attain that end. But throughout the summer and autumn of 1944 the American presidential campaign placed an almost insurmountable obstacle in the way of such a conference. It was only after President Roosevelt's inauguration for a fourth term that the way was cleared for his long-deferred reunion with Churchill and Stalin.

The meeting took place at Yalta in the Crimea from February 4 to 11, 1945. The announcement at the close of the conference indicated substantial progress in smoothing over the more acute difficulties which troubled the relations of the leading Allies. A formal acceptance of Russia's claims respecting the Polish boundary was accompanied by provisions for compensating Poland at the expense of Germany and for a broadening of the basis of the Russian-supported Warsaw government. Agreement was reached on the terms of surrender to be offered Germany and the allocation of zones of occupation in which France was to be invited to share. Closer collaboration for the future was to be attained by periodic meetings of the three Foreign Secretaries. The principles of the Atlantic Charter were reaffirmed, and the signatories asserted their determination "to build, in co-operation with other peace-loving nations, world order under law, dedicated to peace, security, freedom and the general well-being of all mankind". As an earnest of these benevolent intentions, a conference of all the United Nations was called for April 25 at San Francisco to discuss the Dumbarton Oaks proposals and to draw up the charter for world organization.

Behind these published pronouncements lay secret agreements which added considerably to their scope as well as their precision. Outstanding in importance was the definite provision that Russia would join in the struggle against Japan within a period of two to three months after the end of the war in Europe. In return, Russia demanded a price which was not revealed until the secret agreement was published exactly a year later. The terms meant that Russia would regain the position she had held in the Far East at the height of the Tsarist regime, before her defeat at the hands of Japan. This involved not merely the restoration of the Kuriles and southern Sakhalin, but also the regaining by Russia of her special economic position in Manchuria and Chinese recognition of the autonomy of Soviet-dominated Outer Mongolia. President Roosevelt undertook to secure Chinese acquiescence to these sacrifices; and after six months of negotiation they were embodied in a series of agreements which included a Soviet-Chinese treaty of alliance and which were signed in Moscow on August 14.

By that date the collapse of Japan had changed the whole perspective. In view of the brevity of Russian participation in the war in Asia, it was easy to see in the planting of permanent Russian influence in Manchuria a concession which was needlessly high and which held grave consequences for the future. But at the time of its conclusion the agreement offered advantages which it was impossible to over-estimate. "It was made," Churchill reminded the world, "at a time when no one could say that the German war might not extend all through the summer and autumn of 1945, and when the Japanese war was expected by the best judges to last for a further eighteen months from the end of the German war." In the light of these calculations, the promise that the tremendous military power of Russia would be thrown into the scale against Japan was one which

transformed the whole strategic outlook; and if military considerations had made it possible to reveal this fact at the time of Yalta,
rejoicing in the Allied world would undoubtedly have overshadowed
whatever qualms might have been felt about the price.

The initial outburst of enthusiasm which greeted the report of
the Crimea conference showed how deep an anxiety had been created
by the prospect of Allied disunity, and how profound was the relief
at this evidence of renewed cordiality. In actual fact, the area
covered by precise agreements at Yalta was small compared to the
magnitude of the problems which must ultimately be settled. The
few positive decisions applied to limited and short-range matters, and
even then the wisdom of some of them—so far as their nature was
revealed—was open to question. Yet the compromises and evasions
implicit in the report were rightly overshadowed by the reaffirmation
of broad principles which it contained. If actual progress was small,
the direction of future policy was clearly charted. The course would
inevitably be marked by further compromises, and the need to resolve
conflicting views and aspirations would result in decisions that were
the best obtainable rather than ideally perfect. The professions
embodied in the Yalta declaration had yet to be tested in action; but
to the extent that they were put forward in good faith, they showed
an encouraging determination on the part of the Allied leaders to
continue their united efforts toward a sound as well as a victorious
peace.

For the immediate future the most significant accomplishment
was in the military sphere. It was this that was placed in the very
forefront of the report. It was clearly implied that Russia's former
reluctance to share her plans with her allies had now been overcome,
and that complete unity of strategy had been attained. The military
staffs had met daily and exchanged the fullest information, and
arrangements had been made for further meetings should necessity
arise. The results were summed up in one pregnant sentence: "The
timing, scope and co-ordination of new and even more powerful blows
to be launched by our armies and air forces into the heart of Germany

from the east, west, north and south have been fully agreed and planned in detail." It was a welcome promise of final and decisive action after the winter of strain and delay which had been imposed by a doomed but stubborn Germany on the forces of the Allies.

THE WESTERN FRONT

The approach of winter saw the Allied armies in the west brought to an abrupt halt after their sweeping advances of the early autumn. The speed of their drive through France and Belgium brought inevitable supply difficulties which rapidly diminished the impetus of the offensive. The consequence was seen in their inability to rush the defences covering the German frontier before the enemy could recover his balance; and their failure transformed the prospects which had seemed so bright during their headlong advance.

The setback at Arnhem was especially critical for the whole subsequent campaign. The bare five miles by which the Allies fell short of their goal made all the difference between an early defeat of Germany and a new and protracted effort against a reorganized German resistance. Victory at Arnhem would not in itself have been immediately decisive. Existing supply difficulties would still have hampered its full exploitation, particularly when the spearhead was at the apex of a narrow and vulnerable corridor served by a single main road. Yet even with these limitations, Arnhem would have offered a base for a deadly threat against Germany beyond the flank of the Westwall. It would have opened the way to the plains of northwest Germany and forced a drastic redisposition of the harried German forces, with the most profound strategic consequences in favour of the Allies.

Failure in this gallant and tragic enterprise was not retrieved by success on other sectors. The diminishing power of the offensive, which deprived the Allies of the power necessary to outflank the Westwall, also left them too weak to overrun the defences before they were fully manned. The rush of the American First Army carried it through the first line of fixed defences on either side of

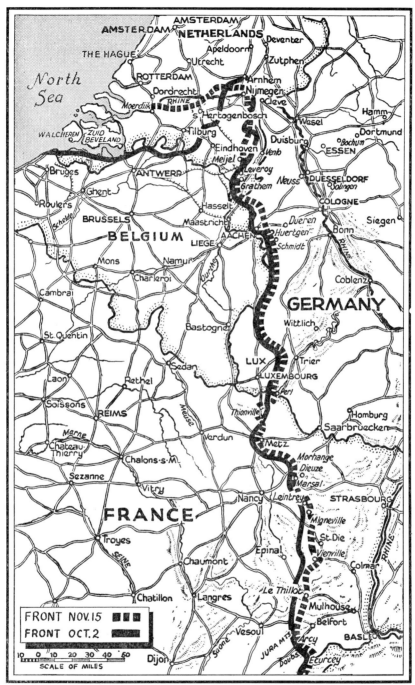

By permission of the New York *Times*

THE WESTERN FRONT, AUTUMN 1944

Aachen, but the spearheads were checked by stiffening German resistance before they could break out into the plain before Cologne. The armoured forces of the American Third Army outran their fuel supplies and were brought to a halt on the Moselle between Metz and Trier. The impetus of the pursuit ebbed in the latter part of September, and the Germans gained a temporary breathing space in which to gather their strength for a new and desperate effort to defend the approaches to the Rhine.

At the heart of this situation lay the Allied need to overcome their supply difficulties and to build up their material resources preparatory to a new assault. Once they were checked by the fixed defences along the German frontier and stiffening resistance on either flank, the necessity was imposed on them of mounting a full-scale effort against these barriers. The task was made more formidable by the devastation of the French railway system, first by Allied bombing and then by the Germans during their retreat, and by the limited nature of the port facilities available to the Allies. The German tactics of prolonging the defence of the Channel ports and wrecking the harbours before surrender had contributed to the exhaustion of the Allied offensive. There was still a German garrison in Dunkirk; Bordeaux was neutralized by a German force at the mouth of the Gironde; and other garrisons remained in the Channel Islands and the smaller ports of the Breton peninsula and the Bay of Biscay. All told these isolated forces were estimated at over 130,000. It was an expensive procedure for the Germans with their desperate need for trained troops to defend the frontiers. But as a short-run investment it served the purpose of delaying a full-scale Allied assault on the Rhineland, and so gave the Germans time to construct new defences and to train new levies for the defence of the Reich.

The battered German forces which turned to confront the Allies along the new defence line were desperately in need of replenishment. At the disposal of von Rundstedt were the remnants of five armies which had been involved in the disasters of Normandy and southern France. Along the northern part of the line, one army group under

Model contained the Fifteenth and Seventh Armies backed by the Fifth Panzer Army. The southern group, commanded by Balck as successor to Blaskowitz, consisted of the First and Nineteenth Armies. The effective strength of these formations had been reduced by nearly half. In four months since the landing in Normandy the Allies had taken over half a million prisoners, and Churchill estimated that German losses in killed and wounded were in the vicinity of 400,000. With this depleted strength, von Rundstedt had to hold a front of some 450 miles, nearly six times the length of the Normandy front before the Allied breakthrough.

To fill these yawning gaps the Germans acted swiftly and ruthlessly. Divisions which had been withdrawn from the eastern front for rest and regrouping were thrown into the defence of the west. The navy and the air force were drawn on for reinforcements for the army. A drastic comb-out of civilian occupations provided recruits for the *Volksgrenadier* units which were incorporated into the army, and the general levy of all remaining males between 16 and 60 created a Home Guard or *Volkssturm* as a final line of defence.

The mixed quality of these forces was stark testimony to the plight of the German army and the deterioration of its standards. None the less, the measures served their immediate purpose of raising adequate forces to hold the Westwall. The untrained and physically inadequate *Volkssturm* was not intended as a regular fighting force. It was to be used in emergencies to help stem a breakthrough and gain time for the troops to reconstitute a defence line, although some of its units were employed in brief rearguard actions to cover withdrawals along the front. The *Volksgrenadier* units, on the other hand, were an active part of the army. They were composed chiefly of older men or of those who had hitherto been exempt because of physical defects such as deafness or stomach ulcers. But most of them had some military training, and they were stiffened by a sprinkling of younger men and led by experienced non-commissioned officers. In spite of their deficiencies in skill and stamina, they showed fighting qualities which made them highly useful in the defence of fixed positions, particularly when they were mingled among regular army units and both types of troops were backed by elite S.S. Panzer divisions. At the price of this measure of dilution, von Rundstedt in a short time gathered forces which enabled him not only to garrison the Westwall but to build up a mobile reserve for both defence and counter-attack.

At the beginning of October the front was briefly stabilized on a general north-south line. The exception was in Holland and Belgium, where the Germans held the south bank of the Scheldt to the outskirts of Antwerp, while north of Antwerp the narrow Nijmegen salient thrust to the lower Rhine. From the Rhine at Arnhem the front followed the general line of the German frontier to the southern border of Luxembourg, and continued south along the border of Alsace-Lorraine.

It was with the northern half of this front that the Germans were most acutely concerned. In the south, Alsace and Lorraine formed a territorial buffer, and there it was still possible for the Germans to sell a limited amount of space in order to conserve their forces. An advance by the Allies in Alsace would bring them to the gorge of the upper Rhine, which was easily defensible and beyond which there were few vital objectives. The conquest of Lorraine would threaten the industrial Saar basin and the Lorraine gap leading toward Mainz, but these objectives were still covered by the deep defences of the Westwall. But in the Aachen area the Americans had already driven a wedge into the defences which covered the most direct route to Cologne, and farther north the British were within a few miles of the frontier where the northern end of the Westwall covered the approaches to the Ruhr. At all costs the Germans must hold at these points if they were to avoid irretrievable disaster.

By the end of October seven Allied armies were arrayed along the front. In the north was the Twenty-First Army Group under Montgomery, containing the First Canadian and Second British Armies. Bradley's Twelfth Army Group contained the Ninth as well as the First and Third United States Armies, covering the

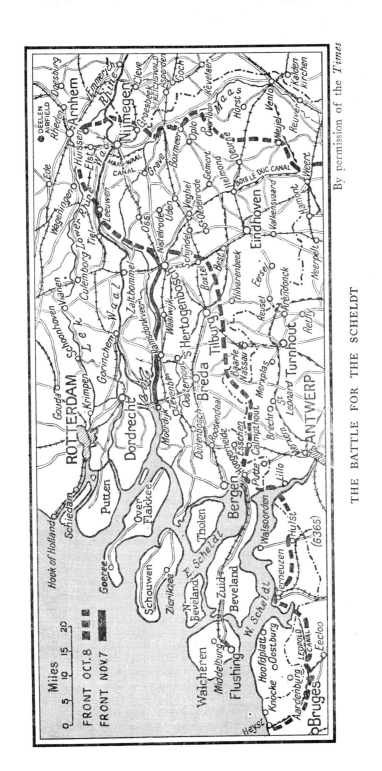

THE BATTLE FOR THE SCHELDT

By permission of the *Times*

sector from about Venlo to the Rhine-Marne canal below Metz. In the south, where Devers commanded the Sixth Army Group, the Seventh United States Army was closing on the passes of the Vosges, and the First French Army was pressing toward the Belfort gap. On all these sectors the autumn was a period of preparation, of regrouping forces and accumulating supplies and gaining the necessary springboards for the coming general assault.

THE BATTLE OF THE SCHELDT

The success of the Germans in stabilizing a linear defence, much of it based on fixed fortifications, lifted Antwerp to a paramount place in Allied calculations. The ports already captured were now far behind the existing battlefront. Most of those that remained in German hands were reduced in potential value by the same factor of distance and by the certainty that they would be wrecked before they were surrendered. But the swift dash of a British armoured column had secured the great prize of Antwerp with its harbour facilities undamaged. This was the second largest port on the continent, with an annual capacity of over 20 million tons. It was within easy reach of the whole northern half of the front, to which supplies could flow over Belgian railways which had suffered far less than those in France. Its complete liberation would break the shackles which at the moment constricted the Allied lines of supply.

It was of the utmost importance to the Germans to delay this achievement as long as possible. Though they had been prevented from destroying Antwerp, they were still in a position to deny its use to the Allies. They were firmly planted along both banks of the lower Scheldt whose 55-mile channel connected Antwerp with the sea. Until they were dislodged, the port was useless. When therefore the setback at Arnhem ended all prospects of a continued advance beyond the Rhine, the breaking of the enemy grip on the approaches to Antwerp became an immediate and urgent Allied objective. "Right now," wrote General Eisenhower on September 21, "our prospects are tied up closely with our success in capturing the approaches to Antwerp. All along the line maintenance is in a bad state . . . but if we can only get to using Antwerp it will have the effect of a blood transfusion."

The enterprise was arduous and complex. It involved a series of co-ordinated local operations by comparatively small forces against highly defensible positions. South of the Scheldt estuary the German foothold was virtually an island bounded by the river and the Leopold Canal. North of the Scheldt were the islands of Walcheren and South Beveland connected by narrow causeways with each other and with the mainland. In these areas the land was low-lying and partly flooded, confining the advance to dikes and causeways and making it impossible to use tanks in any large numbers. Individual German positions had to be reduced one by one. It took an intricate combination of amphibious landings co-ordinated with multiple thrusts by infantry in small bodies to complete the month-long job of dislodging the Germans from their last foothold commanding the approaches to Antwerp.

The task fell in the first instance on the Canadian Army, which included British and Polish troops and was further reinforced by an American division in the final stages of the operation. The complexity of its task was illustrated by the dual effort launched at the beginning of October. On the left, a Canadian division assailed the Breskens pocket south of the Scheldt. Simultaneously, on a sector 40 miles away to the east, another division cleared the Germans from the suburbs of Antwerp and drove north toward the causeway leading to South Beveland, while on the right Canadian and Polish forces struck across the Turnhout Canal in the direction of Tilburg.

The attack on the Breskens pocket opened on October 6 with a thrust from the south across the Leopold Canal toward Aardenburg. The attack met fierce resistance. It was halted after a short distance by massed fire from a heavy concentration of German artillery, and assailed by counter-attacks which split the bridgehead in two. Its unity was restored in hard fighting, but the tenacity of the German resistance prevented its further expansion and led to a temporary cessation of offensive efforts at this point.

To break the deadlock an amphibious effort was launched against the eastern flank of the pocket. On October 9 a thrust was made across the estuary from Terneuzen to a point a few miles from Hoofdplaat. The landing force pushed inland, and eventually linked up with a new thrust across the eastern sector of the Leopold Canal. The German foothold was gradually compressed in hard and dogged fighting. The defenders were strongly entrenched along the dikes which cut up the countryside, and in the towns they had turned the houses into virtual fortresses. The attacking force had to advance virtually without cover across the flat drowned land. But pressure from the east was combined with a new attack from the original bridgehead across the Leopold Canal in a pincers movement which pinned the Germans back against the sea. Their chief stronghold dominating the Scheldt estuary from the south was eliminated with the capture of Breskens on October 22. Fort Frederik Hendrik a short distance away fell on the 25th after a two-day battle. The capture of Cadzand on the 30th eliminated the last guns dominating the estuary from that side, and by November 3 the last of the German defenders had been mopped up and the number of prisoners taken in the course of the operation had risen to over 12,000.

Simultaneously the drive to clear the north bank of the Scheldt was being pushed relentlessly. The dual push north of Antwerp and Turnhout had begun on October 2. Here too the attack met stiff resistance backed by a strong concentration of artillery, and by tanks whose counter-thrusts helped to slow down progress; but by October 11 the Canadians had gained a foothold on the causeway which offered the only path of retreat for the Germans on South Beveland and Walcheren.

The next ten days saw little change in the battle lines. The Nazis held firm on a line covering Tilburg and Breda and Bergen-op-Zoom, and struck with savage counter-attacks which threatened the

Canadian hold on the causeway. On October 20, however, a new thrust inaugurated a more intricate and comprehensive pattern of operations. Forces of the Canadian Army drove north with three spearheads, threatening Breda which was one of the remaining gateways serving the Germans in western Holland. By the 24th the solidifying of the grip on the causeway was followed by a drive along it toward South Beveland. In the interval the British Second Army came into action on the right flank. Since the withdrawal from Arnhem the British had been engaged in widening the Nijmegen salient by pressure which expanded its sides both east and west. Now they launched a strong attack from its western face toward Tilburg and Hertogenbosch, and this move in conjunction with the Canadian drive threatened to trap the bulk of the German Fifteenth Army along the Dutch coast.

The battle for the Scheldt was now approaching its final phase. The Canadians battered their way along the causeway and across a 500-foot ship canal to the main island of South Beveland. The Germans on the island were assailed in a new quarter on October 26 when the Lowland Division attached to the Canadians effected an amphibious landing on the south shore. By the end of October the two forces had linked up to gain control of South Beveland and to launch an attack on the causeway leading to Walcheren.

This island, the last German stronghold commanding the approaches to Antwerp, now became the focus of a triple attack. Already it had been partly flooded by a series of bombing raids which cut the sea dikes and confined the Nazis to isolated points of high ground. On November 1, while British and Canadian forces pressed a determined attack along the causeway, two amphibious landings were made at Flushing and Westkapelle in the face of savage German resistance. It had been intended to soften the defences by a two-day period of bombing; but the weather prevented this operation, and fog grounded the heavy bombers on the morning of the actual attack. In spite of this handicap, the urgent need to complete the opening of the Scheldt brought a decision to launch the two attacks along the causeway and at Flushing as planned, and this in turn resulted in a decision to risk the Westkapelle landing rather than lose the advantage of a concerted assault.

Small as the operation was, it was a minor epic of gallantry and tenacity. The commandos who struck across the Scheldt estuary before dawn effected a landing at Flushing with little trouble, but the infantry which followed became involved in a savage and costly street battle before the town was cleared. At Walcheren, where the focus of attack was the breach that had already been made in the sea wall, the state of the tide forced the commandos to go in in broad daylight without air cover. They were backed by the heavy guns of a battleship and two monitors, but the bombardment failed to knock out the German pillboxes and the gun emplacements in fortified warehouses and hotels. The commandos were met by a curtain of fire which took a heavy toll from the landing force and wreaked havoc among the light support craft which dashed inshore to provide covering fire. By sustained courage and determination a foothold was effected, and the attackers gradually mastered the German positions guarding the sea approaches. Meanwhile the causeway was also forced against stiff opposition, and Allied forces converged on the defenders from three directions. The flooding of the island, which had hitherto inconvenienced the Germans, now seriously hampered the progress of the attack; but the Germans were gradually driven from the coastal rim and pressed back into the town of Middelburg. With the capture of that position on November 7 the Scheldt was at last clear of the enemy, and all that remained was to sweep the channel to open the way for the flow of supplies to Antwerp and the battlefront.

Parallel with these grim and laborious operations on either side of the Scheldt estuary, other operations of a very similar character were in progress against the Germans in the coastal region of Holland south of the Maas. By October 22 these forces had been severed from the German garrisons in the islands north of the Scheldt, and the rough quadrangle which they occupied became the object of a concerted assault by the Canadians from the south and the British from the east.

Here too the going was difficult. Rain and flooded lands placed the main burden of the attack on the infantry which slogged forward through the mud, and whose progress was further hampered by the usual lavish minefields with which the Germans had supplemented their defences. Yet in spite of these obstacles the offensive developed with a power and precision which quickly dislocated the whole German defensive position.

The main weight of the British thrust was directed against Hertogenbosch, an important road junction and a main bastion of the German defence on the west side of the Nijmegen salient. The Canadian attack above Antwerp swung westward toward the coastal flank and the stronghold of Bergen-op-Zoom. The resulting pincers movement threatened the envelopment of that portion of the German Fifteenth Army remaining in southwest Holland. By October 25 the danger was acute. Converging British columns had fought their way into Hertogenbosch, and British and Canadian forces were within two miles of Tilburg and Bergen-op-Zoom. The Germans, with their defences collapsing and their main roads of retreat virtually severed, embarked on a general withdrawal. In an effort to relieve the pressure, an armoured thrust was launched against the eastern side of the Nijmegen salient in the vicinity of Venlo. This attack, which signalized the appearance of the German First Parachute Army in that sector, gained several miles before it was halted and thrown back; but it had little effect on the pressure on the Germans farther west, who were now withdrawing behind stiff rearguard resistance to the line of the Maas.

The operation now moved swiftly to completion. Resistance in Hertogenbosch was crushed on October 27 after four days of street fighting. Farther south the road centre of Tilburg, which had already been bypassed by the advance, fell the same day. On the 28th the Canadians occupied Bergen-op-Zoom. On the following day the Polish armoured division on the right flank of the Canadian Army drove into Breda. Roosendaal, the last important centre of German resistance, fell on October 30. By the 31st the British had reached the Maas north of Tilburg and the whole line was wheeling up toward the river between that point and the sea. The remaining Germans were pouring back across the bridges that remained intact and blowing them up before the Allies could seize them, destroying in particular the great Moerdijk bridge as well as the one at Geertruidenburg.

By November 8 the Allies were in command of virtually all the south bank of the Maas to a point some 20 miles west of Nijmegen, where their line swung north across the Maas and the Lek to the lower Rhine opposite Arnhem. No large bodies of Germans had been trapped in the final phase of this operation; but the German Fifteenth Army, which had been severely mauled in the battle of France, had again been badly cut up. Two divisions had been virtually annihilated in the Breskens pocket and the Scheldt islands. At least two others had suffered heavily. The struggle for the Scheldt and southwest Holland had cost the Germans over 38,000 prisoners, with probably an equal number either killed or seriously wounded. British and Canadian casualties of 40,000 of all categories were not light; but they were far below those of the enemy, and they had attained results of incalculable importance. The great port of Antwerp was available for immediate use, transforming the whole supply situation of the Allies. The Nijmegen salient, at the outset a narrow and precarious corridor, had been expanded into a broad and secure area stretching westward to the coast. The grip on the Maas and the lower Rhine was now solid, and this, together with the unimpeded possession of Antwerp, cleared the way for the resumption of a general offensive against the Siegfried Line.

PREPARING FOR THE OFFENSIVE

Meanwhile a more direct preparation for the offensive, though on a smaller scale, had reached completion with the capture of Aachen. By the latter part of September the initial penetration had brought the Americans to the outskirts of this town which stood at the gateway to the Cologne plain. But stiffening German resistance combined with Allied supply difficulties and shortage of ammunition had imposed a temporary check on the advance. Although Aachen was partly encircled, it continued to bar the way, and its capture was needed to provide a solid springboard for an attempt to crash through the Rhineland defences toward Cologne and the Ruhr.

The assault was launched on October 2 with a thrust on a narrow front north of the city. In two days it drove through a 4-mile belt of permanent fortifications, and tanks were thrown in to exploit the breach. But the attack came up against strong field defences, and stiff counter-attacks by German armour brought progress to a halt. Meanwhile however a second threat had developed to the south of the city, and on October 8 a full-scale and concerted assault was launched from both directions. The southern arm captured a strong switch position on a ridge east of Aachen, dominating the town and the roads leading to it. By October 9 only a gap of 1500 yards separated the northern and southern forces, and the city was virtually isolated.

None the less the Germans fought grimly and desperately to protract the defence to the uttermost. The small garrison remaining in Aachen ignored a surrender ultimatum delivered on October 10. Outside the town the Germans threw in a persistent series of counter-attacks in a vain attempt to break the closing ring. On October 13, after a merciless bombardment from the air and from the ground had reduced Aachen to rubble, a direct assault was launched from the east. It took nine days of sustained fighting against the defenders within the town and repeated counters from without before the last resistance was crushed. But the capture of Wuerselen on October 16 finally closed the ring about the city; the last serious strong points were reduced on the 20th; and on October 21 the final reduction of the garrison was completed and Aachen was in American hands. It was the securing of a pivotal point whose further exploitation now awaited the completion of the final phase of the concurrent operations in the Netherlands.

These preparatory efforts on the ground, so relentless and sustained under the most arduous conditions, showed how urgent the Allies felt it was to resume the main offensive against Germany. Equally revealing was the intensity of the air effort which all during this period was in progress against the Reich. In spite of uncertain weather conditions, October saw the greatest air assault which had yet been delivered against Germany, which now lay completely at the mercy of the Allied bombers.

The objective was nothing less than to wreck the immediate resources on which the Germans depended for defence in the west. The distinction between strategic and tactical bombing had now narrowed almost to the vanishing point. As Germany's production declined and her reserves dwindled, the raids on industrial centres were no longer calculated to have a long-range effect on enemy war potential. They struck at the sources of weapons and supplies which might flow directly to the front. They were thus integrated with the methodical blows by the heavy bombers at the main transportation centres, and these in turn were supplemented by the sustained activity of the lighter forces against traffic and transport arteries in the immediate battle zone.

The assault steadily rose in weight and intensity. The Allies were now able in twelve hours of daylight to put over the Reich more planes than the German air force possessed on all fronts. On October 7 the operations involved 1400 American and 700 British heavy bombers from Britain and 800 from Italian bases, and fighter escorts brought the numbers to a total of between 6000 and 7000. The increasing weight of bombs carried by the heavy bombers made it possible to strike a single target with a saturation raid of 5000 tons. The bombs themselves were growing in size and in destructive power. New 6-ton bombs containing more powerful explosives had effects nine times as great as the earlier 2-ton bombs, and monsters weighing 11 short tons were being developed for use in the following spring. German cities could be subjected in a single day to an ordeal exceeding that which London had experienced in the course of a whole year.

Against the crushing power of this offensive the *Luftwaffe* could now offer only the most spasmodic resistance. Its once formidable offensive power had almost disappeared. A few sharp but limited attacks on Britain in March 1945 were the first raids by piloted bombers since the preceding June. The Germans relied in the interval on the V-1 robot bomb and the V-2 rocket projectile, not only against England but against Antwerp and other bases in the rear of the battle zone. Fearsome as these weapons were in certain aspects, they had not yet reached a stage of accuracy or reliability which would make them an efficient substitute for bombing planes. On the defensive side the decline of German air power was equally striking. The *Luftwaffe* still had a sting; but in the face of attacks against the very heart of the German war potential, the Germans depended more and more completely on their ground defences, hoarding their fighter strength for the most desperate emergencies. There were occasional sharp clashes, such as took place over Berlin on October 6; and there was a full-scale battle on November 2 when the Germans threw in 400 fighters to defend the Leuna oil refinery at Merseburg. But the effort cost them 208 aircraft, including 25 destroyed on the ground, as against American losses of 40 bombers and 10 fighters. The Germans could not afford such inroads into their limited strength; and with German ground defences hampered by the loss of radio-location stations in France and Belgium, Allied losses showed a progressive decline. On October 22, 1400 bombers struck at German targets without the loss of a single plane. On October 26 only 1 was lost out of 1200. The figures were a graphic commentary on German inferiority in the air.

The greatest weight of the assault was directed against German communications. A methodical campaign was carried out against the chief junctions and marshalling yards through which traffic flowed to the Rhineland. The main centres along the Rhine were subjected to particularly heavy attacks, but the assault reached back to the key points on the railway system of western and central

Germany in a studied attempt to seal off the whole Rhineland area from its sources of weapons and supplies.

Closely integrated with the campaign against the railways was the simultaneous assault on oil production. By the beginning of October, German production had already been cut by an estimated 77 per cent. There was a sustained effort to prevent its recovery, and if possible to reduce it still further. The impairing of railway facilities threw a heavier burden on road transport. By denying to the German forces the oil and gasoline necessary for road traffic, a major contribution could be made to the paralysis of the whole transport system. The effects went farther and bore directly on the attempt to paralyze Germany's fighting capacity by denying her the necessary weapons of combat. Shortage of fuel had a direct effect on the mobility of German armoured forces and the fighting potential of the German air force; and the attack on oil centres was thus a bridge between the assault on German transport and the continued attacks on the factories producing tanks and planes.

From all these points of view, the chief cities along the Rhine were outstanding objectives. As vital transportation links and as centres of war industry, they were of key importance to the maintenance of the defence of the Rhineland. Throughout October the bombers slashed methodically at the Rhine valley with devastating blows. Cologne in particular received a terrible battering which left that great city virtually in ruins. Heavy raids by both day and night bombers were interspersed by punishing blows from Mosquito squadrons. During October there were 18 attacks on Cologne, including 8 raids of major proportions, with a total weight of bombs in the vicinity of 20,000 tons. Other Rhineland cities were less frequent targets; but on October 14 a heavy day raid on Duisburg was followed by an even heavier night raid to deluge that city with nearly 10,000 tons of bombs—a far greater weight in less than 24 hours than London had endured during 11 months of *blitz*. By comparison, Duesseldorf's 4000 tons on the night of November 2 was only what her sister cities were undergoing on repeated occasions.

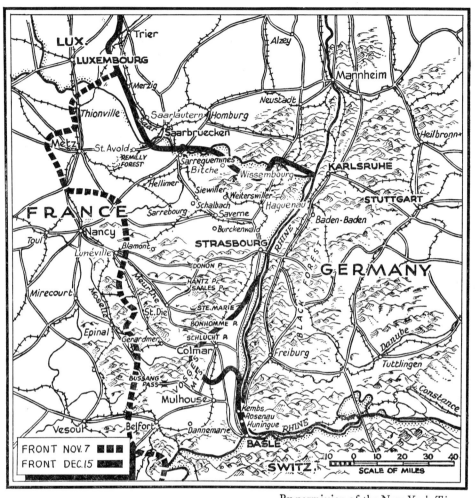

By permission of the New York *Times*

ALSACE-LORRAINE AND THE SAAR

During the month of October, the bombers based in Britain and Italy deluged Germany with 112,000 tons of bombs—almost as much as had fallen on German soil during the whole of the preceding nine months. By the first week in November the objectives of the bombers were becoming more dispersed as they sought to create temporary interruptions of traffic over the widest possible area. It was a sign that the new general offensive was now in the last stages of preparation. Although the season was unpropitious, the Allied command considered it vital to strike at the earliest possible moment. Germany must be denied the time she desperately needed to train her hastily gathered levies and to improve the Westwall defences and the field fortifications behind them. With the assurance that Antwerp would soon be available, and with a reserve of supplies accumulated during a month-long lull on the main fronts, a concerted drive was undertaken against the extended German defences from the Dutch border to the Belfort gap.

THE WINTER OFFENSIVE

The offensive developed as a series of blows in rapid succession on one sector after another, until six Allied armies were fully engaged. The initial move was by the American Third Army against Metz on November 8, followed next day by a thrust across the Moselle in the Thionville area. On November 14 the British Second Army attacked in the north and the American Seventh Army opened a drive in the Vosges. On the 15th the First French Army struck toward the Belfort gap; and on November 16 the American First and Ninth Armies launched a powerful attack in the Aachen sector against the defences guarding the Cologne plain.

The pattern and timing of these attacks suggested the outline of the Allied strategic plan. This was to draw the German strength to the flanks, and particularly to the area south of the Moselle, and then to strike with concentrated force in the centre toward Cologne and the Ruhr. The German forces would be pinned down frontally by the weight of the Allied assault, while behind them the relentless

bombing of communications would sever their lines of both reinforcement and retreat. In spite of bad weather, the Allied bombers
in November deluged Germany with a new record total of 114,700
tons—a tribute to the effectiveness of the instruments and navigational aids which had been developed in the course of the air
offensive. The sustained attack on oil production and rail centres
not only restricted German mobility, but imposed special hazards
if the Germans should be driven to an effort at retreat across the
Rhine. General Eisenhower remarked that this would be almost an
amphibious operation in view of Allied damage to the Rhine crossings,
and expressed his belief that the Germans had been committed to a
decisive battle west of the river, and that the Allies were about to
destroy them there.

In this situation the German opportunities for flexible defence
were seriously limited. On the northern half of the front in particular,
every yard of retreat was a step nearer disaster. The Germans
showed a special nervousness over the possibility of a new British
offensive in Holland. In an effort to impose all possible obstacles,
they breached dikes and opened dams to flood the "island" between
the Waal and the Lek in the Arnhem-Nijmegen area, and below this
they kept strong forces on the alert between Cleve and Venlo. But
the sector from Venlo to Aachen was equally vital. This was the
gateway to Cologne and the Ruhr, and a breakthrough would threaten
the very heart of German war production and bring the Allies within
striking distance of the north German plain.

In Alsace-Lorraine, on the other hand, the Germans still had a
limited amount of space which they could afford to sacrifice in order
to gain time. Beyond the Vosges and the Belfort gap lay the gorges
of the upper Rhine which were easily defensible, and few vital
objectives would be threatened even if the Allies should manage to
force a crossing. North of Metz and Strasbourg was the important
industrial region of the Saar; but it was covered by strong defences,
and on this sector of the Westwall the forces falling back from
Lorraine could still hope to make a protracted stand.

Such were the considerations which determined German defensive strategy. The enemy made skilful use of the slender margin for manoeuvre which remained to him. The professionally expert campaign which he now waged gave clear evidence that the burden of Hitler's military intuition no longer weighed down the commanders in the field, and that Rundstedt was free to use his resources in accordance with the dictates of sound military policy. In the south he conducted a controlled retreat covered by a stiffening rearguard resistance. In the north he concentrated his best troops for a determined stand, yielding ground grudgingly and only after bitter combat. In this phase the German defence was conducted with efficiency and, within inescapable limits, with relative economy. There was no effort to hold positions for reasons of fanaticism or prestige. They were defended as long as was practicable, but given up in preference to the loss or envelopment of any substantial forces, or to the risk of an Allied breakthrough.

These were methods which involved the abandonment of Alsace-Lorraine, but which held the Allies farther north to a slow and grinding advance which was often measured in yards. Progress was further hampered by the weather, which had been persistently un-favourable almost since the landing in Normandy. Rain and snow turned the battle area into a virtual morass. Bad weather failed to halt the strategic bombing of German centres, but it seriously impeded the activity of the tactical forces over the actual front. The Allies thus found themselves deprived of the full use of one of the chief elements in their superiority over their adversaries. On the ground they had no decisive margin over the Germans in actual combat strength. Each side had now approximately 70 divisions available; and while many of the German divisions were under strength or were bolstered by troops of inferior quality, the disparity was not great enough for the Allies to crush the defenders by sheer weight of numbers.

Some of the Allied commanders favoured an attack which would concentrate the maximum weight in a single sector, breaking the

German defences at a chosen point and fanning out to roll up the rest of the Siegfried Line. But this would involve leaving a considerable part of the German armies undisturbed behind fixed defences, and Eisenhower felt that the resulting danger from a counter-offensive was too great to be risked. The alternative which was adopted however involved a certain dispersal of power. The Allies had a powerful concentration on the sector between Venlo and Aachen, but a considerable port of their strength was engaged in Alsace-Lorraine along an extended front and in an area where the enemy could save strength by surrendering ground. Even on the northern sector, the impact of the offensive was qualified by the failure or inability to make use of large armoured forces. The sodden ground, traversed by swollen streams and rivers, and the strength of the German fortifications and field defences—to which might be added the superiority of the newest German tanks over those of the Allies in weight and firepower—were all obstacles to an effort at a breakthrough by a massed armoured assault. With the Allies thus deprived by circumstances of certain significant advantages, the Germans were able to balk the Allied hope of forcing a crushing decision while they prepared a counter-stroke which would further delay the prospect of final victory.

The first blow in the new offensive was struck against Metz, the initial barrier guarding the Lorraine gap. On November 8 the American Third Army attacked with three divisions on a 27-mile front south and southeast of the fortress between Pont-à-Mousson and Chateau-Salins. This implied threat of outflanking Metz to the east was broadened next day to a general converging movement. Two more divisions were thrown in on the western flank of the original attack, while another division struck toward Metz from the northwest. Simultaneously still another division launched a thrust across the Moselle just north of Thionville. By November 11 the Third Army had thrown in 8 divisions, 2 of them armoured, on the sector from the Luxembourg border to the Rhine-Marne Canal east of Nancy.

The arc around Metz was steadily compressed during the week that followed. Although German resistance was marked by repeated counter-attacks against both flanks of the drive, the defence was a delaying action to cover a general withdrawal. Rather than commit strong garrisons to an advanced bastion which was threatened with isolation, the Germans decided to conserve their forces by a retirement to the Siegfried Line. By November 18, American troops had broken into Metz in a frontal assault. Resistance of the German rearguard, which included *Volkssturm* formations, collapsed two days later, and such isolated pockets of resistance as remained were cleaned out by November 22. The outlying forts held out longer, and their gradual reduction was only completed on December 13; but this task did little to delay the advance which pressed on toward the frontier and the defences covering the Saar basin.

At this stage the bridgehead across the Moselle above Thionville took on a new importance. In its first stages it had been assailed by counter-attacks which make the American foothold precarious for several days. By November 15, however, it had been consolidated into a base for a fresh advance. Two fresh divisions were thrown in above Thionville; and while the main advance pressed toward Saarbruecken from the south, these forces launched a strong attack against the Siegfried Line around Merzig.

The strength of the drive was increased by the events which were now in progress farther to the south. On November 14 the American Seventh Army attacked on a 10-mile front to the east of Lunéville. This assault picked up and extended the advance on the right flank of the Third Army, while at the same time it struck at the northern flank of the German positions in the Vosges. On November 15 the other end of the Vosges line was assailed by the First French Army, which drove forward on a 25-mile front astride the Doubs valley toward the Belfort gap.

The Germans, already in process of being ousted from Lorraine, now found themselves being dislodged from Alsace as well. The French forces in the south made rapid progress. On November 20 they entered Belfort and drove spearheads beyond it to reach the Rhine. From the corridor thus created they swung north along the Alsace plain. On November 22, at the other end of the Vosges, the Seventh Army broke through the Saverne gap, and next day their forces were in Strasbourg. On November 26 they drove another spearhead through Saales Pass to increase the pressure on the Germans remaining west of the Rhine. A converging movement from north and south gradually compressed the enemy pocket, until by mid-December it was reduced to an area of 1000 square kilometres around Colmar.

While elements of the Seventh Army were thus pressing south from Strasbourg, the main effort was being exerted against the northern side of the corridor. Here the Third and Seventh Armies were now moving forward on a continuous front stretching from the Luxembourg border to the Rhine. On the left a wedge was driven into the Siegfried Line after stubborn fighting around Saarlautern and Dillingen during the first half of December, and the Third Army had thrust across the Saar river at a dozen points. In the centre it had driven through the Maginot Line at St. Avold and had secured full control of Saarguemines. Farther east the Seventh Army was closing on the stronghold of Bitche. Its right wing, driving through the Wissembourg gap, had taken Haguenau and forced the Germans from their line along the Seltz river and was offering a growing threat to Karlsruhe. The German frontier defences were under mounting pressure, and were showing signs of crumbling before the sustained power of the attack.

Farther to the north meanwhile the Allies were engaged in an even more intensive effort. This was the critical sector from the German point of view. Beyond Aachen the Allied spearheads had already penetrated the border fortifications and were pointed directly toward the Cologne plain. A breach at this point would determine the fate of the whole Rhineland, endanger the main German forces in the west, and place the Allies in position for a decisive assault on the last great barrier of the Rhine.

The operations began with a drive by the left wing of the British Second Army against the bridgehead which the Germans still held west of the Maas along a 40-mile stretch covering the important communications centre of Venlo. This area, behind which lay the northern flank of the Siegfried Line, was one about which the Germans showed acute concern. But while they kept strong forces on guard behind the Maas, it was soon evident that they had decided to economize their strength and to fight only a delaying action in the bridgehead itself.

The attack was launched on November 14 under cover of a heavy artillery barrage. Its main weight was on the southern part of the bridgehead around the junction of the Noorden and Wessem canals. It was opposed by little more than rearguard resistance; but this was aided by lavish minefields and by the water-logged moors split up by a series of canals. In these conditions progress was slow but steady. Four days of fighting brought the British to the Maas opposite Roermond and gave them command of the southern sector of the bridgehead. Pressure from west and south gradually reduced what remained of the salient opposite Venlo. By November 26 it had been cleared of all but a few pockets, and these were eliminated by December 4 to give full control of the west bank of the Maas.

This however was a preliminary operation with limited forces, designed to clear the northern flank and pin down the defenders in that area. The pivot of the main offensive was just north of Aachen on a 9-mile sector between Geilenkirchen and Eschweiler. Here the American Ninth Army, after an air assault which showered the German defences with 5600 tons of bombs, struck in full force on November 16. The right wing of the British Second Army came in on the northern flank, and the American First Army, part of whose forces were engaged in the difficult area of the Huertgen forest, launched a strong attack above that region toward the anchor point of Eschweiler on the southern flank of the Ninth Army.

The two weeks that followed saw a slow but inexorable advance by these concerted forces in the face of bitter opposition. The Allies

THE ROER SECTOR

By permission of the New York *Times*

Inset map labels: NETH. · BELG. · Aachen · GERM. · Metz · FRANCE · Belfort · SWITZ.

Legend: FRONT NOV. 7 · FRONT DEC. 15

SCALE OF MILES

Superhighways · Highways

Map place names: Muelheim · Rhine · Rhine · Laverkusen · Longerich · Rhine · COLOGNE · Brueh · BONN · Grefrath · Worrem · Bergheim · Libiar · Euskirchen · Bedburg · Erft · Elsdorf · Sindorf · Gladbach · Zuelpich · Kommern · GERMANY · Ellbach · Dueren · Bergstein · Juelich · Merzenhausen · Engelsdorf · Aldenhoven · Niedermerz · Laurensberg · Duerwiss · Eschweiler · Heistern · Wenau · Schevenhuel · Kommerscheidt · Schmidt · Linnich · Geronsweiler · Ederen · Ungershausen · Roehe · Kinzweiler · Stolberg · Huertgen · Vossenack · Monschau · Wurm · Geilenkirchen · Roer · NETH. · Wuerselen · AACHEN · BELG. · Roetgen · Eupen · Roer had massed powerful forces on a narrow front in an attempt to batter their way through the thick German defences which covered the approaches to the Roer river, the chief natural barrier west of the Rhine. But the Germans too had gathered their strength to hold this vital area. On a front of some 20 miles from Huertgen to Geilenkirchen they had massed 12 divisions of good quality, half of them armoured. It was a heavier concentration of tanks than that of the Allies, and the advance was assailed by strong and persistent counter-attacks which at times brought it virtually to a standstill.

In spite of this opposition, and of the rain and snow which further hampered the advance, the German defences were gradually beaten, down. A brilliant joint action by British and American troops resulted in the encirclement of Geilenkirchen and its capture on November 19. This eliminated the northern bastion of the defence on the main sector, and the southern one fell when the American First Army, after several days of stiff fighting, dislodged the Germans from Eschweiler on November 22. On the intervening sector the Ninth Army pushed forward against bitter resistance. There were fierce local struggles for the villages which had been turned into defensive strongholds, and sharp armoured clashes in limited strength; but by November 22 the Ninth had penetrated a 5-mile defensive belt and thrust a spearhead to the Roer below Juelich. During the subsequent week its foothold on the west bank was gradually extended northward to the vicinity of Linnich, while on the southern flank the First Army broke out of the Huertgen forest and pressed forward in the direction of Dueren. A new surge along a 10-mile front led to a German withdrawal across the Roer in this sector on the night of December 10, while farther to the south a fresh assault below Huertgen carried the First Army toward the upper reaches of the river.

The Allies now stood opposite the chief crossings of the Roer at Linnich and Juelich and Dueren. The river itself was normally little more than 200 yards wide, but its low-lying banks could be flooded by opening the dams which were still in German hands. There had

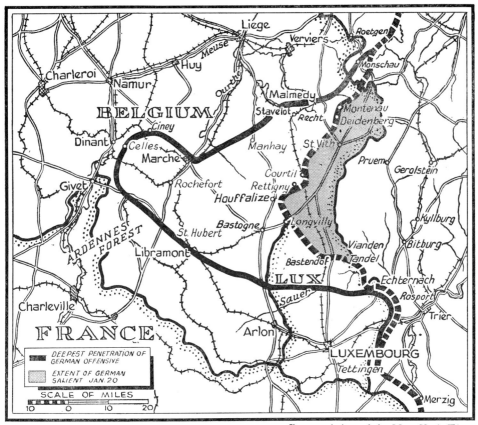

By permission of the New York *Times*

THE ARDENNES BULGE

been persistent efforts to deprive the enemy of these assets by air attacks on the dams; but even the 6-ton bombs of the R.A.F. proved ineffective against these structures, and the floodgates remained in German hands. Their importance was shown at the end of November, when a partial release of the waters they controlled resulted in the flooding of the valley, in some places to a width of nearly a mile. The Allies, having reached the Roer, would need to pause and gather their strength for a new effort against this defensive line.

Thus by mid-December the general offensive had resulted in gains which, though highly significant, were as yet by no means decisive. The Germans had been forced to surrender nearly the whole area which had allowed them a margin for manoeuvre. In the two major areas of the Saar and the lower Rhineland they were under powerful pressure to which they could not yield without an immediate threat of disaster. The Allied offensive had already cost them an estimated 152,000 casualties, including 74,000 prisoners; and while Allied losses were on a comparable scale, the drain of strength was far more serious to the Germans whose replacement problem was now so desperate.

This attrition in space and manpower was of the utmost consequence for the future. Its immediate effect on the situation was more limited in character. The German defences west of the Rhine were still strong and unbreached. The hope of disrupting and destroying the defending armies in that region had not yet been realized. Indeed, the Allied offensive, powerful and extended as it was, had not even forced the Germans to engage their full strength. They had been able not merely to maintain but actually to increase their mobile reserve; and this was now available for the counter-stroke which von Rundstedt launched in an effort to relieve Allied pressure and to disrupt preparations for a new and more decisive offensive.

THE BATTLE OF THE BULGE

The timing of the German blow, shrewd in many of its aspects, was very largely determined by circumstances. Not the least of these was the certainty that a massive Russian drive was preparing in the east, and that this was only too likely to coincide with a renewed and more powerful assault by the Allies in the west. A thrust which would throw the Allies off balance and force them to relax their efforts against the Rhineland defences was urgent if the Germans were to avert a crushing pressure from two directions at once.

Conditions by mid-December were favourable to such an effort. The front along the Roer was temporarily stabilized. The new American thrust below Huertgen was a threat to the flank of that line, but this and the drive against the Saar could be weakened by a counter-stroke which would force a shifting of Allied strength. The respite on the Roer made it possible for the Germans to withdraw the bulk of their Seventh Army for use in the new operation. Two Panzer armies were also available—the Fifth which had served as a mobile reserve, the Sixth composed of various units, some already withdrawn from the Russian front for rest and refitting, which had been assembled in the area around Cologne. Now, with the uncertain December weather bringing frequent overcast which hampered Allied air observation, the opportunity was excellent to move and concentrate these forces unobserved.

The place as well as the timing of the offensive was dictated by the existing situation. Between the Saar and the Roer lay the Ardennes sector which had hitherto been lightly held by both sides. This was virtually the only place along the whole front where Rundstedt could strike with any prospect of profit. The Eifel hills confronting the Allies made the region unsuitable for an offensive on their part, and they believed that the hilly and wooded terrain with its limited communications would be unfavourable to a serious German effort. But this was the path which Rundstedt had taken in 1940 to achieve the breakthrough at Sedan. He had shown that it could be traversed by strong armoured forces, and at this season its high ground was hard and dry and would favour rapid movement. With 24 divisions available, 10 of them armoured, Rundstedt could strike a swift and powerful blow which would threaten not only Sedan, but the vital communication and supply bases of Liége and Namur, and whose full success might even open the way to the recapture of Antwerp, the isolation and envelopment of the northern group of armies, and the disruption of the whole Allied position.

The German attack achieved complete surprise. Although some troop movements had been detected from the air, the Allies had completely failed to realize their extent. Allied intelligence had failed to fill in the gaps. The result was a serious under-estimation of the strength which the Germans had available, and of their ability to mass and move and supply strong forces in spite of the damage to their communications from the air. The terrible bombing assaults, which had slashed methodically down the whole length of the Rhine valley, were still limited in their effects. They had not isolated the Rhineland area from the rest of Germany, nor had they destroyed the mobility which allowed the Germans to mount and sustain a serious offensive operation.

Miscalculations in such matters led to an over-optimism on the part of the Allies which proved of further advantage to the enemy. It was understandable that the Ardennes sector should be comparatively thinly held. The main strength of the Allies was being used offensively in two main areas, and their concentrations on the Roer and the Saar made it impossible to guard the rest of the line in any considerable strength. But they also felt that such a measure was unnecessary, and their over-confidence even led to a neglect of routine defensive measures. The absence of minefields and the lack of prepared road blocks made easier a rapid German penetration, and reduced the delay which the thinly-stretched defenders could impose.

The Germans struck at dawn on December 16 with a series of probing attacks along a 60-mile front between Monschau and Trier. Parachute troops, some in Allied uniforms, were dropped behind the Allied lines. Overhead the *Luftwaffe* made one of its rare appearances in force, throwing in some 500 of its hoarded fighters and fighter-bombers, including a number of fast jet-propelled planes. Simultaneously the Allied rear areas were heavily bombarded by robot missiles. The Germans lost over 100 planes in the course of the first day, but weather during the first stage of the offensive curtailed the full use of Allied air supremacy, and sleet and fog hampered particularly the sort of air concentration against the attacking ground forces which had proved so effective in halting the Avranches counter-attack during the Normandy breakthrough.

By afternoon on the first day the preliminary attacks had uncovered the soft spots in the defence, and German armour was flung in to exploit them. Two elite divisions, the 1st Adolf Hitler and the 12th Hitler Jugend, launched parallel thrusts in the general direction of St. Vith, while farther south another column plunged through a wide gap in the direction of Bastogne. The thin defences crumbled under the weight of the assault. The American 106th Division, which took the chief shock of the armoured assault, lost two-thirds of its effectives. At least two other divisions were overrun, and the front was cracked wide open from Monschau south to Echternach.

By the second day there was perilously little left between the German spearheads and the Meuse. The column driving west from the vicinity of Echternach was headed in the general direction of Sedan—a name which once more took on an ominous sound. An even more acute threat from the Allied point of view was rapidly developing on the northern flank of the expanding bulge. Here the German armour was swinging in a left hook toward the main Allied base of Liége. This was the immediate and paramount German objective, and its successful attainment would be a major blow to the Allies.

The realization of the German aim was prevented first of all by the desperate resistance of the American troops in the path of the advance. By clinging to a number of strategically critical positions, they imposed obstacles which were of decisive importance to the final outcome. Below Monschau and around Echternach the

defenders rallied and held firm, pegging down the shoulders of the
salient and preventing the broadening of its base. Farther west two
vital road centres were held against tremendous odds by troops that
had been hastily rushed to their defence. The American 7th Armoured
Division seized St. Vith and for several days denied the use of this
important road junction to the Germans. At Bastogne the 101st
Airborne Division, reinforced by elements of two armoured divisions
and by the remnants of some units that had been overrun in the
first assault, put up a vigorous defence which, like that at St. Vith,
partially dammed the tide of the German advance.

The seizure of these key points was indicative of a second factor
of the utmost importance. This was the speed with which the Allied
command reacted to the situation. The German thrust, which had
driven through the front of the American First Army, had split the
communications of Bradley's 12th Army Group. In the interests of
co-ordinated action the American First and Ninth Armies were
switched to the 21st Army Group under Montgomery's command,
and Bradley was left to rely mainly on his Third Army to contain
the southern flank of the German drive. This intricate task was
carried out with speed and precision. Parts of 7 divisions were at once
swung from the southern wing of the Third Army and across its lines
of communications to the area between Echternach and Bastogne.
During the next few days the bulk of the Third Army was realigned
along a front extending west to St. Hubert, while the Seventh took
over the Saar front from which these units were withdrawn.

On the northern flank similar measures were taken to meet an even
more dangerous and complex situation. At the first sign of a German
breakthrough, Montgomery shifted the XXX Corps from the British
and Canadian Armies into position to hold the line of the Meuse and
bar the way to Antwerp. With this backstop in place, he rushed
all available forces to head off and channel the German drive away
from the route to Liége. The bulk of the American First Army and
several divisions from the Ninth were thrown into the battle area,
while the remainder of the Ninth took over that part of the Roer

front which had been held by the First. A British force from Holland dashed across Belgium to help check the German frontal advance. It was thrown in on Christmas Eve against the tip of the salient, and helped to batter it back until the contraction of the perimeter led to the withdrawal of these troops in mid-January. Involved in these operations was the British 6th Airborne division, which with the American 82nd and 101st had been called up to help stem the tide. But the bulk of the British forces remained in reserve against more serious contingencies; and out of more than 30 Allied divisions actually involved in the struggle, approximately nine-tenths were American formations.

The critical phase began on December 18. On that day Rundstedt made a serious effort to drive his armoured spearheads north along the direct route to Liége. The 12th Division struck at the hinge of the salient below Monschau, while the 1st swung farther west in an attempt to turn the flank of the defence and break through around Malmédy and Stavelot. Both were checked in fierce fighting by the American divisions which had been rushed up to hold the northern side of the bulge. During the next three days a bitter struggle continued as the Germans hammered at the Allied lines and extended their efforts still farther to the west in an effort to find an opening. It was a race between the two sides along the growing perimeter, with the Allies trying to consolidate fresh barriers before they were outpaced by the German westward sweep. By December 21, however, the situation in this sector had been brought under control, with German expansion checked and the direct thrust toward Liége virtually abandoned.

To this outcome the American stand at St. Vith made a vital contribution. It had forced the German armour thrusting toward Liége to bypass the town on the north. The enemy drive was thus split into two salients, and the northern arm was too confined to have the strength to break through the thickening wall and the massed firepower which it encountered around Malmédy and Stavelot. Below St. Vith however the situation was still dangerous. The

German drive had been channeled toward the west by the barriers which restricted it on both flanks. But frontally it was still meeting with little opposition; and if the defence of St. Vith forced Rundstedt to abandon Liége as his immediate objective, he could still shift the weight of the drive toward the Meuse at Dinant and Namur. There was a brief slackening while he regrouped his armour and gave his infantry time to catch up. Then, striking through Rochefort, he lunged forward on a comparatively narrow front in a new left hook from the apex of the lower salient; and by December 24 his forces had reached Ciney and Celles and were within 4 miles of the Meuse.

This was the peak of the German success. The Allies had now had time to bring adequate power to bear, and the enemy advance was labouring under difficulties which diminished its impetus and impact. The rapid alignment of the American Third Army on the southern flank of the bulge had forced the diversion of several German armoured divisions from offence to defence. The Allied forces around St. Vith, menaced by the German sweep around their flank and rear, had now been withdrawn, thus allowing the Germans to join the two salients and freeing their communications in that area; but the delay continued to have its effect in diminishing the power available at the apex of the bulge, and American resistance at Bastogne continued to constrict German freedom of movement. The town was surrounded on December 19 and thenceforth depended on supplies dropped from the air. Its medical unit was captured almost at the outset, its food and ammunition at times ran perilously low, and its hastily constructed perimeter was under assault by elements of as many as 8 divisions. But to a demand for surrender the American commander replied on December 22 with the inelegant but expressive word "Nuts!" and his troops lashed out briskly against the besiegers during the days that followed. For eight days they held on, until the 4th Armoured Division pushed through a narrow corridor to bring relief on December 26.

The weather too had deserted the Germans. For most of the first week, clouds and fog had protected the advance from any serious

Allied air attack. Communication centres in the rear were hit by the heavy bombers, but the lighter planes were only spasmodically active over the actual battlefield. But by December 23 the weather had cleared considerably, and the tactical forces swung into action. The Germans made desperate efforts to challenge Allied air power, with results that were disastrous to themselves. In three days they lost 375 planes against an Allied loss of 183; and from the air the Allied planes raked convoys and troop concentrations, imposing a serious measure of disruption on the German supply system and further diminishing the power of the offensive.

By Christmas Day the initiative was passing to the Allies. The final German effort had been checked at Celles and Ciney. Rundstedt had thus been headed off from his objectives after a penetration of 50 miles, and the bulge was sealed off by the strengthening cordon which the Allies threw around it. British armour cut in behind the Germans at Ciney, and American tanks drove the parallel spearhead from Celles. The process of compressing the bulge was under way, with a frontal assault against its apex and advances by the First and Third Armies on its flanks.

During the final week in December the Germans fought hard to maintain their gains. They put up strong defences around the perimeter of the bulge, bringing the Third Army to a halt after a gain of 14 miles and holding firm against heavy pressure from the north. But frontal attacks by the Allies battered in the tip of the salient, and there remained the danger of a pincers movement as the Allies sought to cut off and destroy the German forces. Their efforts against the base of the salient made only slight progress; but at Bastogne they held a deep wedge thrusting into the German lines from the south, constricting the enemy's freedom of movement in the western part of the bulge and reaching out toward the Allied forces attacking around Manhay and Grandmenil on the northern flank.

There was little purpose in clinging to the salient if such action involved the risk of serious losses. In itself, the ground which the Germans had won was unimportant. It contained no objectives of any real significance. Its only real value was as a base for a renewed offensive effort, and the prospect that it could be used effectively in this fashion had now disappeared. The Allies had thrown in superior forces and had forced the Germans on the defensive. Rundstedt had no further reserves with which he could afford to embark on a new gamble in the west. The Russian advance up the Danube and the imminence of a major offensive on the Vistula called for the diversion of forces to the east. The chance of even consolidating the gains in the Ardennes faded when strong and persistent German attacks failed to cut the Bastogne corridor, and when the continued frontal attacks of the Allies drove the Germans from Rochefort on December 30. By the end of the year, Rundstedt had decided on withdrawal.

The Germans attempted to ease the pressure during their retreat by strong diversionary attacks against the extended front of the American Seventh Army. In the last days of December they struck in the vicinity of Bitche. This effort was limited in strength, and although it resulted in a gain of several miles, it initially offered no serious strategic threat to the Allies. Farther east however it was supplemented by other attacks which together developed into a dangerous enveloping movement against Strasbourg. The Germans thrust across the Rhine at points some miles on either side of the city, while simultaneously they attacked toward Haguenau in the north and from the Colmar pocket in the south, and from the expanding salient below Bitche they threatened Strasbourg's communications from the west. At one stage the Allies contemplated the possibility of withdrawing from Strasbourg to a line along the Vosges. But while this could have been done without serious strategic sacrifices, the effect on French morale would have been deplorable, and the idea was rejected. The French First Army took over the defence of the city. The Americans north of Haguenau withdrew to the Moder river and stabilized a new line in spite of heavy German attacks. The remaining German thrusts were halted and contained. At the end of the third week in January the Allies attacked the

Colmar pocket in a pincers movement which closed off a considerable part of it on February 5. On February 9 the remainder of the bridgehead was eliminated and the Allied grip on Alsace was again secure.

Meanwhile the liquidation of the Ardennes bulge was proceeding inexorably. On January 3 a concerted offensive was launched against the whole perimeter, which slowly contracted as the Germans pulled out under cover of fierce rearguard resistance. By January 23, with the capture of St. Vith, the elimination of the salient was virtually complete. Once again the Germans had successfully withdrawn from an exposed position, avoiding the encirclement of any substantial body of their forces. But although a return of bad weather during the first week in January gave temporary protection to the retreat, it was an uncertain respite. Tactical forces lashed out at German transport on every favourable occasion, while the heavy bombers kept up their sustained assault against the chief railway junctions serving the Rhineland. The Germans had tried to forestall an Allied tactical air offensive by a surprise assault on Allied airfields on New Year's Day. They did substantial damage to grounded planes that were packed on forward air bases, but the effort cost them over 300 of their precious fighter planes. It was a sacrifice which they could ill afford. The assault was virtually the last offensive effort by the *Luftwaffe*, while Allied losses had little effect on their subsequent efforts. When a new period of good weather set in on January 22, the retreating Germans were at the mercy of Allied air power. On that day the fliers swept down on roads packed with German vehicles, destroying over 1500 trucks and damaging over 1000, in addition to havoc wreaked on heavily loaded railways. Nearly 2000 more vehicles were destroyed on the roads during the following day, and during the remainder of the month the roads and railways behind the front were mercilessly hammered as the Allies carried out the greatest devastation of enemy transport that had yet been achieved from the air.

A balance sheet of the Ardennes battle was not easy to strike. Neither side had been able to realize the full advantages which the situation seemed to offer. "Soldiers of the western front", said Rundstedt at the opening of the offensive, "your great hour has struck. . . . Everything is at stake. . You have a sacred duty to give everything to achieve the superhuman for the Fatherland and our Fuehrer". If Allied sources were correct in their assertion that Rundstedt hoped to cross the Meuse in two days and reach Antwerp in three weeks, he had reason to call for superhuman efforts. On the Allied side there were the hopes expressed by General Eisenhower on December 22: "By rushing out from his fixed defences, the enemy may give us the chance to turn his great gamble into his worst defeat. . . . Let everyone hold before him a single thought—to destroy the enemy on the ground, in the air, everywhere—destroy him!"

Both sides had to be content with much more modest achievements. The German gain was the disruption of Allied offensive dispositions and the imposition of a delay of six weeks. That prevented full co-ordination of offensive operations on the western and eastern fronts. But though they gained that much delay, the Germans were unable to capitalize on it by strengthening their defences to a degree that would more than offset their losses in the offensive. The actual extent of those losses was speculative. German casualties on the whole Western front during December and January were estimated at 220,000, of whom half were prisoners. American casualties during the same period were 136,000, and the Ardennes battle probably accounted for the bulk of these on both sides. The proportion was not unfavourable to the Allies, particularly in view of their superior power of replacement. In its outcome the Battle of the Bulge was another phase in the struggle of attrition; and as such it might ultimately be counted as an asset to the Allies in spite of the loss of time which it imposed on their offensive plans.

CAMPAIGN ON THE DANUBE

The progress of the Allied campaign in the west had always to be viewed in the light of one cardinal factor. That was the limited strength which Germany had available for the defence of her western

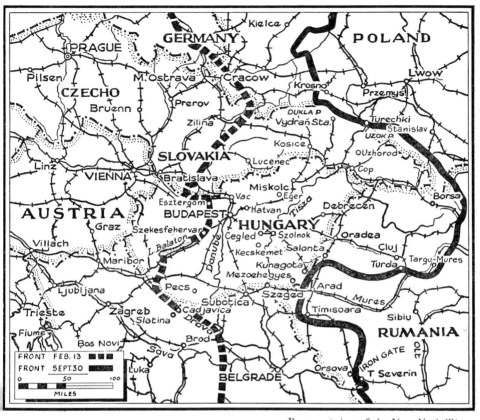

By permission of the New York *Times*

HUNGARY AND SLOVAKIA

frontier. As the ring closed about her, Germany had to stand guard
along almost her whole perimeter. Her mounting losses, and the
steadily rising power of her adversaries, made the task increasingly
difficult. Her dwindling manpower had to be distributed with the
aim of establishing a firm defence at every major danger point.
But it had now become virtually impossible for her to provide even
the minimum strength that was needed to stabilize each separate
front; and with the disappearance of her strategic reserves, her
distribution of forces tended to become more and more inflexible.
She still had a slight margin which allowed her to draw a few
divisions from inactive sectors, or to shift some forces from one front
to another, but her freedom of choice was now too limited to have
any decisive effect on the strategic situation.

It was thus impossible for Germany to mass superior forces in
the west without risking disaster in the south or east. In spite of the
vital importance of the struggle in the west, it never absorbed more
than one-quarter of the estimated 300 German divisions which were
still in existence in the autumn of 1944. Nearly two-thirds of these
were stretched out along the eastern front from the Baltic to the
Danube. Scandinavia and the Balkans each absorbed something like
a dozen more, and between 25 and 30 were pinned down in Italy.

Thus in spite of the dwindling area held by German arms, it was
still vast enough to impose a grave burden on Germany's defensive
strength. She clung tenaciously to the remaining buffers which
protected the soil of the Reich. The divisions isolated in Latvia
maintained a stubborn defence. Garrisons remained in Denmark
and Norway to guard Germany's northern flank. There was a
withdrawal from Greece and Serbia, but the Germans maintained their
hold on Croatia. In Italy, where no major operations were undertaken
during the winter, the Allied threat was still active enough to
immobilize at least 25 divisions of good quality. And in Hungary and
Czechoslovakia a conflict raged during the autumn and early winter on
a scale and with an intensity not very far short of the struggle on the
western front.

This area was the scene of the main Russian effort during the closing months of 1944. On other sectors of the eastern front there were bursts of fierce activity, but no such sustained operations as those along the Danube. The tremendous surge of the summer offensive which carried the Russians to the Vistula and the borders of East Prussia had created immense supply problems on the main front in Poland. In the face of stiffening German resistance the Red Army needed to restore or construct communication routes across Poland, and build up forward bases, and mass the troops and supplies necessary for a new major effort. Months would be needed for these tasks, and during that period only limited operations could be expected.

These operations were chiefly directed toward improving the situation on the Baltic flank in preparation for the winter offensive. In one aspect the operations below the Carpathians served a similar purpose in relation to the flank in south Poland, although other objectives were also involved. In the north however the aims were limited; and when they could not be attained with limited forces, the Russians abandoned the effort rather than compromise their preparations for a more comprehensive assault.

The Russian breakthrough to the Baltic coast above Memel, followed by the capture of Riga on October 13, cut off the German forces in western Latvia. A strong body, which the Russians said included the remnants of 30 divisions, was hemmed in on the peninsula of Courland west of the gulf of Riga. But although this group had been severed from the main German armies, it was not effectively isolated. The Germans still held the ports of Libau and Windau, through which they could draw supplies and from which they could be evacuated in case of need. They succeeded in stabilizing a defensive line running southwest of Riga and south of Libau, and their retention of this position tied down important Russian forces and represented a potential threat to the whole northern flank.

An initial attempt to dislodge the Germans was launched on October 27. The first blow was struck southeast of Libau against the base of a German salient which extended down the coast, and the attack was broadened a few days later by a thrust in the vicinity of Auce some 20 miles farther east. Little progress was made against stiff German resistance, and at the end of a week the assault subsided except for minor actions. A stronger effort was undertaken on November 19 with little more success. A simultaneous drive dislodged the remnants of a German garrison which had clung stubbornly to the southern tip of Oesel island, and this success freed the sea approaches to the port of Riga. On the mainland, however, local Russian gains were checked short of a real breakthrough, and on November 25 the offensive was broken off. The struggle was renewed in the latter part of December, but on a more local scale and with an equal lack of decisive results. All reports of these actions came from the German side, and the complete silence of Moscow was adequate indication of the absence of any important success on the part of the Russians.

The struggle on the borders of East Prussia, though comparatively brief in duration, was a much more serious affair. The expulsion of the Germans from their strong positions in that region would be of incalculable value to the Russians in their preparations for a new attack along the Vistula. From the German point of view, East Prussia was not only a bastion of the highest strategic importance, but also the point at which the sacred soil of Germany itself was now menaced by the advancing tide of Bolshevism. Emotional as well as military considerations were involved, and the Nazis showed a frantic desperation in their efforts at defence. A million conscript workers, foreigners and German civilians, were mobilized to dig trenches and construct fortifications. Large contingents of *Volkssturm* were thrown in to assist in the work and to bolster the defence. The Russians were confronted with formidable barriers in a region where lakes and forests restricted the route of advance, and where deep defence lines of concrete fortifications supplemented by earthworks barred the chief avenues of approach.

The prelude to the drive was Bagramian's breakthrough to the Baltic on October 10. Swinging his weight against the southern side of the corridor, he drove down the coast, encircling Memel and pushing on to the line of the Niemen. This advance, which by October 22 brought the Russians to the Niemen opposite Tilsit, threatened East Prussia from the north; and at the same time Rokossovsky in the south was maintaining a local pressure along the Narew. With the menace of a pincers movement thus pinning down German forces on the flanks, the main drive was launched in the centre on October 17 by the Third White Russian group under Chernyakhovsky.

The attack was directed toward the Insterburg gap which lay between the Niemen and the Masurian lakes. Its axis was the railway running west from Kaunas to Insterburg and Koenigsberg. The main weight of the offensive was concentrated on a 50-mile stretch between Schirwindt and Suwalki, with operations on the left flank extending southward against the fortress of Augustov. In five days of heavy fighting the Russians broke through the strong defences along the border and drove 20 miles inside East Prussia to take the town of Goldap and menace the strongly defended railway centre of Gumbinnen.

This promising success however proved to be the maximum gain in this phase of the offensive. Russian spearheads which pushed westward during the next two days were said by the Germans to have reached Angerapp, 33 miles inside the frontier, but they were unable to consolidate their advance. There were still powerful defences to be overcome, with almost every village turned into a fortress which had to be reduced before further progress was possible. German troops, many of them natives of East Prussia, battled fanatically in defence of their homeland. Behind the front lay a good network of communications which enabled the Germans to rush reinforcements and supplies to the threatened area. By the second week fresh troops had been thrown into the struggle, including 4 Panzer divisions, and the Germans had seized the initiative with heavy counter-attacks. The Russians were pushed back from their maximum penetrations. A prolonged and savage struggle ended with the German recapture of Goldap on November 6. Long before that the Russians had abandoned their offensive efforts as it became clear that success would call for the use of far greater strength than they were prepared to commit at this stage. They consolidated their limited gains, and the front in East Prussia settled down to an uneasy stalemate as the Russians shifted their chief weight to the area south of the Carpathians.

THE INVASION OF HUNGARY

The autumn offensive which swept over Rumania and Bulgaria was a drive which carried the Russian armies away from the direction of the German frontier. It achieved important objectives, both strategic and economic. It not only deprived the Germans of the help of some 20 Rumanian divisions, but even turned part of that force against Germany and Hungary. It freed the shores of the Black Sea, secured control of the lower Danube, and virtually forced the Germans to withdraw from Greece and Serbia. It cut off important sources of the grain and oil which Germany needed so desperately. But it presented no direct threat to Germany itself; and it was only in the latter part of September, when their great wheeling movement carried the Russians around the eastern flank of the Carpathians, that their spearheads were once more pointed in the direction of the Reich.

Even then their basic objectives lay far ahead. The ultimate goal was the southern fortress area in which the Nazis were planning to make their final desperate stand. The arduous task of clearing Hungary and Slovakia was merely a preliminary operation which would bring the Russians into position for an assault on the more vital areas of Austria and Bohemia. When that stage was reached, two points would become pivotal for future progress. The capture of Vienna would open the way to the conquest of Austria. The capture of Moravska Ostrava would give the Russians command of the Moravian gap and tremendously facilitate a drive into Bohemia. With Austria overrun, with the mineral resources and war industries of Czechoslovakia in Russian hands and the Bohemian bastion taken from the rear, the Germans in the Bavarian Alps would be assailed by the Russians from the east as well as by the British and Americans closing upon them from the north and west.

This was a long vista from the positions in which the Russians stood at the beginning of October. Three army groups were engaged in a slow and stubborn effort to dislodge the Germans from the defences guarding Slovakia and barring the way into the Hungarian plain. The Fourth Ukrainian Group under Petrov was closing on the Carpathian passes from the north. The Second Ukrainian under Malinovsky was pushing through Transylvania and had thrust a broad spearhead across the Hungarian border on either side of Arad. On the southern flank, the Third Ukrainian under Tolbukhin stood at the Iron Gate on the Danube and along the western border of Bulgaria.

This extended front rested on strained and tenuous communications which limited the power and duration of individual offensive thrusts. To offset this, the defence too was under severe strain. The German supply system might be more advantageous, but on this as on other fronts the available manpower was inadequate to hold the whole line against attacks in strength. So long as the Russians held the initiative, they could choose their points of assault, shifting their weight from one sector to another as each blow in turn was checked by a stiffening defence. The pattern of their advance was marked by repeated powerful blows in one quarter after another, with each successive gain contributing to the success of the effort which followed it.

At the heart of the broad strategic plan lay the need for control of the Danube. As the Russians advanced westward, the river became increasingly essential as a route of supply. The result was to make Budapest a focal point in this phase of the campaign. This city was the main supply and distribution point for the German forces in southeastern Europe. From it radiated a network of roads and railways which, together with its commanding position on the Danube, made it the strategic nerve centre of the whole region. Its possession was essential to the Russians as a base for their further advance toward Vienna. Its retention was vital to the Germans as an advance bastion guarding the approaches to Austria. The ensuing campaign, with its complex operations over a wide stretch of territory from Ruthenia to Yugoslavia, centred on Budapest as the major immediate objective.

The first blow was struck on the southern flank. In the last days of September, Tolbukhin broke through the German defences on either side of the Iron Gate, forcing a bridgehead across the Danube and expanding it by September 30 to a breadth of 60 miles. His southern wing, aided by Bulgarians and Partisans, fanned out rapidly toward the Morava valley, where progress was crowned by the capture of Nish on October 16; and the main force drove westward toward a junction with the forces of Marshal Tito and a concerted assault on Belgrade.

The drive made rapid progress. It was aided by a strong armoured thrust which Malinovsky launched from his left wing north of the Danube on October 3. Advancing 45 miles in two days, this force broke through the German defence arc to outflank Belgrade from the north while Tolbukhin and Tito closed on the city from east and south and west. By October 14 Belgrade had been pocketed and the assault was under way, with combined forces of Russians and Partisans already through the outer defences and fighting their way into the city from the south. There were several days of fierce street fighting as the garrison clung to positions in the heart of the town and the Germans launched a strong relief column to their aid. But the relief effort was halted within sight of Belgrade; another strong force that had been trapped southeast of the city was pinned up against the Danube and wiped out after it lost most of its tanks in an effort to break clear; and on October 20 the last resistance in Belgrade itself was overcome, and the Yugoslav capital which had suffered so much at Nazi hands was free once more.

By this time a radical change had come over the situation in Hungary. Malinovsky's breakthrough to the Danube north of Belgrade had cleared the southern flank of the broad salient beyond Arad; and together with Tolbukhin's advance it gave a firm base for a lunge westward to the Tisza valley, the chief natural obstacle protecting the middle Danube below Budapest.

The drive opened on October 6. On a front of over 90 miles which extended into northern Yugoslavia, the Russians broke through German and Hungarian resistance for gains of over 30 miles. Three days of fighting carried them to the Tisza on a 15-mile front which was rapidly broadened during the next few days. On the southern end of the drive the impetus of the assault carried the Russians across the Tisza to capture Szeged on October 11 and to take the Yugoslav communication centre of Subotica next day. On the northern flank the Russians bypassed Oradea, and on the level Hungarian plain they drove a powerful spearhead northward between Oradea and Szolnok to the outskirts of Debrecen.

This last move placed the German forces in Transylvania in a highly precarious position. They were now in a deep salient which was under pressure from Malinovsky's forces in Transylvania and from Petrov's dogged advance into the Carpathians, while the new Russian thrust threatened their communications from the rear. The Germans fought desperately to hold open the road of retreat. They threw in strong armoured forces at Debrecen, and a 10-day tank battle raged before that city while the Germans pulled back from Transylvania under sustained Russian pressure. Cluj was taken on October 11. Oradea fell on the following day. On October 18, with the eastward bulge almost eliminated, Petrov seized control of seven Carpathian passes and drove into eastern Czechoslovakia on a front of 170 miles. On October 20 Debrecen fell, and Malinovsky drove north toward a junction with Petrov. The two armies linked up on October 26. Next day the capture of Uzhorod cleared the last German defenders from Ruthenia, and Petrov's forces plunged into a bitter struggle for the railway centre of Cop, around which the Germans were striving to stabilize a new defensive line.

Meanwhile the remorseless advance of Malinovsky was carrying his armies rapidly toward the heart of Hungary at Budapest. The spearhead which captured Subotica pressed on to reach the Danube on October 21, and to extend Russian control over the whole of the east bank to a point 84 miles below Budapest. This success gave

the Russians a firm grip on the southern part of the corridor between
the Tisza and the Danube—a broad foothold from which they could
turn north and drive along the high ground between the two rivers
to the gates of the Hungarian capital.

With only a short pause to adjust his dispositions, Malinovsky
wheeled his left flank up the east bank of the Danube. At the same
time, on October 30, he thrust another spearhead across the Tisza
farther north in the direction of Kecskemet. This town, 44 miles
southeast of Budapest, commanded the avenue between the Tisza
and the marshlands bordering the Danube. Its fall on November 1
not only eliminated an important obstacle, but allowed this Russian
force in its turn to slash across the corridor and to close a trap on the
Germans caught between it and the columns advancing from the south.
The whole German defence along the middle Tisza collapsed. Its flank
was rolled up as the Russians drove rapidly northward until by November
6 they were little more than 4 miles from the outskirts of Pest.

Here their progress was checked for the moment. At the beginning
of November the drenching autumn rains set in, turning the plains
into a sea of mud and slowing down the tanks and motorized
transport of the Russian spearheads. German shock troops were
thrown in to save the Hungarian capital and to stabilize a line
running east from the city along the railway and highway leading to
Szolnok. The latter effort was only partly successful. The Russians
thrust a wedge between Szolnok and Cegled and drove the Germans
from those two cities on November 4. Farther west toward the
capital however the advance was brought to a temporary halt, and
the Germans announced that counter-attacks against the Russian
flanks had relieved the immediate pressure.

The Russian response to this check was characteristic of the
whole campaign. Malinovsky promptly swung his weight to his
right wing against the German lines along the upper Tisza. On
November 9 the river was forced on a broad front. The Russians
advanced toward Eger and Miskolc, placing the Germans directly
east of Budapest in a steadily deepening salient. The peril to the

defenders in this sector was increased by strong Russian thrusts against the southern face of the salient which threatened to pocket the troops at its apex above Szolnok. Under this converging pressure the whole German line was pushed back like a swinging door whose hinge was Budapest. On November 15 the strongly defended road and rail centre of Jaszbereny, 17 miles southeast of Hatvan, fell after three days of fighting, and the Germans were driven back to a new line based on Hatvan and Eger and Miskolc.

The Russians gave the enemy no respite which would allow him to consolidate. The offensive was sustained through a month of autumn weather during which rain and mud continued to hamper the mobility of the attackers. At the end of the third week in November the area of assault was extended by a renewal of Petrov's operations in Slovakia. The stronghold of Cop, which had changed hands several times in bitter fighting, was at last secured on November 23. With this obstacle eliminated, Petrov pressed slowly westward, aiming at Kosice and offering a growing threat to the flank of the German defence line in Hungary.

That line meanwhile was being hacked to bits by Malinovsky's relentless attacks. His forces gradually closed on the three main centres of resistance, severing the roads and railways which connected them and drawing a siege arc around each one individually. By the end of November the German positions had collapsed. The loss of Hatvan was announced by the Germans on November 25 and confirmed next day by the Russians. Eger fell on November 30; and on December 3, after two weeks of stubborn resistance, the Germans were driven from Miskolc. They fell back to a new line based on the Matra and Buekk mountains northeast of Budapest— a line which in its turn was soon undermined by the unremitting pressure of Malinovsky's offensive.

THE STRUGGLE FOR BUDAPEST

The steady swing of the Russians around the Hungarian capital from east to north had placed the eastern section, the modern industrial town of Pest, in increasing jeopardy. The Russians had gradually drawn an arc from south to east and northeast, leaving only a corridor along the east bank of the Danube above the city. With the fall of Hatvan and the Russian advance beyond it, the encirclement of Pest was almost within sight. It was now the turn of Buda, the ancient city on its hills west of the Danube, to come within the grip of the forces which converged upon it.

The basic pattern of the Russian thrust up the east bank of the Danube was repeated west of the river. Both were adaptations of the "hammer and sickle" tactics whose combination of proved effectiveness with happy symbolism had rightly endeared them to Russian leaders. The region between the Danube and Lake Balaton on the west was in its broader strategic features comparable to the corridor between the Danube and the Tisza on the east, and offered the same opportunities for a broad wheeling movement co-ordinated with a westward thrust which would shatter the enemy's hold on the area and open the way to Buda from the south.

The point of the sickle was first driven in just below the Yugoslav border. An initial crossing was reported at Apatin early in November. It was not immediately developed, but behind this initial penetration a strong force of men and armour was massed during the next three weeks. In the final days of November, Tolbukhin drove in strength across the Danube on a rapidly expanding front. On November 29, two days after the first report of the drive, he had swept over Mohacs and captured Pecs, 25 miles west of the Danube, and his columns were fanning out in three main directions. His left advanced parallel with the Drava toward the gap south of Lake Balaton; his centre struck in a broad sweep toward the lake and the area north of it; and on his right a spearhead thrust up the Danube valley toward Budapest.

The bulk of the area below the capital was rapidly overrun. On December 7, Tolbukhin's southern spearhead captured Barcs; and with their left flank protected by the Drava, the Russians now stood before the gap between that river and Lake Balaton. The southeast shore of the lake was by this time under Russian control, and on the right the column sweeping northward was joined by the hammer stroke which Malinovsky delivered across the Danube.

The base for Malinovsky's operation was Csepel island, a low-lying stretch of 30 miles in the middle of the Danube. A Russian landing on the island was reported on November 23. During the next fortnight the Germans were pressed back toward the northern tip which lay in the very heart of Budapest. With a firm foothold thus secured, the Russians prepared a daring surprise stroke. Pontoons were dragged by hand across the muddy terrain and secretly massed for the assault. On the night of December 5 the attack was launched across the river 13 miles below Budapest. The German defences on the west bank were pierced, and by dawn a 10-mile bridgehead had been established. Fierce German counter-attacks failed to dislodge the Russians or to prevent a complete break-through. Malinovsky's forces beat down all opposition and drove west to link with Tolbukhin's spearhead at Lake Velencze, half-way between Lake Balaton and Budapest.

Simultaneously Malinovsky struck with other forces north of the city in a blow which set the stage for the final encirclement of the Hungarian capital. The deep Russian advance beyond Hatvan had seriously strained the German forces guarding the corridor east of the Danube above Pest. Against this sector Malinovsky massed powerful forces of tanks and artillery under cover of fog and rain which grounded planes on both sides and prevented German air reconnaissance. The attack, covered by a powerful artillery barrage, took the Germans completely by surprise. A broad gap was torn in the defences, and through this the Russians swept forward to the Danube. Vac on the Danube elbow above Budapest was taken by December 9, and the Russians drove down toward Pest from the north while other forces closed in from east and south.

With the inner defences of Pest lashed by dive-bombers and crumbling under Russian assault, the Germans fought desperately to hold open their communications with Buda from the west. For a fortnight Tolbukhin was halted by strong defences covering the gap between Budapest and Lake Balaton as the Germans threw into battle reserves that had been drawn from Italy and the west. In the last week in December however a new assault was launched which broke the German defence line on either side of Lake Velencze. The pivotal stronghold of Szekesfehervar, guarding the gap above Lake Balaton, fell after stiff fighting on December 24. Next day Tolbukhin's forces captured Esztergom and reached the south bank of the Danube where only a narrow corridor separated them from Malinovsky to the north. On December 27 the ring was finally closed when another spearhead swept to the Danube just north of the capital, pocketing the remaining German forces in the bend of the river and setting the stage for a final concerted effort to crush the German garrison in Budapest.

In the interval the Russian forces north of the Danube had maintained their slow but relentless progress. Above the Danube elbow at Vac, Malinovsky broadened and deepened a salient which carried him west to the Ipel river and which threatened the right flank of the German positions in the Matra and Buekk mountains. Their left flank was similarly menaced by Russian progress on a broad front northwest of Miskolc; and here the Russians were drawing close to the border of Slovakia and placing the stronghold of Kosice in jeopardy from the rear. A more immediate threat to that base was offered by Petrov's renewed offensive in mid-December. His frontal advance from the east had been held, but the hardening of the ground allowed him to swing strong armoured forces secretly to the south and to strike from that direction on the flank of Malinovsky's advance. By the end of December the Russians were battling on the approaches to Kosice; the Germans had been dislodged from the Matra mountains and had fallen back on new positions covering Lucenec; Malinovsky had advanced from the Ipel river to the Hron, and his forces massing on that line had already established bridgeheads across the Hron and were on the plain leading to Bratislava. South of the Danube meanwhile

Tolbukhin was broadening the corridor west of Budapest and had reached a line running directly north from Szekesfehervar.

Hungary was now virtually lost to the Germans, not only territorially but politically. Admiral Horthy had failed in his effort to spare his invaded country from the ravages of war. On October 15, in a broadcast which bitterly reproached the Nazis for their infringements on Hungarian sovereignty and their failure to keep their repeated promises of aid and redress, Horthy announced that Germany had lost the war and that he had decided to ask for an armistice. The Germans acted promptly to prevent this desertion by their last remaining satellite. Horthy was deposed as Regent, and a new government was set up under Ferenc Salazi, leader of the Nazi-type Arrow Cross party. But the step was only partially successful. Several Hungarian military leaders, including General Miklos of the First Army, went over to the Russians. The Hungarian troops which continued to fight on the German side did so with mixed enthusiasm. A conspiracy against the Nazis and their puppet government was uncovered and suppressed with ruthless severity. As the Russians swept forward, the Hungarian population showed considerable readiness to accept them as liberators. This attitude made it possible in the latter part of December to hold elections for a provisional assembly in the greater part of the country which had now been freed from the Germans. The assembly, meeting at Debrecen on December 21, set up a provisional government under General Miklos. The new government declared war on Germany on December 29, and on January 20 armistice terms were signed with the United Nations. In broad outline the terms followed those already accepted by Rumania and Bulgaria, with Hungary agreeing to give up the territory she had taken from her neighbours, to provide 8 divisions against Germany, and to pay reparations amounting to $300 million.

In spite of these developments, the Germans were not ready to give up Hungary for lost. The vital strategic importance of Budapest —which a German military spokesman described on December 7 as "the principal storm centre of military operations on all fronts"—impelled them to an effort to save it from its impending doom. The garrison defended the city street by street. Resistance in Pest was at last crushed on January 18, and by that time the greater part of Buda was in Russian hands; but the German remnant in the area around the castle fought desperately on, and from outside the Germans launched a powerful attempt to break through to their rescue.

It was significant of the importance the Germans attached to this enterprise that, even with the great Russian winter offensive impending in Poland, tank forces were shifted from that area to Hungary. When the Sixth Panzer Army was withdrawn from the west after the Ardennes offensive, it too was reported south of the Carpathians. The German blow was struck on January 2 with strong infantry forces spearheaded by 6 tank divisions, and the effort was sustained for a month before it was finally frustrated.

The first thrust was directed along the south bank of the Danube. At the outset it met with considerable success. Esztergom was recaptured on January 6; but beyond that point the drive was halted, and persistent attempts to break through due west of the capital were halted in a week of fighting some 15 miles from the outskirts. Balked in their direct approach, the Germans struck farther south in a flanking attempt. They broke through above Lake Balaton, capturing Szekesfehervar on January 21 and driving on to reach the Danube. But here too they were checked short of their goal. The Russians established a line between Lake Velencz and the Danube 15 miles below Budapest and held firm against all attacks. By the end of January they had regained the initiative. Counter-attacks on either side of the corridor dislodged the Germans from the Danube and forced them back toward Szekesfehervar. Meanwhile their temporary success south of the Danube was being offset by continued Russian gains north of the river, where Malinovsky and Petrov maintained their dogged advance. German efforts to stabilize a firm line in Slovakia and northwest Hungary were unavailing.

Lucenec was taken by the Russians on January 14. Kosice, after a prolonged struggle, fell on January 20. Immediately north of the Danube, Malinovsky swept across the Hron in strength and drove to the outskirts of Komarno. With the steady advance below the Carpathians and the mighty offensive in progress farther north, the failure of the German thrust toward Budapest could not be retrieved by drawing strength from other fronts for a renewed effort. The check was decisive, and sealed the fate of Budapest. On February 13, after seven weeks of fighting, the remaining Germans in the castle area surrendered and the ruins of the once lovely city were completely in Russian hands. By Russian estimates the defence had cost the Germans 49,000 killed and 130,000 captured, in addition to heavy losses in the abortive effort at relief. The costly effort to bar the road to Vienna had ended in failure, and at a price which the Germans could ill afford.

ADVANCE IN THE PACIFIC

When Roosevelt and Churchill and their advisers met at Quebec in August 1943, one of their basic tasks was to define the relation between the operations in the European area and those in the Far East. At an earlier stage, when the defeat of Germany was accorded first priority, it was assumed that this would restrict the effort against Japan to little more than a holding war. But the expansion of American war production and the increasing flow of power that was becoming available seemed to open up wider prospects. The initiation of an offensive against Japan no longer needed to wait on the end of the struggle in Europe. The crushing of Germany remained the first objective, but the decision was taken to prosecute the war in Orient with the fullest vigour compatible with the demands of the European theatre.

This was a decision of basic importance. It was amplified and expanded at a second conference at Quebec in September 1944. With the collapse of Germany in sight, detailed plans were discussed for the shifting of the full weight of Allied power against Japan. Britain successfully pressed for a larger share in the coming operations in the Pacific than had previously been contemplated by the United States; and the relative rôles of these two Powers, as well as of Canada and Australia and the Netherlands, were defined with greater precision.

The plans thus laid, and the consequent assignment of strength to the Pacific, were based on somewhat optimistic calculations about the progress of the European war. This was particularly true at the second Quebec conference which met while the Allied armies were sweeping through France and Belgium and the collapse of Germany seemed assured before the year's end. The stiffening of German resistance behind the Westwall, followed in December by Rundstedt's offensive in the Ardennes, falsified the high hopes that were entertained at the beginning of September. The revelation of how slender a margin of strength the Allies possessed in the west came as a further shock to the public at large. One result was a tendency to blame the Quebec decisions for these developments, and to feel that victory in Europe had been delayed by the decision to prosecute a full-scale offensive in the Pacific.

Such views had at most a limited validity. The Pacific absorbed men and supplies, and above all shipping. But in Europe during the autumn the dominating problem was to provide the existing forces with an adequate amount of the available supplies, and this resulted not from a shortage of shipping, but from the disruption of land communications and the lack of adequate ports. It was only after the capture of Antwerp that these difficulties were overcome. There may then have been a certain time lag occasioned by a shortage of shipping in the Atlantic; but by the end of the year this had been remedied, and fresh divisions were pouring in to provide the power for the final offensive. From then on the remaining stringency had its chief effect in curtailing the supplies available to the civil population in the liberated lands rather than in restricting military operations.

There was in fact a strong case for prosecuting the war against Japan with all possible vigour, perhaps even at the price of a limited delay in achieving victory in Europe. It is true that some of the considerations were political, but even these could not be ignored. Account had to be taken of the considerable body of opinion in the United States which refused to recognize the paramount importance of an early defeat of Germany and felt that the national effort should be directed chiefly against Japan. Even more critical was the desperate state to which China was reduced after seven years of war. Her accumulated economic and political problems had all but eliminated her as a military factor in the struggle. But her formal continuance in the war absorbed Japanese strength; and to sustain this, it was of the highest importance to keep her hopes of ultimate victory alive by tangible evidence that every possible effort was being made by her allies and that her rescue was fast approaching. Beyond such considerations, however, lay motives of fundamental strategy. The more time Japan was allowed to consolidate her gains, the longer and harder would be the task of subduing her. It was vital to subject her to the maximum pressure, to undermine her strength by a steady process of attrition, to accelerate the process of penetrating her outer defences, so that when the end of the European war allowed a full concentration against her the preliminary stages would be passed and everything would be prepared for an effort at a knockout blow.

A determining factor in the situation was the steady increase in Allied naval power, which included air power as an integral component. By the autumn of 1944, Allied superiority had reached overwhelming proportions. American forces, including a score of carriers and nearly as many battleships, served alternately as the Third and Fifth Fleets. Admiral Nimitz in August described the organization of duplicate command teams which provided each of the two fleets with its own amphibious corps, and made possible a continuous offensive in which one group carried out the current operations while the other was planning and preparing for the next in the series. In addition, the strong British force of modern battle-ships and aircraft carriers which had been assembled in Far Eastern waters was now to be employed chiefly in the Pacific in co-ordination with American operations. This overwhelming might represented an asset which could no longer be employed with advantage in the European theatre. The only question was whether it should be restricted to limited operations in the Pacific, or whether an effort would be made to exploit it to the utmost by the provision of the necessary means. With such a weapon at hand, it was almost inconceivable that the leaders at Quebec should refrain from a decision to use it to the full.

The result was an impressive demonstration of mounting offensive power. In the year that followed the first conference at Quebec, the Allied forces in the Pacific overran New Guinea and swept from the Solomons to the Marianas. Powerful Japanese bases such as Truk were bypassed and neutralized. Strong Japanese garrisons in the Pacific islands were left stranded thousands of miles behind the Allied advance. In spite of their isolation, these enemy forces maintained a stubborn resistance, and the task of mopping them up was arduous and inglorious. Australian troops met bitter and sustained resistance on New Guinea and Bougainville. Even after the Americans established effective control over the Marianas, it took months to root out the surviving Japanese from hills and caves. But these tasks detracted nothing from the power of the main offensive, which went forward with lengthening strides. By the end of the third year of the war in the Pacific, the Allies were poised before Japan's inner defensive ring and their air power was striking with growing weight against Japan itself. Though the monthly total of bombs dropped by the B-29's had only recently reached the modest figure of 1500 tons, the experimental stage was almost over, and the establishment of the big bombers on new bases in the Marianas heralded a methodical campaign of increasing weight against the chief cities and production centres of Japan.

These developments transformed the whole strategic outlook in the Far East. The weakness of Japanese sea and air power was glaringly revealed. The breaking of Japan's grip on her sea com-

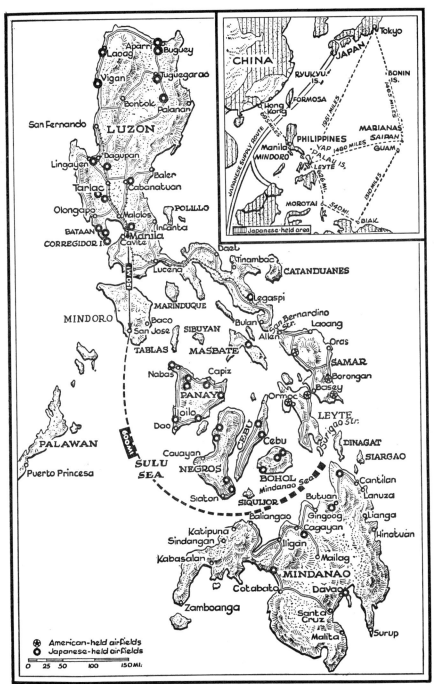

By permission of the New York *Times*

THE PHILIPPINES

munications with her recently conquered empire was already in sight; and with the cutting of the supply lines, the task of regaining the lands which Japan had seized dwindled in magnitude. The reconquest of Burma from the north, which had once seemed a hopeless enterprise to all but a few enthusiasts, now entered the realm of practicability. The inability of Japan to control the sea approaches to the mainland of Asia, or even to her home islands, brought nearer the day when the final struggle would be joined; and the advocates of a direct attack on Japan found increasing support from the growing possibility of an invasion without waiting for the prolonged softening-up from air bases in China which more cautious strategists had once envisaged as essential.

ADVANCE TO THE PHILIPPINES

With the conquest of the Marianas and the advance to the western tip of New Guinea, the Philippines were clearly the next major goal. There were still however intermediate steps which were felt necessary before a direct attack could be launched on that strongly garrisoned position. Japanese forces and air bases on such islands as Yap and Palau and Halmahera stood across the approaches to the Philippines from the south. But with these eliminated or neutralized, the way would be clear for a converging attack from the central and southwest Pacific against the main objective.

During the late summer, Allied land-based planes conducted a wide-ranging offensive against Japanese island air bases in the western Pacific. Halmahera was attacked with special persistence, and with such effect that by the third week in August a considerable number of its airfields had been rendered inoperative. The assault was extended to the Japanese air bases on southern Mindanao, and smaller but repeated attacks were kept up against other bases from Palau to Truk.

On August 31 the navy joined in an offensive designed to isolate the next invasion objectives. Operating over a wide arc from Wake to the Philippines, carrier forces attached to the Third Fleet struck at air bases and ravaged shipping in the chief Japanese island strong-holds. The Bonin and Volcano islands were hit on three successive days, and this was followed by a three-day assault on Yap and Ulithi. On September 9 an attack on Mindanao inaugurated a series of blows against aircraft and shipping in the Philippines. From the 12th to the 14th the carriers struck at the islands of Cebu, Negros, Panay and Leyte. In these three days 198 Japanese planes were destroyed in the air or on the ground, and strong air opposition encountered at the outset had vanished by the final day. While Japanese supporting air power was thus being crushed, the immediate objective of Palau was being softened up for invasion. A fighter strafe on September 6 was followed by a bombardment by warships next day; and on September 10 there began a concerted series of daily attacks which formed the prelude to invasion.

The blow fell on September 15. In two co-ordinated operations, MacArthur's forces bypassed Halmahera and seized the smaller adjacent island of Morotai, while the 1st Marine Division, by-passing in their turn the stronghold of Babelthuap, drove ashore on Peleliu in the Palau group. Two days later the Palau invasion was broadened by a landing on the island of Angaur a few miles south of Peleliu; and on the 23rd, far to the northeast, the island of Ulithi was occupied to complete the outflanking of Yap.

Peleliu was the chief centre of the subsequent struggle. On the other islands control was established with comparatively little difficulty, but the attack on Peleliu met resistance as fierce as any yet encountered in the Pacific. The garrison, which had sheltered in caves against the covering naval bombardment, dashed out to meet the landing forces with a storm of fire. In fierce fighting the marines established a narrow but firm beachhead during the first day, and from this foothold they pushed on to surround and capture the island's airfield. But the Japanese fought back desperately from the ridges beyond, and it was only on September 23 that the deadlock was broken. The marines, reinforced by the 81st Division which had captured Angaur, swept the length of the 6-mile island during the next three days, and trapped the remnants of the Japanese garrison in the hills and caves of Bloody Nose Ridge. By October 7 all serious opposition had been crushed, with Japanese losses of 11,083 killed and 214 captured as against fewer than 1000 American dead; yet for another two months the few survivors of the garrison kept alive a dwindling resistance while the grim process went on of eliminating them one by one.

Throughout the struggle the navy continued its vigorous activities which prevented any effective Japanese aid to the invaded islands. The bombardment which covered the landing was followed by a resumption of the attack on air and naval bases in the Philippines. On September 21 and 22, carrier aircraft struck in force at Cavite and the airfields in the area of Manila bay, sinking 40 ships and destroying over 350 Japanese planes in the air or on the ground. A further blow was struck on September 24 against airfields on Cebu and Negros as well as on Luzon and against shipping in the waters adjacent to those islands. The naval operations were supplemented by continued raids by land-based planes, whose extended range was illustrated by attacks on the important oil centre of Balik Papan and by the bombing of Batavia from bases in Australia. These attacks brought to a climax a month that was disastrous for the Japanese. Nearly 2000 planes were destroyed during September. The front line of Japanese air defence was pushed back to the northern Philippines, and fresh inroads were made on both shipping and naval facilities. "The operations of the Third Fleet", said a communiqué on September 24, "have forced the enemy to withdraw his naval forces from their former anchorages in the Philippines and to seek new refuges in the same general area, have disrupted inter-island communications, and have broken his air force in the Philippines."

These results opened the way for thrusts still deeper into the Japanese zone. On October 10, after a diversionary bombardment of Marcus island the previous day, a carrier force struck at the chief bases in the Ryukyu islands stretching between Japan and Formosa. A still more daring stroke followed. There was a covering attack on Luzon on October 11; then on the following day the carrier forces swept boldly in against Formosa. For three successive days they battered at this strongly defended base, the main bastion guarding the approach to the coast of China. On October 14 the B-29's took over the attack, and they struck again on the 16th and 17th. Meanwhile the fleet had turned its attention once more to the Philippines. On the 14th its fighter planes strafed Aparri in northern Luzon; and on the 18th a fresh blow at the Manila area inaugurated a sustained and comprehensive assault on the main bases throughout the Philippines.

The results were shattering to the Japanese. In the operations from October 10 to 18 inclusive they lost over 1000 planes, and they had shown themselves completely impotent to prevent the incursion of powerful forces into the very heart of their island defences. They had thrown strong forces of planes against the ships attacking Formosa and Luzon, but the effort had only added to their losses. That did not prevent them from putting out claims of an overwhelming victory. By October 18 their mythical total reached 11 carriers and 2 battleships sunk and 8 carriers and 2 battleships damaged, as well as a heavy toll of smaller ships and the virtual extinction of the Third Fleet. But in fact no major unit received more than superficial damage, and the reported death of 22 Japanese admirals during the past seven weeks was a profound indication of the discouragement which recent setbacks had spread in the circles most directly affected. Part of the Japanese fleet, perhaps misled by propaganda claims, did in fact issue from its Formosa base at the height of the attack; but the sight of the unimpaired strength of the Third Fleet was enough to dissipate its desire for combat and to send it scurrying once more into hiding.

The success of these bold thrusts confirmed the weakness of Japanese air and naval power which had already been revealed by the operations in September, and which had led to a significant change in invasion plans. Initially the invasion of the Moluccas and the Palaus had been intended as a converging operation preliminary to a landing on Mindanao in November. But the situation now disclosed made it possible not only to advance the date, but to strike at a more advanced point. It was decided to bypass Mindanao and the southern part of the Philippines, to abandon a projected attack on Yap, and to advance by two months the date for the invasion of the central island of Leyte. Together with the adjacent island of Samar across a narrow channel to the north, Leyte controlled the only passages through the Philippine chain; and a firm foothold in that area would threaten to split the Japanese forces defending the larger islands and provide a pivot from which American forces could strike in several alternative directions against the main parts of the archipelago.

The carrier raids in a wide arc from the Ryukyus through Formosa to the Philippines were thus calculated to pave the way for the new invasion by pushing back Japanese supporting air power. The assault on Formosa impeded, though it did not wholly prevent, air reinforcement of the Philippines. The sustained attack which followed on Philippine bases was meant to blanket Japanese air power throughout that area. Further preparatory steps were taken when three islands guarding the approaches to Leyte gulf were seized on October 17 and minesweepers boldly cleared the channel for the invading force. Then on October 20 the attack struck, and General MacArthur accomplished the first step in his promised return to the Philippines from which he had been driven nearly three years before.

THE STRUGGLE FOR LEYTE

The landing caught the Japanese by surprise. They had apparently expected it on Mindanao, and even the preliminary operations at the entrance to the gulf had not put them on guard. The garrison was chiefly composed of a single division, supplemented by other units which brought the total strength to around 24,000 men. The American invading force was composed of 4 divisions of the Sixth Army, organized in two corps of 2 divisions each. The 24th and 1st

Cavalry Divisions landed just below the town of Tacloban. The 7th and 96th went ashore 15 miles farther south in the vicinity of Dulag, while a small force was detached to seize the southeastern tip of the island and the adjacent island of Panaon.

The two forces drove inland against initially light opposition, except from an enemy concentration at the lower end of the northern beachhead. By October 22 they had taken the towns of Tacloban and Dulag with their adjacent airfields, and during the next few days they extended their control over the island of Samar. By this time however the Japanese had rallied from the shock and were fighting back fiercely. Whatever Japanese propagandists might say about the imminent destruction of the invaders, the Japanese leaders had no illusions about the critical nature of the struggle which had now been joined. Leyte was a stark and inescapable test of their ability to bring the continued American offensive to a halt, and into that effort they threw not only fresh troops, but also the bulk of their long-hoarded fleet.

The immediate aim of the Japanese counterstroke was to wipe out the transports and supply ships in Leyte gulf. Having failed to intercept the invasion expedition, the Japanese fleet now embarked on a belated effort to smash it before its task was completed. The full strength of the American force was not yet ashore; and if the ships could be destroyed—and still more if the Japanese could regain naval ascendancy in the waters around the Philippines—the American troops already on Leyte would be temporarily isolated and exposed to destruction by the Japanese ground and air forces.

The outcome of the plan depended to a very considerable extent on the success of the preliminary air attack on the American covering forces. This was one main task of the Japanese force which struck down from the north between Luzon and Formosa. It included 4 carriers, one of them of the large *Zuikaku* class, and 2 hybrid carrier-battleships of the *Ise* class fitted with flight decks aft, in addition to 5 cruisers and 6 destroyers. The plan was to strike with strong forces of planes from land bases on the Philippines; then, with American air strength fully engaged, the planes from the carriers would be sent in at long range against the unprotected American carriers. After the completion of their mission they would land at bases in the Philippines to refuel and to join in the subsequent attack which would finish off the shipping in Leyte gulf. Meanwhile, and even more important, the northern force would draw off the covering strength of the Third fleet, sacrificing itself if necessary to expose the beach-head to a decisive blow.

The main attack was to be delivered by a powerful surface force striking from two directions. The smaller of the two divisions headed to the south of Leyte toward Surigao strait. It consisted of 2 battleships of the elderly *Yamashiro* class, 4 cruisers and 13 destroyers. This presented the most immediate threat to Leyte gulf and would draw American surface strength to oppose it. Simultaneously a stronger force would drive through San Bernardino strait above Samar and strike down from the north. This division had 5 battle-ships, including 2 of the new *Musashi* class of over 40,000 tons, a dozen cruisers and 15 destroyers. From its size and composition it was clear that this was the force designed to deliver the decisive blow.

The plan, though bold and skilful, represented a desperate gamble in the face of the overwhelming strength of the American naval forces in the area of attack. The attack on Leyte represented the converging of the Central and Southwest Pacific Commands and brought two fleets into action. The Seventh under Admiral Kincaid was engaged in direct support of the landing. The Third under Admiral Halsey had the broader task of covering the whole operation from inter-ference by air as well as by sea. In spite of its carrier sweeps against Japanese air bases in the Philippines, the enemy fields had not been put out of action. Japanese land-based planes struck persistently against the landing forces and their convoys, and the attacks had to be met by American carrier planes. It was not until October 27 that the first land-based fighters were set down on Leyte's rude airstrips. Until that date the whole task of providing air cover rested on the navy.

The approach of the main Japanese surface fleet through the South China Sea was detected by American submarines early on October 23. Word was flashed back, and submarine attacks were launched which sank 2 cruisers and damaged 2 others. Next day carrier planes made contact with the Japanese; and in spite of the heavy air attack which the Japanese launched on that day against American ships and positions, the Americans struck heavy air blows against the approaching Japanese ships. The battleship *Musashi* was sunk. The enemy air attacks were beaten off. The light carrier *Princeton* was lost in the course of the battle, but even attacks by Japanese suicide pilots failed to inflict serious damage on the rest of the fleet. The American carrier forces remained almost intact, both as to planes and to ships.

Meanwhile the Japanese forces had already suffered serious attrition from submarine and air attacks. By the afternoon of October 24, damage of varying seriousness had been inflicted on at least 3 battleships and 7 cruisers as well as a number of destroyers, and hits had been scored on nearly all the ships involved. In spite of these attacks, the southern force kept on toward Surigao strait; but the central force heading for San Bernardino strait was so seriously mauled that it turned back on its course, and it looked as though this part of the attack had been abandoned.

It was just at this stage that Admiral Halsey received word of the approach of the northern force of carriers and battleships. Leaving Admiral Kincaid to deal with the threat from the south, Halsey swung his whole force away from the Leyte area and raced north to intercept the approaching Japanese. To guard San Bernardino strait there remained only a handful of light carriers detached from the Seventh Fleet, with a few destroyers in support.

During the night a part of the southern Japanese force consisting of 2 battleships, a heavy cruiser and 4 destroyers steamed ahead through the narrow waters of Surigao strait toward the ambush that had been prepared for it. Across the mouth of the strait to the east lay 6 American battleships, 5 of them salvaged from the disaster at Pearl Harbour, with cruisers in support. Ahead of them were two squadrons of destroyers lying in wait on either side of the narrows, and still farther down the strait the PT boats were alert for the enemy. Contact was made shortly after midnight by the smaller craft, which launched a torpedo attack and disappeared into the darkness. Three hours later the Japanese ran into the destroyer ambush and were again attacked with torpedoes; and almost at once they also came under the fire of the cruisers and battleships lying in wait for them. Hopelessly outmatched and with little room to manoeuvre, the Japanese tried to turn and escape. Almost none of them succeeded. A damaged light cruiser made its way out of the straits only to be caught and finished off by planes after daylight. The rest of the Japanese force went down under the guns of the American ships.

Within a few hours the northern carrier force had also met with disaster. Their planes had been sent off to take part in the air attack on October 24, and had not yet returned from refuelling on Luzon. When Halsey located the Japanese carriers after dark their decks were virtually bare. This force too turned and retired once contact was made, but pursuit was continued into the morning of October 25. Three carriers were sunk from the air. The fourth carrier was crippled and was later sunk by a cruiser. A damaged Japanese cruiser was sunk by a submarine during the following night. Almost all the remaining ships, including the two battleships, received hits of varying seriousness, and there were prospects that the whole force could be destroyed if pursuit were maintained.

But the complete victory which seemed in sight at dawn on October 25 was suddenly jeopardized by a new and alarming development. This was the reappearance of the central Japanese force, the most powerful of the three. After retiring on the previous day, it reversed its course under cover of darkness and made its way at high speed through San Bernardino strait. The *Musashi* had by this time disappeared, but 4 other battleships with strong accompanying forces issued from the straits at dawn, to find themselves confronted only by 6 American escort carriers and 7 destroyers and destroyer escorts.

The Japanese still had nearly 200 miles' sailing before they could reach Leyte gulf, and there they would find stronger opposition awaiting them. They had lost time by their double reversal of course and could no longer hope to co-ordinate their attack with that of the southern force. Admiral Kincaid had already won his victory and was free to turn against the new threat. But the Japanese force was not far inferior to his own, which was now almost out of ammunition, and his fleet was too distant and dispersed to come to the immediate aid of the light forces off San Bernardino strait. Calls at once went out to Admiral Halsey for help, obliging him to abandon air pursuit of the northern force. Leaving part of his surface force to mop up the stragglers, he turned his carriers about and raced toward the new scene of action.

Meanwhile the small American ships were undergoing a terrible ordeal. Confronted with an overwhelming enemy force, the light carriers and their accompanying destroyers tried to escape by flight. But the superior speed of the Japanese ships enabled them to head off the Americans and to close the range rapidly. The small force was battered by the heavy guns of battleships and cruisers. Planes from the carriers struck at the Japanese ships but were unable to hold them off. One of the carriers was hit and lost speed. Two destroyers and a destroyer escort, in a final desperate effort to save the wounded ship, hurled themselves at the Japanese in a suicide torpedo attack. Though they went down under heavy fire, as did the damaged carrier, the fury of their assault caused the Japanese to waver and temporarily checked the attack. But the pursuit was shortly resumed, and by mid-morning the range had been closed to 12,000 yards and the remaining American ships seemed doomed to annihilation.

Then suddenly the Japanese broke off the battle and turned in retreat. The rearguard forays of the American planes and destroyers had already cost the enemy 2 cruisers and possibly 1 destroyer. His force was by no means fatally weakened; but in the light of the disaster to both the northern and southern forces, a continued advance would risk encounter with the full combined strength of Halsey and Kincaid. The Japanese were unprepared for this particular suicide venture. They turned back through San Bernardino strait, and it was only after their retreat had begun that the first planes from Halsey's carriers came into action to harry them during their flight and to add still further to their losses.

The defeat cost the Japanese heavily. The battleships *Fuso* and *Yamashiro* were sunk in Surigao strait. The modern battleship *Musashi* from the central force was also lost. All 4 carriers of the northern force were destroyed, and further losses from the first contact on October 23 to the final aerial blows on October 27 totalled 10 cruisers and 9 destroyers. Other ships were so heavily hit that even if they were able to make port they would be out of action for a protracted period. Out of the three forces engaged, only a handful of destroyers escaped without damage. American losses were 1 light carrier, 2 escort carriers, 2 destroyers and 1 destroyer escort.

Japanese sea power had failed in its attempt to save Leyte, and its crippling losses forbade any renewal of the effort. The burden fell squarely on the shoulders of the land forces supported by air power from the neighbouring islands. The task was taken up with desperate energy. For almost the first time since their expulsion from the Solomons, the Japanese were in a position to reinforce their embattled garrison in spite of American naval ascendancy. Fresh troops were thrown into Leyte, and the braggart General Yamashita, the conqueror of Singapore, took command with the avowed intention of repeating his triumph against MacArthur.

The Americans countered with renewed efforts to isolate Leyte. With the danger of interference from the main Japanese fleet now removed, the Third Fleet resumed the work of interdicting Japanese reinforcements and air support. Six times during November the carriers of Halsey's fleet struck at Luzon in an attempt to wreck Japanese air bases. Nine convoys carrying troops and supplies to Leyte had been heavily attacked by mid-December. But in spite of substantial Japanese losses in planes and ships and men, embittered resistance continued on Leyte. Elements of 5 Japanese divisions were involved by November, and the garrison was maintained at a strength of between 40,000 and 50,000 men. Admitting the seriousness of the situation, the Tokyo radio described the struggle as "the decisive battle in which we cannot withdraw even a single step, for we have burned our bridges behind us".

As a result, the Americans after the initial success of their landings were confronted by a fierce and sustained resistance which imposed a deadlock for nearly two months. American forces on Leyte were steadily increased to a total strength of 7 divisions. They pushed the Japanese back from the eastern and southern portions of the island, but the defenders established themselves in strong hill positions stretching from Ormoc bay to Carigara bay, covering the northwest part of Leyte and the port of Ormoc into which reinforcements continued to flow. Against this Yamashita Line the attacks made slow progress. Typhoons lashed the island, deluging it with 24 inches of rain in the course of a month and turning the ground to mud. Airfields that had been painfully repaired or improvised had to be abandoned. The Japanese tactics of fighting it out on this advanced line held prospects of imposing a serious delay on the campaign to reconquer the Philippines.

The deadlock was broken by an amphibious outflanking move. Unable to break the defence by frontal attack, MacArthur boldly sent an expedition around the southern end of the island to land at Ormoc and threaten the garrison from the rear. It struck almost simultaneously with a Japanese effort to disorganize the Americans by dropping parachute forces behind their lines. But the airborne attackers were quickly wiped out, and the landing just south of Ormoc took place on December 7 with little difficulty. Ormoc itself was taken on December 10, depriving the Japanese of the supply port on which they were so dependent; and by this time the southern part of the defences had been nipped off between the landing force and the Americans attacking from the east. There was another fortnight of hard fighting as the Japanese line was assailed from both ends; but the line was broken on December 21 and the remnants of the garrison were herded into the peninsula to the west of Ormoc bay. Although the usual tedious process of mopping-up remained, the capture of the coastal village of Palompon by amphibious attack on December 25 virtually ended the Leyte campaign. It had cost the Japanese over 77,000 dead on the island in addition to heavy losses in convoys, against 2630 Americans killed; and the way was now cleared for a more vigorous prosecution of the campaign against the main Philippine islands which had already been carried a step further by the invasion of Mindoro on December 15.

2

JANUARY TO APRIL 1945

FROM THE VISTULA TO THE ODER

THROUGHOUT the autumn of 1944, one vital sector of the siege arc that was closing on Germany lay in ominous quiet. From Warsaw south to the foothills of the Carpathians, no action of importance took place between the early part of August and the close of the year. The Russian armies were far from idle during this period. In the north they cleared the whole of the Baltic States except for the Courland peninsula. In the south their formidable and sustained offensive swept up the Danube and closed the ring around the doomed garrison in Budapest. Yet these achievements, important as they were, could not obscure the fact that the real area of decision lay beyond the Vistula. Friend and foe alike hung on the anticipation of a new and massive blow along the front which stretched from the Baltic to the Carpathians. This, and this alone, would mark the full unleashing of Russia's offensive power. By comparison with past performances and future prospects, even operations on the scale of those in Hungary seemed secondary in scope and significance.

This protracted pause on the main part of the eastern front, broken only by the brief and limited thrust against East Prussia in October, was in one sense a legacy of Russia's very success during the previous months. The summer offensive had carried the Red Army across the vast stretch of territory between the upper Dnieper and the Vistula. It had exhausted its impetus before Warsaw and the borders of East Prussia. The Germans had rallied to make a stand on one of the major natural defence lines guarding the eastern approaches to the Reich. It was bolstered by strong fortified positions, and behind it lay an efficient network of communications and supply bases. The Germans in retreat had lessened the distance between their armies in the east and their centres of war production, particularly the relatively undamaged centres in Silesia as well as the more battered industrial area of Berlin. The Russians in contrast were once more beset by the problem of lengthening supply routes and the relative scantiness of communications and bases in eastern Poland. Time was needed to overcome these difficulties and to mass the weapons and resources necessary for the resumption of the offensive.

The magnitude of the task was increased by the tremendous scope of Russia's offensive plans. The objective was not merely to dislodge the Germans from their existing positions, but to overwhelm their whole defensive system in one crushing assault and to sweep forward in an irresistible tide which would brush aside all efforts by the shattered enemy to rally on new lines short of the German border. Marshal Rokossovsky, commenting on the German stand at Warsaw and on the middle Vistula, stressed the Russian determination to avoid any such wearing battle of attrition as that which had proved so ruinous to the Germans at Stalingrad. Berlin was the ultimate goal of the Red Army, and it had no intention of compromising its main offensive effort by exhausting its forces against more limited objectives. His remarks were illustrated not only by the Russian halt before Warsaw, but by the abandonment of the autumn drive on East Prussia as soon as it became clear that its success would involve a major effort. The Russians preferred to accept a temporary check on these sectors rather than to seek prestige victories at the risk of compromising their wider aims.

The preparations for breakthrough and pursuit on such a scale called for the massing of vast resources. Both on the Vistula and in East Prussia the Germans had thrown up extremely strong defences which must be forced in the first shock of assault. To achieve this the Russians relied heavily on artillery. The use of concentrated firepower, which had long been traditional with the Russian armies, had been an increasingly marked feature of the previous campaigns. For the new offensive the Russians gathered a greater weight of artillery than ever before, and the accumulation of guns and ammunition on an unprecedented scale was itself a major task during the months of preparation.

Yet even this was overshadowed by the preparations that were necessary for the full exploitation of the breakthrough. In the past two years the Germans had become expert in disengaging their main forces once their lines were broken, and in carrying out a rapid retreat which gradually shook off pursuit and enabled them to rally in new positions. The very swiftness with which the advance moved forward in their wake meant that the supply services had difficulty in keeping pace, and the diminishing power of the offensive gave the Germans the time they needed to consolidate. Once the Russian drive was set in motion, the urgent task was to maintain its momentum at the maximum for the longest possible period.

This called first of all for strong tank forces. West of the Vistula there were no major natural barriers between that river and the Oder. There were strongly fortified centres which the Germans might turn into pillars of a new defence system if they were allowed a breathing space. But the open Polish plain was ideal for a massive armoured sweep which would keep the enemy on the run and out-flank the chief strongholds before they could be linked in a coherent defensive line. The process of accumulating the thousands of tanks needed for this aspect of the offensive was in itself enough to account for the comparative quiescence of the Russians in Poland throughout the autumn. The weather added another and highly significant factor. In Poland the Russians were unable to count on the sustained cold which had hardened the ground during their previous winter campaigns; but it was at least desirable that the operations should be launched at a time when frosts offered the most favourable conditions for mobility.

It was not only the tanks to which these conditions were important. One of the features of the ensuing drive was the closeness with which mobile infantry followed up the armoured spearheads, consolidating their gains and minimizing the danger from counter-attacks. Such tactics were only possible on the basis of a vast and efficient system of communications and supply. The Russians in their previous offensives had astonished the outside world by their ability to keep large armies moving over long distances under the most difficult conditions. A Russian general, asked for the secret of their success, replied: "It is very simple—we just put a lot of people on the job and the supplies get forward." But while manpower was one explanation, it was far from the whole answer. Resources and facilities and organization all had to be available in abundance. Tremendous stores had to be accumulated in bases immediately behind the front, and great fleets of transport vehicles had to be gathered in readiness for the surge toward the west.

The eve of the offensive found the Russians with forces that were vastly superior to the enemy in both men and *matériel*. At the beginning of the year it was estimated that the Germans had approximately 160 divisions north of the Carpathians. Against them the Russians were credited with some 300 infantry divisions and 25 tank corps, and with strong cavalry formations in addition. Roughly two-thirds of these forces were thrown into the initial stage of the offensive. The rest were fed in rapidly to sustain and broaden the pursuit. With such a margin of strength the Russians were able to engage along virtually the whole front simultaneously. Their opening blows were struck at selected points, but on broad sectors which tore gaping holes in the German defences and brought the collapse of the entire line.

This crushing offensive power was increased by Russian superiority in the air. At the opening of the offensive, bad weather grounded planes on both sides, and the decisive rôle fell to the artillery; but by January 17 the air arm came into play, and fierce combats raged over the battlefront. The Russians maintained their mastery of the skies; and although the Germans shifted a large part of their hoarded reserves from the west, their desperate efforts failed to redress the balance in the air or to blunt the Russian spearheads on the ground. Their plight in the east was aggravated by the activities of the Allied bombers striking from the west. As the Russians advanced, Allied planes struck at the centres through which German supplies and reinforcements were directed toward the front. Strong forces of Mosquitos harried Berlin with nightly attacks. Fortresses subjected the capital to its most concentrated raid of the war on February 3. Dresden was hit by a paralyzing succession of night and day raids between February 13 and 15, and the important junctions of Chemnitz and Cottbus were heavily bombed during the same period. A less direct contribution, but one that was even more telling in its ultimate effect, was the sustained offensive which by mid-February had all but wiped out German oil production. The Russian claim to have captured 345 grounded planes in the Glogau area on February 12, and over 500 more at various airfields during the two following days, gave striking proof of the extent to which the *Luftwaffe* had been crippled by the destruction of its sources of fuel.

The offensive was launched by four great army groups. On January 12 it opened with an assault by the First Ukrainian group under Marshal Konev which struck from the upper Vistula toward Cracow and Silesia. On the same day General Chernyakhovsky on the Third White Russian front opened a preliminary attack which was the prelude to a full-scale drive toward Koenigsberg.[1] With

---

[1] The career of the brilliant young Chernyakhovsky was cut short by a fatal wound in February. He was succeeded in his command by Marshal Alexander M. Vasilevsky.

the assault in progress on both flanks, the armies in the centre struck two days later. Marshal Rokossovsky, who had replaced Zakharov in command of the Second White Russian front, attacked toward East Prussia from the southeast in an enveloping assault that was co-ordinated with that of Chernyakhovsky. His previous command, the First White Russian Front, was now under Marshal Zhukov whose simultaneous attack swept around Warsaw and opened the way for a massive and expanding drive toward the Oder and Berlin. Meanwhile in the north the Germans isolated in Courland were pinned down by holding attacks; and on Konev's southern flank the dogged advance of Petrov astride the Carpathians protected the advance on Silesia and formed a link with the operations in Slovakia and Hungary.

In the existing circumstances the Russians could have little hope of achieving strategic surprise. The actual timing of the attack could be concealed until it was loosed, but the main points of assault and the major objectives were implicit in the situation. The Germans fully expected a dual drive on East Prussia and an effort against Warsaw and an offensive by Konev from the Sandomierz bridgehead. The element of surprise which was actually attained lay in the magnitude of these operations. The Germans recognized that they might have to give way before the first shock, but they believed they could contain the offensive for limited gains. The unprecedented speed and power of the Russian offensive scattered all their calculations to the winds. Within a few days the German commentators were openly admitting that all hope of a successful stand against the overwhelming Russian might had for the moment been abandoned. "What is going on on the eastern front has no parallel in the whole history of the war", said one of them. "Things have happened which have brought the war to a stage which can be called downright decisive." General Dittmar put it even more plainly when he spoke of the situation as being balanced on a razor's edge. The crushing weight of the new Russian blows swept the Germans in one furious rush from the last broad belt of territory guarding their borders in the east, and left them starkly confronting the doom which was rapidly closing on the Nazi Reich.

BREAKTHROUGH IN POLAND

Before Konev was brought to a final halt in the early autumn he had succeeded in establishing a roughly triangular bridgehead across the upper Vistula with its base resting on the 20-mile stretch from Sandomierz to Baranov. This position was of acute concern to the Germans. They had succeeded in containing the Russians and blocking their immediate threat to Cracow and Kielce; but they were unable to wipe out the bridgehead itself, and its existence constituted an ever-present threat, not merely to the industrial area of southern Poland and to Silesia beyond, but to the security of their whole Vistula line.

On January 12 Konev opened the winter offensive with a powerful attack along the southwest face of this salient. On a 25-mile front a tremendous concentration of over 300 guns to the mile shattered the German defence positions. The first two lines were overrun in a single day. The third and strongest line, with its trenches and fortified gun positions protected by a deep belt of minefields, was overcome in another 24 hours. In two days of fighting the Russians had torn a broad gap in the German defences, expanding their front to 37 miles and sweeping forward 25 miles from their starting point. The next German line along the Nida river covering the approaches to Cracow was stormed on January 14 before the Germans had time to man it properly. This meant a deep penetration below Kielce; and Konev, turning flank to front along the northern face of the salient, struck out from his right wing to take that stronghold on January 15. His front was thus broadened to over 70 miles; and while his left wing drove rapidly toward Cracow, his right struck directly west toward Czestochowa.

Meanwhile the line of the Vistula, seriously undermined by Konev's breakthrough, was giving way completely under the impact of the assault which Zhukov launched on January 14. This was a

double attack from two narrow bridgeheads which had been established across the Vistula some distance north and south of Deblin,
and its immediate task was to link the two prongs in one broad solid
front. In three days the aim was achieved. With the aid of massive
artillery support, Zhukov's forces broke through 12 miles of deeply
staggered defences and swept forward 38 miles on a front of 75 miles.
On the southern flank the fortress of Radom was captured on
January 16. On the northern flank the spearheads struck northwest,
overwhelming a German tank concentration and fanning out in a
sweep which rapidly outflanked Warsaw from the south and west.

The fate of the Polish capital was now sealed. To meet the main
drive which was swinging past and around it, another thrust struck
across the Vistula north of the city, its flank protected by
Rokossovsky's drive toward East Prussia which was simultaneously
in progress. The converging forces swung inward in a concerted
movement from north, west and south. Cut off from the rear and
with its strong frontal defences bypassed, Warsaw fell with hardly
a struggle on January 17, and Zhukov's triumphant forces swept
westward in a drive parallel with that of Konev to the south.

The tremendous scope and weight of these operations wrecked
all hopes that the Germans may have entertained of establishing a
new defence line in central and southern Poland. The natural pillars
for such a line were the fortresses of Torun and Lodz and Cracow.
As late as January 18 a German commentator was describing Cracow
as "the cornerstone of the present German rallying position". But
with the Russian tide rolling forward at a speed of up to 40 miles
a day, the Germans were overwhelmed before they could organize a
fresh stand. On January 17, the same day that Warsaw fell, Konev
thrust a broad wedge above Cracow with the capture of Czestochowa.
On the 19th his forces captured Cracow itself; and on the same day
Zhukov's capture of Lodz eliminated the chief barrier to the plains
of western Poland over which his armoured and motorized forces
could range almost at will. While the spearheads of the two army
groups continued their rapid westward advance, which by January 19

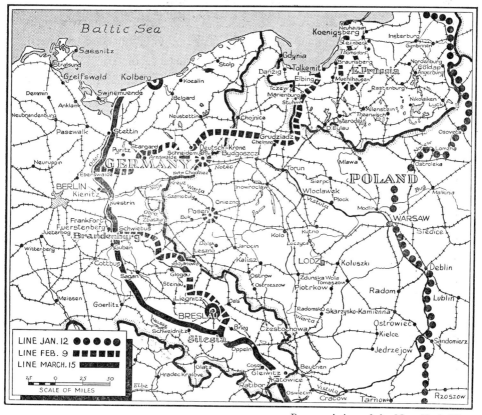

By permission of the New York *Times*

THE RUSSIAN WINTER OFFENSIVE

had already brought Konev to the Silesian border, Zhukov's right wing struck off in an immense wheeling movement to the north. Torun was outflanked and bypassed; the fortress of Bydgoszcz was overwhelmed on January 23; and beyond that point Zhukov's forces linked with the expanding left wing of Rokossovsky's armies to complete the encirclement of Torun on January 27.

This swift expansion accompanied by rapid shifts of direction kept the Germans continually off balance. West of Lodz they had brought up a considerable force of armour to meet the Russians frontally. But while Zhukov's left wing drove on along the railway through Kalisz and Ostrow, his powerful thrust on the right carried him around the flank of the German concentration. Before the enemy could take advantage of this manoeuvre by launching a counterstroke, part of the force advancing toward Bydgoszcz had wheeled again to the west. Breaking through a chain of lakes west of the Vistula, the tanks fanned out across open country, while the main body drove down the general line of the railway from Torun toward Poznan.

Poznan was a prime objective. The chief road and rail centre of western Poland, it was also a centre of war industries, including a large aircraft plant, and the Germans fought desperately to save it. Zhukov was checked in a furious three-day tank battle on its approaches, and it became evident that the defence was too strong for the town to be taken by immediate assault. Pinning down the main German forces by strong pressure from the east, Zhukov thrust two powerful columns across the Warthe north and south of Poznan. By January 26 the city had been bypassed on both sides, the line of the Warthe was broken in that sector, and the Russian spearheads drove toward the German border. Next day the ring was closed around Poznan on the same date that Rokossovsky completed the encirclement of Torun.

The isolation of these two centres had a double significance. In one aspect it showed that Russian offensive power was still unchecked, and that important strongholds could still be bypassed with impunity in view of the German inability to establish a coherent defence line.

Yet the fact that they were bypassed and not reduced was a sign that German resistance had begun to stiffen. In the first stages of the onslaught the chief centres had been stormed before their garrisons could organize an effective defence. Neither the fortified towns nor the German formations which the armoured spearheads had bypassed in the open were able to impose a serious delay on the Russian advance. Now for the first time since the offensive started the Germans retained their grip on important communication centres behind the main front. The effort was to use them as rocks in the stream, partially damming the flood and aiding in the task of erecting a permanent barrier farther to the west.

For the moment, however, neither frontal opposition nor the existence of hedgehogs in their rear imposed any serious check on Zhukov's armies. Their expanding sweep continued in a great arc which roughly paralleled the curving eastern frontiers of Brandenburg and Pomerania. West of Poznan they rolled forward on a broad front along the direct route toward Berlin, while to the north and northwest the powerful spearheads thrusting into Pomerania offered an increasing threat to Stettin.

Guarding the approaches to Berlin was the strong defensive zone of the Oder quadrilateral. Its western base was the Oder from Kuestrin south to a point some miles below Frankfort. There the river made a right-angle turn, its east-west course forming the lower side of the quadrilateral. The northern side was formed by the parallel course of the Warthe river which joined the Oder at Kuestrin. The smaller Obra river formed the fourth or eastern face. Along the Obra were strong permanent fortifications, and behind them the Germans had massed a concentration of tanks and infantry to halt the Russian advance.

The outcome showed that Russian offensive power was still in full vigour. Swinging part of his forces above the Warthe, and crossing the Netze some miles farther north, Zhukov thrust a powerful armoured spearhead across the German border to outflank the main forces defending the quadrilateral. At the same time he struck a crushing blow with tanks and infantry which shattered the Obra defences and drove the Germans in retreat toward the Oder. On January 30 his left wing reached the Oder at Kleinitz, 55 miles east and slightly south of Frankfort. Next day the heavily armoured forces advancing north of the Warthe took the fortress of Landsberg which guarded the approaches to Kuestrin. By February 5 the Russians had virtually cleared the last Germans from the quadrilateral, swept up to the Oder on a front of 73 miles, and thrust an initial bridgehead across it 15 miles northwest of Kuestrin.

Accompanying this westward advance, and adding to the solidity of its gains, was the northward pressure on an expanding front which steadily broadened the base of Zhukov's operations. From the areas of Bydgoszcz and Poznan his columns fanned out toward the Pomeranian border. Their impetus carried them through the frontier defences, where a double flanking movement resulted in the encirclement of the pivotal base of Schneidemuehl on February 1. Above that point, spearheads drove toward Deutsch Krone and Neustettin. Farther west, the strong force that advanced along the Warthe and Netze launched a thrust from its right flank in the direction of Arnswalde and Stargard. Its continued advance beyond Landsberg brought still another thrust toward Stettin in the direction of Pyritz. The Germans were menaced, not merely with the loss of Stettin, but with the encirclement of the whole of northern Pomerania and with a series of thrusts which threatened to cut that area itself into isolated pockets.

Against these dangers the Germans offered fierce resistance. The early part of February, which saw the German defence stiffening along the Oder, also brought bitter fighting in Pomerania which gradually imposed a check on the Russian advance. German counterattacks were still on a local scale, but they were fierce and persistent enough to slow the Russian spearheads and give the Germans a chance to stabilize a new line. Deutsch Krone, on which the Russians had converged from three directions by February 3, was finally taken after stiff fighting on the 11th. Arnswalde was encircled on February

9. But beyond these points the Russian progress was brought to a halt. The Germans held firm at Pyritz and below Stargard and on the approaches to Neustettin. A coherent defence was established in the Baltic lake region covering the railway running from Stettin to Danzig through the key centres of Stargard and Neustettin and Chojnice; and against this line the Russians kept up probing attacks while they strengthened and regrouped their forces for a renewal of major operations.

While Zhukov was carrying out his spectacular sweep across the plains of western Poland, Konev on his southern flank had closed up to the Oder on a swiftly expanding front. Above Czestochowa the weight of his drive was slanted toward the northwest to bring his armies ultimately to the middle and upper Oder along a stretch of over 200 miles. By January 20 his spearheads were across the Silesian border on a front of nearly 60 miles in the area east of Breslau and were fanning out rapidly on either flank. Two days later his forces reached the Oder on a 37-mile front between Breslau and Oppeln. On January 24 Oppeln was captured, and Berlin reported the Russians already across the Oder on either side of Breslau. In the course of the next few days, Konev's whole right wing swept up to the middle reaches of the Oder between Breslau and the bend below Frankfort.

Simultaneously his left wing was flinging a net around the great industrial basin of Silesia. The thrust to the Oder at Oppeln already threatened the communications between that region and Berlin. Below Oppeln one claw of the pincers curled south to capture the mining centre of Gleiwitz on January 25 and outflank the great Dabrowa coal fields from the west. At the same time Konev's extreme left flank, supported by Petrov's armies which since January 15 had been moving forward on a broad front, thrust a second prong south of Cracow to surround and constrict the main area of Upper Silesia. On January 28 the capture of Katowice and Beuthen sealed the Russian mastery of that vital region, and carried the Russian armies almost within striking distance of the Moravian gap.

Three weeks after the launching of their winter offensive the Russian spearheads stood nearly 300 miles west of their starting point. The Germans had been swept from the whole of Poland, except for the neck of the corridor leading to Danzig. The Russians stood inside the pre-war German frontier along a great arc stretching from Chojnice in the north to the vicinity of Ratibor in the south. The great industrial region of Silesia, second in importance only to the Ruhr in the German war economy, had been overrun. With it the Germans lost the sources of 100 million tons of coal annually, some 8 million tons of steel, and the production of tank and aircraft munition factories which had hitherto been relatively little touched by the Allied bombing campaign. Such disasters were irretrievable, and increased the prospect of others still to come. The line of the upper Oder was already crumbling as Konev thrust successive bridgeheads across it. Within the Oder bend, Zhukov was establishing footholds on the west bank and closing on Frankfort and Kuestrin which were the eastern bastions of Berlin. The city itself was in imminent jeopardy, and every available able-bodied German was being rounded up to dig fresh trenches and man the defences before the capital. Even the German grip on the Baltic coast between Stettin and Danzig was now precarious; and while the massed might of two Russian army groups was sweeping over western Poland, two others had simultaneously isolated East Prussia and were grimly and methodically battering into submission the last remnants of its garrisons.

THE INVASION OF EAST PRUSSIA

The reduction of East Prussia was a formidable enterprise. This region of lakes and forests was far more defensible than the open plains of western Poland. The main invasion routes were covered by permanent fortifications, and these had been supplemented during the past five months by extensive field defences with the aim of turning the whole province into an impregnable fortress. It was estimated that enough trenches and anti-tank ditches had been dug in that period to reach from the Baltic clear across Europe and Asia to the Pacific. They were manned by nearly 30 divisions in addition to the *Volkssturm* levies that had been called up to defend the soil of their homeland.

In the face of these barriers the Russians had little prospect of overwhelming East Prussia by a massed armoured onslaught such as that which swept over the Polish plains. Strong tank forces were used to exploit each successive breach of the defences, but their area of penetration was limited by the system of fortifications in depth. The tanks were rarely able to break free over a wide area. The major strongholds were too closely linked to be bypassed and invested while the main drive swept confidently beyond them. Each line had to be battered in by artillery and carried by massed assault. It was the overwhelming superiority of the Russians in numbers and fire-power as well as their strength in armour that enabled them to maintain the impetus of the offensive and to close the pincers on East Prussia with such remarkable speed.

The twin drives were launched along the classic routes of invasion. In the north a corridor between the Niemen river and the Masurian lakes led westward through Insterburg toward the Baltic at Koenigsberg. From the south a gap in the Masurian lakes offered a route through Allenstein toward the Baltic between Koenigsberg and Elbing. Through these gaps the Russians drove two army groups, each of which had a strength far superior to that of the whole German force in East Prussia; and the swift envelopment of that province was followed by the remorseless crushing of the Germans who were trapped in the intervening pocket.

The initial attack which Chernyakhovsky opened near Goldap on January 12 spread northward along a rapidly expanding front. By January 15 a full-scale offensive was under way along a curving arc from Goldap to the Niemen in the vicinity of Tilsit. In five days of fighting the German defences were shattered. The Russians broke through on a 37-mile front for a gain of 28 miles, forcing the Niemen east of Tilsit and wheeling westward below that town. Tilsit was captured on January 20. Insterburg was outflanked by the spearheads thrusting toward the Baltic. The anchor fortress of Gumbinnen was stormed in fierce house-to-house fighting which ended with its capture on January 21. Next day Insterburg fell, and Chernyakhovsky battered his way forward astride the railway leading to Koenigsberg.

Simultaneously the armies of Rokossovsky crashed through the southern gateway of East Prussia. The assault was launched on January 14 from two bridgeheads across the Narew on either side of Pultusk. In this sector the Germans had built strong defences, thick with concrete fortifications and extensive minefields. It took four days of intensive fighting backed by a massive artillery bombardment to join the two initial footholds into a single bridgehead and to break through the German defensive zone. On January 17, however, Moscow announced that success had been achieved. Rokossovsky's troops had torn a 62-mile breach in the German line and advanced up to 25 miles. Coming on the same day as the capture of Warsaw, this meant that the whole German defensive system along the Vistula-Narew line was finally shattered; and while Zhukov drove westward in his great armoured sweep below the Vistula, Rokossovsky thrust a broad corridor northward on either side of the Warsaw-Danzig railway.

The impetus of his assault carried him rapidly through the defences guarding East Prussia from the south. The strongly fortified bastion of Mlawa was overcome on January 19. Next day Rokossovsky's advance forces had thrust across the border on a front of 37 miles which was rapidly broadened during the succeeding days. On January 21 they swept across the historic battlefield of Tannenberg and into the region of the Masurian lakes. On the 22nd, with Insterburg falling to Chernyakhovsky, Rokossovsky captured the pivotal centres of Allenstein and Osterode and Deutsch Eylau, seizing a 40-mile stretch of the main railway linking Torun and Insterburg and driving beyond the lake region toward the Baltic.

The envelopment of East Prussia was now in its final stage. Against stiffening resistance the two Russian prongs pressed inexorably toward the coast. Above Deutsch Eylau, Rokossovsky's left flank fanned out toward the lower Vistula while his spearheads drove north toward Elbing. On January 25 the Germans reported that Russian advance guards had already reached the Baltic. Next day the Russians officially announced the capture of the coastal village of Tolkemit east of Elbing. The latter town, bypassed by the main thrust, was under closing siege from the south as well as the east as the Russians captured Marienburg and pressed toward the estuary of the Vistula along the Nogat river which forms its eastern arm.

East Prussia was now effectively isolated. The Germans managed to contain the corridor to a narrow wedge at the point where it actually touched the Baltic, but it rested on a broad and solid base which held against all efforts to break it. Above Allenstein the Germans launched furious attacks with strong armoured forces; but while they gained some ground, they were unable to achieve a breakthrough. Meanwhile the armies of Chernyakhovsky were closing a second prong around the port of Koenigsberg. By January 27 his steady hammering had brought him to within 4 miles of that city, around which he had drawn a 26-mile arc. Far to his rear the German garrison in Memel, which had clung stubbornly to that port during three months of siege, at last succumbed on January 28. By the 31st the Russians had succeeded in temporarily cutting the last roads out of Koenigsberg south along the coast to Braunsberg and west along the Samland peninsula to the port of Pillau. By desperate efforts the Germans eventually succeeded in restoring communications with these points; but the corridors remained precarious, and Koenigsberg henceforth was under sustained siege and bombardment while the Russians proceeded methodically to assail the Samland peninsula to the north and to reduce the German garrison which had been pocketed between their two main forces.

The corridor which Rokossovsky thrust to the Baltic, and the coordinated advance on Koenigsberg by Chernyakhovsky, pressed the Germans in the intervening sector into a long sack extending to the

lake region in the southeast corner of East Prussia. The bottom of
the sack was closed by the rapid expansion of the front as the two
Russian army groups reached toward a junction with each other.
When Rokossovsky crossed the border he flung his right wing eastward
below the Masurian lakes, while Chernyakhovsky's left simultaneously
expanded toward the south. On January 24 the capture of Lyck
by Rokossovsky and Angerburg by Chernyakhovsky indicated a
concerted assault by their forces on the last main sector of East
Prussia's defences. In this area the deep zone of the lakes, pierced
only by narrow and winding causeways, was particularly favourable
for defence. The natural obstacles were strengthened by a deep
system of fortifications which dated back to the first World War,
and which the Germans viewed as an impregnable barrier. Under
the power of the Russian onslaught it crumbled in a few days. On
January 27, Moscow triumphantly announced that the two army
groups had broken the German line, captured the important rail
junction of Rastenburg, and completely shattered the defence system
based on the Masurian lakes. With these natural obstacles eliminated
the Russians drove steadily forward, rolling up the German pocket
from the southeast and pressing the remaining defenders into a
steadily dwindling area along the Baltic coast.

While East Prussia was thus being overrun, an increasing threat
was developing against the Polish corridor. The Germans had not
only failed to hold Rokossovsky's frontal drive toward the Baltic.
They were equally unsuccessful in their efforts to confine it by holding
the shoulders of the expanding salient. Behind his northward
advance, Rokossovsky's armies were simultaneously pushing west to
overrun the area between the Vistula and the southern border of
East Prussia. This was a movement parallel to Zhukov's swing
beyond Torun to Bydgoszcz and ultimately converging toward it. By
January 27, Rokossovsky's left wing had driven across the Vistula
above Bydgoszcz to link with Zhukov's forces. Farther south he
closed the ring around the fortress of Torun, while his continued
advance along the Vistula menaced the fortified centre of Grudziadz.

By the beginning of February the drive toward the Baltic, like the advance to the Oder, was showing signs of temporary exhaustion. The siege of Torun, pressed vigorously since January 27, was crowned by the capture of that important stronghold on February 1. The German anchor position at Elbing maintained a stubborn defence for a fortnight, but on February 9 the Russians succeeded in flanking and surrounding the town, and a fierce assault carried it next day. Their grip on the coast, already strengthened by its extension 20 miles eastward with the capture of the strongly fortified locality of Frauenburg on the 9th, was thus solidified, and the elimination of Elbing weakened the German defence against a threat to Danzig from the east. Meanwhile the capture of Preussisch Eylau by Chernyakhovsky on February 10 marked the steady dwindling of the German pocket in East Prussia. The main area had now been reduced to less than 600 square miles, and the Germans had been driven from all but a narrow foothold on the Samland peninsula above Koenigsberg. But Koenigsberg itself continued to hold out, and the final clearing of East Prussia awaited the new phase of the offensive which was by this time in prospect.

CLEARING THE FLANKS

By the first week in February the difficulty of maintaining the impetus of the offensive was increased by a change in weather conditions. A thaw at the beginning of the month softened the frozen ground which had favoured the massive armoured sweep from the Vistula to the Oder. Supply lines, already strained by the rapid advance, were even harder to maintain. Faced by stiffening German resistance all along the front, the Russians were temporarily reduced to relatively local operations while they built up their strength for a resumption of large-scale efforts.

Their rapid success in this process was due in very great measure to their effective use of the Polish railway system. The excellent rail network in western Poland had been overrun with such rapidity that the Germans had no time to carry out extensive demolitions. In addition, Polish workers had largely succeeded in preserving the main junctions from serious damage, and their energies were thrown whole-heartedly into the work of repairing such destruction as the Germans had managed to accomplish. A large amount of rolling stock was taken intact, and the Russians were able to use the railways for military traffic with a minimum of delay.

One modifying factor however was now assuming considerable importance. The German tactics in the west of clinging to ports in order to deny their use to the Allies were paralleled in the east, not only by the tenacity with which they defended the chief ports along the Baltic, but also by their efforts to set up hedgehog defences which would keep the main rail centres out of Russian hands. In its early stages the Russian offensive was too swift and overwhelming for the enemy to be able to organize effective resistance at such strategic points. Even Torun, the first centre at which a real stand was attempted, fell after six days of siege. But at Schneidemuehl, and still more at Poznan, there was stiff and protracted fighting before the Germans were dislodged from these important junctions. Schneidemuehl, surrounded on February 1, was not finally cleared until the 14th. Poznan was encircled on January 27, but the Russians had to fight their way into it street by street; and although the main town was cleared by February 17, the remnants of the garrison took refuge in the strongly fortified citadel and held out until the 23rd. The further advances which were under way by that date encountered similar obstacles, and the Russians found themselves committed to a series of arduous and costly siege oper-ations at key centres far behind the front.

The main concern of the Russians in February, however, was with the situation on their flanks. One feature of the offensive was the way in which each of the main thrusts fanned out along a wide front as soon as a breakthrough had been achieved, thus forestalling any serious threats from such local counter-attacks as the Germans were able to launch. Hitherto the Germans had been incapable of mounting a real counter-offensive. They had been kept off balance by the weight and speed of the Russian drive, and they were further hampered by their comparative weakness in armour. On the very eve of the offensive, strong tank forces had been shifted from Poland to take part in the futile effort to relieve Budapest, and these were retained and even reinforced for a renewed blow in Hungary at the beginning of March. With highly dubious wisdom the Germans had committed a large part of their limited armour to the defence of the Danube and Vienna at the expense of the Oder and Berlin.

None the less, the Russians showed no signs of underrating the enemy's power of recovery or the opportunities which the situation now offered him. Zhukov's thrust to the Oder at Frankfort and Kuestrin represented the blunt point of a deep salient with dangerously extended flanks. The virtual conquest of East Prussia had eliminated the most powerful and dangerous position from which the Germans might have launched a counter-offensive to threaten the whole of the Russian gains. But the enemy had partially stabilized a line across Pomerania and the Polish corridor in spite of Russian pressure, and Konev on the upper Oder had been checked on a line which slanted back to the southeast. If the Germans could consolidate these positions, they could rally their reserves for counter-blows against the exposed sides of the wedge. For full security the Russians needed to forestall such a move by pushing out the shoulders and bringing their wings into line with their dangerously advanced centre.

The first blow was struck by Konev on the sector between Breslau and Oppeln. Here the forces which reached the Oder found the river unfrozen, the bridges destroyed, and the left bank defended by strong permanent fortifications. By tenacious efforts, advance units established small footholds across the river near the towns of Ohlau and Brieg and clung to them while the main forces massed on the opposite bank. Russian artillery battered the German fortifications and helped to beat back enemy attacks on the bridgeheads. The engineers built bridges under fire to carry reinforcements across and prepare the way for a full-scale attack. On February 4 the assault was launched. In three days of fighting the river defences were broken. The strong

points of Ohlau and Brieg were surrounded and stormed, the bridgeheads were joined into one, and through a breach of 22 miles the
Russians struck west and southwest to a depth of over 12 miles.

This however was not a complete breakout. The Germans,
fighting back stubbornly, held the Russians to slow progress, and by
February 8 had virtually brought them to a halt. But even while
a check was imposed on the flanking move against Breslau from the
south, a more formidable blow was delivered from the north. Here
the Russians in hard and fluctuating fighting had succeeded in
establishing themselves across the Oder in the vicinity of Steinau.
Striking from either side of that town on February 8, the Russians
crashed through the Oder defences and fanned out on a broadening
front. While the centre drove directly west, the right swung northwest behind the Oder toward Glogau, and the left curled around
west and south of Breslau to meet the spearhead below that city.

Here too the Germans fought hard to contain the Russian advance,
but with much less success. By February 11 the Russians had
captured the industrial and railway centre of Liegnitz and swept west
to the Bober river, the chief natural barrier between the Oder and
the Neisse. The sickle curving around Breslau was checked 15 miles
short of a junction with the southern prong; but five days of hard
fighting broke this last corridor, and on February 16 the ring was
closed around Breslau and the Russians embarked on the grim and
prolonged task of reducing that city block by block. Meanwhile
Konev had continued his expansion west and northwest, thrusting
a spearhead to the Neisse in the direction of Goerlitz, bypassing and
encircling Glogau, and driving up the corridor between the Neisse
and the Oder toward their confluence near Guben.

By the 16th however the pace was slowing. The Germans threw
in fierce counter-attacks to beat back the advance spearheads and to
gain time for the stabilizing of a new line. The Russians were held
along an arc some 20 miles south and southwest of Breslau. Hard
fighting gave them a gradually spreading front along the Neisse which
by February 25 extended for 60 miles; but the Germans continued to

hold a bridgehead covering Guben, and the general line of the Neisse marked for the moment the limit of Konev's advance.

This left the Russians holding a broad curving front which from a point some miles northeast of Goerlitz ran back roughly parallel to the frontier of Czechoslovakia. At the southeastern tip of Silesia, southward pressure by Konev toward Ratibor combined with a westward thrust by Petrov toward Teschen threatened to close the pincers on the approaches to the Moravian gap. Progress however was limited in the face of the stout German defence of this vital position. In the third week in March a surge southeast of Oppeln carried the Russians almost to the Czech frontier. But Ratibor was not taken until the last day of March, and the Moravian gap itself remained in German hands almost to the end.

In the south therefore Konev still presented an extended flank to the enemy. The danger from this direction had however been reduced to almost negligible proportions by the advance beyond the Oder. The prospect that the Germans might mass enough forces in the region of the Sudeten mountains for a successful counter-offensive was slight at the best. The chance that such an attack could seriously threaten the broad-based Russian bulge was even slighter. By driving to the Neisse, Konev had brought his main front into line with that of Zhukov in the Oder bend; and by the time his advance was halted, Zhukov himself was on the verge of eliminating the northern flank by a joint offensive with Rokossovsky against Pomerania.

In this area the situation was almost deadlocked by mid-February. Zhukov had surged through a strong defence line to take Deutsch Krone and surround Arnswalde, but his advance was halted a few miles beyond those points. During the latter part of the month he was chiefly occupied in consolidating his gains and eliminating the German garrisons in his rear. Encircled Schneidemuehl was taken on February 14. The Germans fought stubbornly to relieve Arnswalde, and even claimed to have restored temporary contact by February 17 as a result of attacks whose strength amounted to a limited counter-offensive. But the Russians struck back and restored their position, and on February 23—the same day as the fall of Poznan—they announced the liquidation of the Arnswalde garrison. For a short time the struggle on this sector subsided while both sides gathered their strength for new efforts.

Meanwhile the forces of Rokossovsky farther to the east had achieved tangible though still limited results in their drive up the Polish corridor. The anchor points on either flank of this sector were the fortified towns of Chojnice and Grudziadz, and the whole area was covered by a deep system of defences protecting the approaches to Danzig. By dogged and sustained efforts, Rokossovsky battered his way into the first fortified zone. Chojnice was taken on February 15, along with the strong point of Tuchola 13 miles to the east. A breach in the defences covering Grudziadz was followed by a thrust through the difficult marshes along the Vistula which outflanked the town and closed the siege ring around it on February 18. The advance was pressed along the intervening front during the next few days; but progress was slow, and it was evident that a direct drive on Danzig would be an arduous and costly enterprise.

The result was a shift of direction and purpose. On February 24, Rokossovsky swung the main weight of his efforts to his western flank with the object of striking through to the Baltic coast and cutting off the Polish corridor and eastern Pomerania. Using Chojnice as a pivot, he drove west and northwest against the German defences in the Baltic lakes. Here too there were formidable obstacles. The Germans held a series of fortified positions, around which they had grouped mobile forces that were strong in tanks and artillery, and the marshes and forests of this region gave added advantage to the defence. There was hard fighting during the initial stages of attack, and for some time the issue hung in the balance. The turning point came when a flanking sweep around the lakes which covered the pivotal stronghold of Schlochau carried the Russians through the defences and into the town. The whole German line began to crumble. The remaining strong points were overcome, and through a 36-mile gap the tanks and mobile infantry poured northwest in the direction of Koeslin. The announcement of the breach on February 27 revealed that the spearheads had already reached Bublitz halfway to their goal. Neustettin, bypassed in the first rush, was taken on the following day, and Rokossovsky continued to push out the shoulders of the salient while he drove its point toward the Baltic.

On March 1 this thrust received fresh and powerful support from a new offensive by Zhukov. It came just when the threatened German counter-offensive in Pomerania seemed imminent. Having checked Zhukov's advance below Stargard, the Germans massed a powerful force of élite units in that area, backed by strong air concentrations at Stargard and Stettin. Zhukov moved swiftly to forestall the blow. Shifting a tank army as well as infantry reinforcements to this sector, he lashed out with explosive force along the whole perimeter of the bulge above Arnswalde. While he renewed his direct pressure toward Stargard, he drove west below that town toward the Oder on a front which extended on either side of Pyritz, and simultaneously he struck north of Arnswalde in a thrust which was aimed at bypassing Stargard from the east.

This last move completed the disruption of the German hold on Pomerania. The strong positions which the Germans had constructed along the small Ihna river crumbled under the weight of the assault. Fortified strong points and trenches and anti-tank obstacles were battered down by massive artillery fire. In two days of fighting, Zhukov's forces broke through the German line and drove north on a course parallel to that of Rokossovsky farther to the east.

The dual thrusts progressed with remarkable speed in the face of hard going. The difficulty of penetrating this region of lakes and forests was increased by thaws which softened the ground and confined the tanks to the roads. The corridors were narrow and vulnerable to flank attacks. The Germans rushed reserves to halt the advance, and counter-attacks by forces brought up from the area below Danzig were launched in an attempt to cut off Rokossovsky's advanced units. But the impetus of the Russian advance kept the enemy off balance. The assaults on the flanks were beaten off. The most dangerous centres on the shoulders of the salients were overwhelmed before they could be organized for defence or counter-blows. The Germans were unable to halt the powerful armoured spearheads, and their attempts to cut off the tanks from the supporting infantry were unavailing. On March 4 the Russians announced that the double penetration to the Baltic had been achieved. Rokossovsky had captured Koeslin and reached the coast nearby. Zhukov had thrust a spearhead to the sea just east of Kolberg. Pomerania was split into three segments, and the final conquest of that province was at last in sight.

The task was pursued inexorably throughout the remainder of March. While part of Zhukov's forces struck eastward to achieve the swift elimination of the German pocket between the two corridors, other strong units wheeled westward along the coast toward the mouth of the Oder. These now formed the right flank of an extended arc which was closing toward the focal port of Stettin. On March 4, the same day that he reached the Baltic, Zhukov's forces which had driven through Pyritz arrived at the Oder in the vicinity of Schwedt. Next day the bastion of Stargard fell, clearing the way for a steady extension of the Russian grip on the Oder to the southeastern approaches of Stettin. On March 6 a two-day tank thrust carried the Russians to the Oder mouth, and below that point the whole northern flank was pushing forward to the estuary. Behind the front there remained only a German pocket around Kolberg, which stood a 13-day siege before it was eliminated on March 18. Meanwhile the advance toward Stettin was pressed against stubborn resistance as the Germans sought to stabilize a line covering the east bank suburb of Altdamm. Hard fighting carried the Russians through the outer defences by March 17, and on March 20 the converging Russian assault carried Altdamm itself. The last German bridgehead east of the Oder was thus wiped out, and only the width of the river separated the Russians from Stettin.

Simultaneously Rokossovsky was closing on Danzig along a broad but steadily contracting arc. From Koeslin his left flank pressed eastward along the Baltic coast. In the centre, while one group drove northeast from Chojnice along a broad front, another resumed the northward advance above Grudziadz whose fall on March 6 after 17 days of siege greatly eased their supply situation. From the vicinity of Elbing still other forces drove along the coast and across the network of waterways between the mouths of the Vistula. Two weeks of unremitting pressure crushed the Germans back into a narrow strip of coast covering Danzig and Gdynia. On March 23 the pocket was split by a thrust which drove a 3-mile wedge to the coast between the two towns. Against these the Russians converged in a final assault. Gdynia fell on March 28. On March 30 the columns which had battered into Danzig from three directions completed the conquest of that port, capturing 10,000 of its garrison and wiping out the last German foothold between Koenigsberg and Stettin.

By this time the days of Koenigsberg too were numbered. Steady pressure during February had reduced the East Prussian pocket to a narrow triangle extending below Koenigsberg to Zinten and Braunsberg. On March 14 the opening of a new assault against this position was officially reported. Spring thaws had flooded the low-lying coastal lands, and the Germans had fortified the whole area and sown it thickly with minefields. But on March 15 a Russian breakthrough to the coast 5 miles southwest of Koenigsberg once more cut off that port from the main pocket, and two days later the capture of Braunsberg dislodged the Germans from their western anchor. By March 26 the last effective resistance had been crushed, and the Germans were confined to Koenigsberg and their remaining positions on the Samland peninsula. The garrison held out stubbornly against the sustained bombardment to which the city was subjected; but on April 6 the besiegers opened a full-scale assault which broke through the defences in the north, and after savage street fighting the defence was crushed on April 9. Over 90,000 prisoners fell into

Russian hands; and except for the isolated German forces in Courland, the Russians were now in full control of the Baltic coast east of the Oder.

The operations of February and March had thus brought drastic changes in the strategic situation. The conquest of Pomerania and East Prussia freed two full army groups for action on the main front. The long and dangerous flanks stretching back from the Oder had been eliminated, and Konev and Zhukov had established a coherent north-south line along the Neisse and Oder. From the flanks they were in position to launch a great enveloping movement against Berlin. Frontally the peril to the German capital had been intensified by a new Russian success in the early part of March. During the previous month, Zhukov had established several bridgeheads across the Oder from Fuerstenberg below Frankfort to Kienitz north of Kuestrin. This northern flank was strengthened by the extension of his grip on the east bank as a result of his breakthrough below Stargard, and he struck almost at once to expand his foothold on the left bank and to eliminate one of the chief German bastions. In a two-pronged drive he broke through a strong triple defence belt to flank Kuestrin from the north, while other forces struck from the bridgeheads below that city to threaten it from the south and west. The Germans threw in heavy counter-attacks with strong air support; but while they beat back the deepest penetrations, they were unable to prevent the ring from closing around the main part of Kuestrin on the east bank. A week of bitter fighting ended with the capture of the town on March 12, though it was not until the end of the month that Berlin acknowledged the end of all resistance. Beyond the fallen stronghold and on either side the Russians linked and consolidated their footholds on the west bank, protecting the river crossings while they built up a powerful springboard for the next phase. The foremost spearheads were now barely 30 miles from Berlin; and while the shadow of doom hung over the capital from the east, the last hopes of Germany in the west were being shattered by the Allied drive across the Rhine.

ADVANCE TO THE RHINE

By the latter part of January the Allies in the west were moving toward a resumption of the offensive which had been so rudely interrupted by von Rundstedt's drive in the previous month. The last of the German gains in the Ardennes was gradually liquidated. The British, attacking on January 16, extended their hold on the Roer by wiping out the small triangle which the Germans held between the Maas and the Roer near Roermond. Farther south the American First Army in the Monschau area pressed toward the upper Roer and the dams which controlled the level of that river, while the Third hammered into the Westwall defences toward Pruem. The Allies had completely regained the initiative and were occupying the springboards from which to launch a full-scale assault.

The delay imposed by the need to regroup for offensive purposes was lessened by the fact that the dispositions forced on the Allies by the Ardennes battle were actually favourable to a powerful and concentrated attack. The American Third Army had been shifted north to contain the southern flank of the German drive, leaving the American Seventh and French First Armies to cover the extended front from Luxembourg to the Swiss border. The bulk of the Allied strength was thus massed north of the Moselle, on the very sector where the Germans could least afford to give ground.

Here was a situation which offered an opportunity to strike with great power in a selected area, with the possibility of achieving a decisive result. The previous effort in November, with its attempt to engage the Germans along almost the whole of the front, had involved a dispersal of strength whose consequences were seen in the limited achievements of the drive. Now the situation lent itself to the application of the principle of the concentration of force. By throwing the bulk of their strength against the northern Rhineland, the Allies had good prospects of breaking through and overwhelming the defenders; and the destruction of the enemy in that region would turn the flank of the Germans in the southern Rhineland and bring their destruction as well.

The plan unfolded as a series of three overlapping operations, each of which depended on the ability of the Allies to break through at selected points and create exposed flanks from which the Germans could be rolled up and enveloped. The pivot in the first instance was the front which the American Ninth Army, along with part of the First, had established along the Roer. It was significant for the coming operation that when the American First Army was transferred back to Bradley's 12th Army Group on January 19, the Ninth was left with the 21st Army Group under Montgomery. A breakthrough on the Roer would carry these two armies to the Rhine, splitting the German forces; and simultaneously they would wheel away from each other to right and left to meet the opposite wings of their respective army groups and complete the rout of the enemy north of the Moselle. This in turn would expose the Germans in the Saar, where the Westwall would be completely outflanked; and a thrust by the Third Army down the Rhine combined with a frontal attack by the Seventh Army would complete the third phase of the operation and deliver the whole of the Rhineland to the Allies.

There was hard fighting in prospect before this result was attained. The Westwall had been pierced by the advance to the Roer, but beyond this there were still strong field defences, and along most of the front the permanent defences still had to be overcome. The Germans were still fighting hard and skilfully, and they too had concentrated the bulk of their forces north of the Moselle. After the battle of the Scheldt, the German Fifteenth Army had been shifted to the Aachen sector, leaving the Twenty-fifth to defend northwest Holland. The Fifteenth was now on the Roer sector, with the Fifth Panzer Army in reserve. South of it lay the German Seventh Army, while on its northern flank the élite troops of the First Parachute Army guarded the most direct approach to the Ruhr.

In total strength, however, the Germans were now far more markedly inferior than they had been in December. The Sixth Panzer Army, after heavy losses in the Ardennes, had been withdrawn

to be refitted and to strengthen the hard-pressed eastern front.
German strength in the west was now in the vicinity of 60 divisions,
many of which had suffered severely in recent fighting. The Allies
in contrast were receiving a steady stream of reinforcements. They
now had over 80 divisions, and the number was still growing. A
new American army, the Fifteenth, was shortly added to Bradley's
group. The American Seventh Army was being strongly reinforced.
Faced with fresh troops in superior numbers, the Germans had
almost lost what little flexibility they had hitherto possessed. They
had no further reserves available. They could only shift divisions
from one part of the front at the expense of endangering another.

The plight of the Germans was aggravated by their mounting
supply difficulties. Behind their armies lay a battered war industry
whose key centres were now in ruins, and a transportation system
which was disintegrating into fragments under the relentless and
increasing blows of Allied air power.

By the beginning of February the campaign against German oil
production was close to final success. All major sources of natural
oil had been overrun, and virtually all natural oil refineries had been
put out of action. Russian occupation of the Silesian coal fields,
coupled with the growing transportation difficulties in the Saar and
the Ruhr, had greatly curtailed the available supply of coal for
synthetic fuel. Only 4 synthetic oil plants remained in operation.
During February these were repeatedly attacked, as were the
refineries which the Germans were trying to get back into production.
Mobile repair gangs had been organized in an effort to speed the work
of restoration, and it was difficult to put a plant permanently out of
commission or to bring German production entirely to a halt. None
the less, the sustained destruction continued to outrun German ability
to make repairs, which was further hampered by a growing shortage of
tools and equipment. At the beginning of March it was officially
stated that output had been cut to 25 per cent. of the oil and 15 per
cent. of the gasoline that Germany was producing when the full-scale
campaign was inaugurated in April 1944. Germany had been forced

to live on her reserves, and these were now virtually exhausted. With damage to the railways throwing an increasing burden on road traffic, Germany was being deprived of the essential means for maintaining both military and industrial transportation.

The assault on the railways had by this time assumed top priority. Through January and early February the main attack was delivered against the network feeding western Germany and the Rhineland in an attempt to strangle the supply lines to the latter area. But even this involved a reaching out to important rail centres such as Magdeburg and Berlin, while attacks on such targets as Chemnitz and Leipzig were also calculated to impede German troop and supply movements toward the eastern front.

In mid-February the development of the offensive completed the strategic merging of east and west from the point of view of Allied air operations. In a comprehensive campaign the bombers embarked on an effort to paralyze the whole German railway system. The drive was inaugurated by a double night raid on Dresden on February 13, followed by daylight raids on the 14th and 15th which left that city shattered and prostrate. During the week that followed the bombers struck methodically at the main junctions and marshalling yards from Cologne to Chemnitz and from Hamburg to Munich. In the week beginning February 13, the Allies showered Germany with 23,000 tons of bombs. In the following week the figure rose to 42,000. By February 22 the destruction of the main traffic centres had proceeded so far that the planes could strike out at secondary points, and a "buckshot blitz" by numerous forces of 100 or so bombers hit at multiple targets scattered over areas of thousands of square miles. Through March and April the offensive was sustained, its intensity slackening only on rare occasions and seldom for more than a few hours' duration as a result of bad weather. As in the case of oil facilities, the German repair organization prevented the complete interdiction of rail traffic which was the ultimate aim of the campaign, but could not offset the steady deterioration in transport facilities that these massive operations imposed.

The weight of the attack was carried by the heavy bombers based in Britain, though Italian-based bombers made a useful contribution with raids against Austrian rail and oil centres. The R.A.F., which retained sole responsibility for major night raids, also made its full contribution to the daylight attacks in which it had taken an increasing part since the invasion of Normandy. On March 11, British bombers hit Essen in daylight with 5000 short tons; and next day they showered 5500 tons on Dortmund in the heaviest attack of the war. Specially equipped Lancasters had been evolved to carry the new 22,000-pound bomb against targets that had hitherto stood up to blows from lighter missiles; and its first use against the Bielefeld viaduct on March 14 was followed by other attacks on traffic bottlenecks of a similar kind. And while the heavy bombers were carrying out their work of devastation, the Mosquitos continued their nightly harrying activities against German centres. Berlin was their most persistent target during this period. Beginning with a raid on February 20, they struck the German capital for 36 nights in succession with blows that ranged from less than 100 tons to a raid of 1000 tons on March 9. This series of attacks was only broken for a single night on March 28, and on that night Berlin was still reeling from a daylight blow by American bombers—its fourth major daylight attack in a month. These persistent raids not only contributed to the damage to a main rail and industrial and administrative centre, but helped to pin down strong ground defences in the German capital and to keep down the losses—now averaging only slightly over 1 per cent.—which the heavy bombers suffered over other targets.

In addition to these attacks on railways and refineries, as well as on occasional aircraft and armament plants, two other types of target claimed a measure of attention. With the Germans still in possession of the Dutch coast, the launching sites for V weapons had to be kept under persistent attack. The need was all the more urgent because the Germans were already preparing their V-3—a system of multiple-barrelled rocket projectors designed to deluge London with shells at the rate of ten a minute. And while the Germans were thus planning a last desperate effort to annihilate the British capital, they were also preparing an even more desperate attempt to strangle Britain by a new submarine campaign. Stronger and more efficient U-boats with apparatus for under-water breathing and with more deadly torpedoes in their holds were in German pens and shipyards, and the bombers were again called on to strike at these weapons at their source and frustrate the final counter-blows from which Germany had anything to hope.

By the latter part of March the bombing offensive had achieved an appalling record of devastation. In captured Cologne, four-fifths of which was virtually destroyed, the Allies could see full testimony to the work of air power. Berlin, which had been hit by over 75,000 tons of bombs, had had its centre gutted by explosives and incendiaries and its chief industrial districts partially demolished. Industrial Essen lay paralyzed after the great raid on March 11. Devastation extended over three-quarters of Dresden, and in a dozen other cities, including Hanover and Kassel and Frankfort, the damage was on a major scale. Air power had not yet crushed the will or the ability of the Germans to continue fighting, but it had paved the way for the final victory by the Allied ground forces which was by this time within their grasp.

BREAKTHROUGH IN THE RHINELAND

The offensive opened on February 8 with a drive by the Canadian First Army from the area of Nijmegen against the northern end of the Westwall. Originally scheduled for the first week in January, the attack had been delayed by the German offensive in the Ardennes which had forced the shifting of British forces to hold the line of the Meuse in case of a German breakthrough toward Antwerp. There was an uneasy situation on the Canadian sector during the latter part of December, for the German forces in Holland stood ready to join in the assault once von Rundstedt achieved a clear breakthrough. But the success of the Allies in containing the

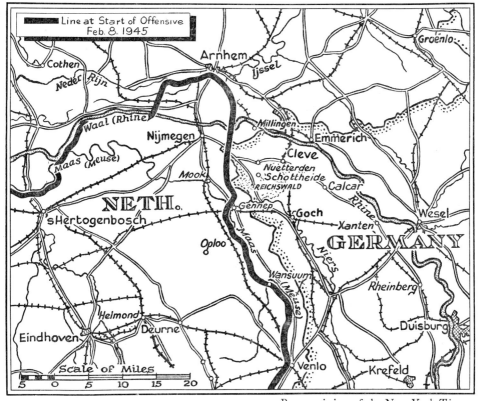

By permission of the New York *Times*

THE CLEVE-GOCH SECTOR

German thrust ended the plan to drive on Antwerp from the north, and by mid-January the Allies had resumed their preparations for attack.

The British Second Army was intimately though not formally associated with the new drive. Canadian forces in the west still consisted of only a single corps. The transfer of the I Corps from Italy was decided on early in February, but this force only came into action in the later stage of the battle beyond the Rhine. By that time the British and Canadian armies under Montgomery had virtually been integrated into a single formation. On the eve of the offensive the XXX British Corps was added to other British units already serving under Canadian command, and still other divisions were fed in during the drive until the bulk of the Second Army was involved in the new push.

The delay of the offensive by a month meant that it was launched under less favourable conditions than might have been encountered earlier. In January the ground was frozen, offering a firm surface to tanks and heavy supply vehicles. By the beginning of February, thaws and floods turned the attack into almost an amphibious operation. In many places the troops had to be carried by amphibious vehicles from one island of land to another. Water and mud restricted the use of armour and slowed down the movement of heavy equipment and supplies. Against the slender opposition that was at first encountered, light mobile forces might have effected a more rapid and extensive penetration, though it would have been another matter to exploit or even to hold their gains. But the plans called for an attack with massive weight on a narrow front, and progress was held to the place at which supplies and heavy weapons could be brought up.

This gave the Germans time to move strong reinforcements to the danger area and to impose still further delay. At the outset the opposition consisted of elements of 2 divisions. But the attack threatened the German northern flank and the anchor of their whole Rhineland position. In a broad sense the situation was comparable to that around Caen in the early summer, where the hinge had to be held or the whole German position would collapse. To protect this vital point the Germans threw in strong forces of both armour and infantry, including several divisions of élite parachute troops. Within a week the defending force had risen to 7 divisions, and elements of 11 divisions were ultimately involved.

In the face of these obstacles the British and Canadian forces found themselves committed to a bitter struggle for slow and hard-won gains. The first blow was struck on a 5-mile front after a heavy air bombardment and an 11-hour artillery barrage. The front was steadily broadened as the attack wheeled down the widening corridor between the Maas and the Rhine. The flank of the Westwall was anchored at Cleve and Gennep and covered by a strong belt of defences in the Reichswald. These positions were overcome in five days of stiff fighting. Cleve and Gennep were captured on February 12. On the following day the last of the Reichswald defences was mastered, and the attack was well through the second belt of the Siegfried Line in this area. Against stiffening resistance marked by strong counter-attacks the right flank pushed down the Meuse, while the left seized the Rhine ferry crossing opposite Emmerich. The Germans fought hard on the approaches to the next defensive line based on Goch and Calcar, and were only slowly overborne. A wedge was driven in between the two towns. Goch was taken after a three-day struggle on February 21; but the drive was temporarily checked on the outskirts of Calcar, and on February 23, after an advance of 17 miles in 15 days, the Canadian forces halted to regroup for a fresh effort.

This period was marked by still another dislocation of the original Allied plans. It had been intended to follow the Canadian attack with a drive by the American Ninth Army across the Roer on February 10. This was frustrated by the delay in securing the Roer dams which controlled the flood level of the river. A partial release of water from the dams in December showed how this step could be used to increase the Roer's effectiveness as a barrier. The Germans could either use it to forestall an offensive, or wait until the first wave of attackers had crossed the river and then let loose a flood which would cut them off from support. Air attacks with 6-ton bombs had failed to demolish the dams and so deprive the Germans of control of this defensive asset. A stubborn defence along the Westwall delayed the American thrust east of Monschau which aimed at the capture of the dams. By February 6 the Americans had taken the second largest of the five main dams and had the others almost within their grasp, but they were unable to prevent the Germans from playing their final card. On February 9 the Nazis opened the flood-gates, and next day they blew up the control gates of the large Schwammenauel dam just before its capture. The waters roared down the valley, raising the river level by several feet and flooding the land on either side of its banks. The projected attack was held up for a fortnight until the floods began to subside.

The delay however was not a complete loss. The Germans had gained a little more time; but as the aftermath of their Ardennes offensive showed, they were no longer able to turn time to positive use. They had failed either to strengthen their defences or to increase their forces to a degree which would offset both their losses in the drive and the steady expansion of Allied power. Although the blowing of the Roer dams delayed a full-scale attack, the interval saw the Germans forced into dispositions which favoured the ultimate aims of the Allies. The enemy strength was drawn to the flanks, weakening the centre and paving the way for a swift breakthrough. On the north the pressure by the Canadian Army absorbed an increasing number of divisions. On the south the American Third Army captured the pivotal strong point of Pruem on February 12 and brought mounting pressure on the Westwall defences guarding the approaches to Trier. By February 22 it had captured Saarburg and cleared the Saar-Moselle triangle in this vicinity, and the Germans had committed 10 divisions including crack Panzer units in an effort to prevent further progress. When the Allies struck across the Roer on February 23, only 6 German divisions were left to oppose them on this front.

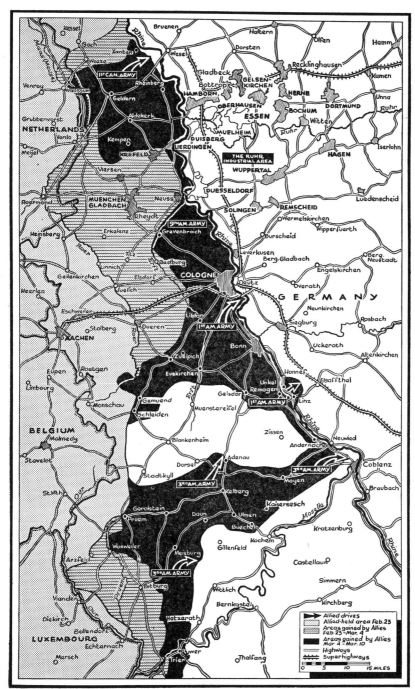

By permission of the New York *Times*

ADVANCE TO THE RHINE

The attack was launched in the darkness of early morning on a front of 22 miles after a concentrated air and artillery barrage. The chief weight was born by the American Ninth Army, using 7 infantry and 3 armoured divisions and supported on its right by one corps of the First. In three days of battling against thick field defences they penetrated 7 miles beyond the Roer, capturing Juelich and Dueren and occupying a strategic ridge northeast of Juelich. While the advancing spearheads drove toward Cologne and Duesseldorf against crumbling opposition, steady pressure on the left flank of the advance presented an increasing threat to the German forces between the American Ninth and the Canadian First Armies.

The Allied offensive plan was now unfolding with a crushing power and precision. The Germans tried to stiffen the defence by shifting two armoured divisions from the Moselle area, but the move failed to halt the progress of the First and Ninth Armies while it weakened the opposition to the Third. By February 27 a complete breakthrough was in sight. The main advance had reached the small Erft river on which the Germans had tried to establish a defensive line, and the expanding left wing in a sudden 10-mile surge was approaching Muenchen-Gladbach and threatening to bypass it to the west. Within two days the Erft defences were overrun, Muenchen-Gladbach was in American hands, and the flanks were fanning out toward Duisburg and Bonn. On March 2 the forces in the centre reached the Rhine, capturing Duesseldorf's west bank suburb of Neuss and spreading out along the river. Within two days the Ninth Army held a 20-mile stretch, its thrust through Krefeld had carried it to the Duisburg suburb of Homburg, its southern flank was secured by the arrival of the First Army at the Rhine a few miles north of Cologne, and on its extreme left a new thrust had taken Venlo and Roermond on March 2 and paved the way for a junction with the Canadian Army.

This last development was an indication that the maximum results which had been hoped for as a result of the breakthrough were still out of reach. The prospect of closing the jaws of the pincers along the Rhine above Duisburg was frustrated partly by stiffening resistance at that point, and still more by the bitter and tenacious opposition which the Germans had maintained against the Canadians. The struggle to hold the flank along the Rhine centred particularly on the Hochwald, where a strong fortified position covered the approach to the Rhine crossing at Wesel. The resumption of the Canadian offensive in a pre-dawn attack on February 26 carried the attack beyond Calcar and into the Hochwald defences. A corridor was driven in along the railway line between Goch and Xanten, but progress was slow and costly, and it was only on March 5 that the Canadians finally fought their way through, to confront a continued and bitter German defence before Xanten. By that date a more limited junction with the Americans had been effected. While troops of the Ninth Army drove northeast from Venlo, British troops from the Canadian Army drove south to meet them. On March 3 the two forces linked up in the Geldern area. The Germans were thus dislodged from the sector they had held along the Maas, and were pressed into a pocket covering the Wesel crossing. Under attack from all sides, they pulled back slowly behind a protective crust of armour. On the night of March 10 the last German troops in this area were withdrawn across the Rhine, and the Allies gained control of almost the whole of the west bank from Arnhem to Coblenz.

CLEARING THE RHINELAND

The elimination of the Wesel pocket marked the end of one of the three main operations of the Rhineland offensive. In contrast with the bitterness of the struggle on the northern sector, and the limits which the enemy had been able to impose on Allied success, the other two phases moved to a swift and spectacular conclusion once the initial breakthrough had been achieved, and inflicted upon the Germans west of the Rhine a disaster that was to prove irretrievable.

By the time the thrust to the Rhine had split the Germans north of the Moselle, operations aiming at the crushing of the Germans facing the American First and Third Armies were already under way. By reaching the Rhine north of Cologne, the left wing of the First Army had opened the flank of the German defences below that point. While swift operations against Cologne brought the capture of that city on March 6, the right wing of the First Army swung into full action, driving south behind the shattered Westwall defences and fanning out with fresh spearheads toward the Rhine in the vicinity of Bonn; and farther south the remaining German positions north of the Moselle were giving way under the frontal assault of the Third Army.

All through the period of the Roer drive the Third Army had kept up a relentless pressure in the Moselle sector. Following the capture of Pruem and the clearing of the Saar-Moselle triangle, two spearheads drove forward on either side of the Moselle. The northern one aimed at Bitburg, a key road junction on which the Germans depended for lateral communications. The southern one, striking across the Saar near its junction with the Moselle, rapidly developed into an imminent threat to Trier.

The success of this twin operation seriously weakened the German position covering the Eifel hills. On February 26 a powerful attack with 10 divisions on a front of 30 miles broke through the defences along the Pruem river. The Americans surged forward for a gain of 7 miles, converging on Bitburg and making it virtually untenable. Leaving a small garrison to fight a delaying action during the next two days, the Germans pulled back the remainder of their forces for a new stand along the Kyll river a few miles farther east.

By this time Trier also was tottering. While one column threatened to flank the city to the north, an armoured force drove across the Saar to the south. Then in a sudden wheel it drove directly toward Trier, risking the exposure of its flank but taking the Germans by surprise. Infantry followed up to fill in the angle created by this shift of direction and to make the advance secure. One spearhead drove into Trier from the south. Another swung around it to attack from the east. In spite of its hopeless position the

German garrison refused to surrender, and its brief and useless stand brought a heavy bombardment and sharp street fighting which left the ancient city largely in ruins when it fell on March 2.

The stage was now set for a decisive effort on the whole sector between Pruem and Trier, where the Americans were through the Westwall defences. On March 4 an attack by two divisions established a bridgehead across the Kyll beyond Bitburg. Next day General Patton struck from this foothold with his crack 4th Armoured division. Lashing out toward the northeast, the tanks reached the highway running from Pruem to Coblenz and drove eastward astride it, while at the same time other forces attacked along the remainder of the bridgehead and along another sector east of Pruem. The Germans fought stubbornly to hold what was left of their defences, but the armoured breakthrough made their stand completely hopeless. Behind the crust of resistance along the Kyll they had almost nothing in support. The tanks plunged into the difficult Eifel region and sped eastward without meeting serious opposition. Another tank column, after harder fighting at the outset, drove east of Pruem to broaden the corridor and make it secure. On the evening of March 7, after travelling 65 miles in 58 hours, the armoured spearhead reached the Rhine just north of Coblenz.

A junction was now in the making between the First and Third Armies. Only 25 miles separated them, and the gap was rapidly closing. One force of the First was 2 miles above Bonn. Another, driving southeast through Euskirchen, had reached the Rhine at Remagen and was expanding south along its bank. On March 9 Bonn itself was captured, and on the same day the First and Third Armies joined hands between Remagen and Coblenz. They thus sealed a ring around elements of some 5 German divisions whose liquidation was accomplished in the course of the next five days to complete the clearing of the whole of the Rhineland north of the Moselle.

This triumph however was almost overshadowed by another achievement resulting from the speed of the First Army's advance.

This was the seizure of the Ludendorff bridge at Remagen on March 7. The Allies in the course of their bombing offensive had wrecked or damaged most of the Rhine bridges north of Bonn. Those that remained were blown up by the Germans in the course of their withdrawal to the east bank. But an American tank force arrived at Remagen to find the bridge still standing, though its destruction was timed for ten minutes later. Prompt action prevented the demolition. Tanks and troops rushed the bridge and drove across to the east bank of the Rhine. One charge was set off, damaging the structure, but the others were located and dislodged or disconnected before they could be exploded. By nightfall the Americans had established a bridgehead across the Rhine, and were pouring in men and tanks and artillery to make their foothold secure.

This was a fatal lapse which the Germans found it impossible to retrieve. They shot four officers for negligence, and they embarked on desperate efforts to demolish the bridge by bombing and artillery fire. But they were unable to check the buildup of the American force on the east side. General Eisenhower ordered 5 divisions to be thrown across the river; and when mounting damage ultimately brought the collapse of the bridge on March 17, other structures were in place to maintain the flow of reinforcements and supplies. It was highly significant of German weakness that no effective counter-attacks were mounted during the early period. The Americans were able not only to consolidate their foothold, but to expand it steadily. By March 12 they had taken the initiative, striking inland to seize the high ground commanding the river and to cut the Frankfort-Cologne super-highway, while they also extended the bridgehead to north and south. By March 14 hard fighting had won an area 25 miles long by 10 miles deep, and their northern flank was planted firmly along the Sieg river on the southern approaches to the Ruhr. The Allies were across the Rhine in strength, and their prospects for a major drive beyond that barrier were transformed by this unexpected initial success.

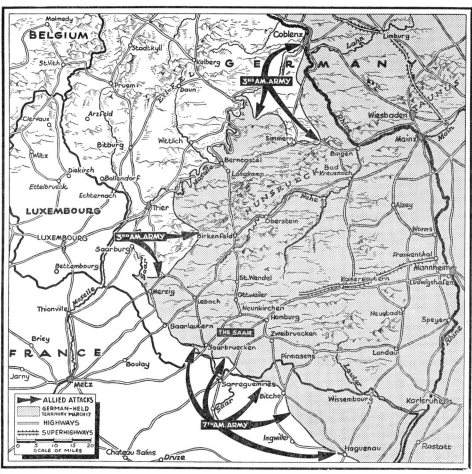

By permission of the New York *Times*

THE SAAR OFFENSIVE

Meanwhile the third and final phase of the battle for the Rhineland had moved swiftly to completion. The Third Army's breakthrough had again created an open flank, this time along the Moselle. In the Saar and the Palatinate the Germans held a rough triangle whose base rested on the Rhine. Along its southern face the Germans still had the fortifications of the Siegfried Line behind which to make a stand. But on the northern side, where a German bridgehead above the Moselle was pinched out during the second week in March, the river itself was the chief barrier, and the western tip of the triangle had already been blunted and driven in by the earlier American penetration southeast of Trier.

Thus the launching of a concerted Allied assault on March 15 found the Germans in a precarious position. In darkness shortly after midnight the reinforced American Seventh Army, with French support on its right, struck without preliminary barrage along a front of 50 miles. On the same day the Third Army increased its pressure from the Saarburg area toward Merzig, and from a new bridgehead which it had established across the Moselle just west of Coblenz it struck out with a powerful armoured thrust down the Rhine valley and across the base of the whole German position.

The Germans tried to meet the danger by a controlled withdrawal from the western Saar. They fought a stubborn covering battle along the Westwall, and particularly on the eastern sector in front of the Wissembourg gap on which they tried to pivot their wheeling movement back toward the Rhine. But the western flank of their border defences was being turned by the Third Army's attack toward Merzig, and their deliberate withdrawal was disastrously outpaced by the speed with which Patton's armour slashed across their lines of retreat. Below the Moselle, as above it, the crust of German resistance had nothing behind it. The tank forces which broke out of the Moselle bridgehead, sealing off Coblenz and plunging into the rugged terrain of the Hunsrueck, met little serious opposition. By March 16 they were through this natural barrier and had reached the Nahe river at Bad Kreuznach, while multiple columns were fanning out to extend their grip on the Rhine and to broaden the wedge below the Moselle.

A number of traps were now in the making as the Germans struggled to extricate their forces. One of these was represented by the two wings of the Third Army whose armoured spearheads were wheeling to meet each other below the Moselle. By the time this set of pincers closed at Merzweiler on March 19, the Germans had drawn clear except for a small group of about 2000. Another trap now threatened the forces remaining in the tip of the salient, for the Seventh Army had driven a gap through the Siegfried Line east of Saarbruecken and its tanks were thrusting toward a junction with the right wing of the Third Army. Contact was established on March 20 about 12 miles west of Kaiserslautern. The Germans in the apex of the salient were cut off, and were split up by a second and simultaneous junction farther west near Ottweiler. Kaiserslautern itself was captured, depriving the Germans of the main road and rail junction in this region and giving the Americans a pivotal centre for their continued advance.

Meanwhile the Germans fought desperately to avert the third and greatest threat of envelopment presented by the advance of the Third Army's left wing down the Rhine. Around Bad Kreuznach the Americans ran into fanatic resistance, but this improvised effort was swiftly beaten down. On March 20, the day of its junction with the Seventh Army farther west, the Third Army broke through beyond the Nahe. While one column wheeled to attack Mainz, another drove straight across the base of the Rhine loop at this point to capture Worms. On March 21 another thrust brought the capture of Ludwigshafen. The Rhine crossings were falling one after another, and the exposed German pocket was being disrupted by multiple stabs as the troops struggled back toward the remaining bridges. With the capture of Speyer on March 23, all that remained was a dwindling salient west of Karlsruhe, and that was liquidated by March 25. The conquest of the Rhineland was complete. The cities on the left bank, including Coblenz and Mainz, were now in

the hands of the Allies. Across the Rhine the steadily expanding
bridgehead at Remagen was supplemented by another foothold when
a surprise night attack on March 22 carried the Third Army over
the river below Mainz; and far to the north the British Second Army
was poised for the main assault which would shatter the German
defences beyond the Rhine.

When the attack across the Roer signalled the unleashing of the
full offensive, General Eisenhower reiterated his hope for a decisive
battle in the Rhineland. "Given a continuation of the conditions as
we see them now and a reasonable break in the weather—and I am
not asking for July in Kansas—the attacks we are now seeing
should mark the beginning of the destruction of the German
forces west of the Rhine." On the surface these hopes were only
partly realized. In spite of their heavy losses, the Germans had
succeeded in withdrawing a considerable part of their forces across
the river. The Allied aim of complete annihilation had not been
achieved, and more hard fighting had to be contemplated east of
the Rhine.

Yet the sequel was to show that the fate of the Germans in the
west actually had been decided in the Rhineland. The available
forces had been committed in that region, and had suffered irretrievable defeat. Five armies had been ripped to fragments by the
devastating power of the Allied offensive. The First Parachute
Army, by tough and skilful fighting, had saved a considerable part
of its strength. But the Fifteenth, the Fifth Panzer and part of the
Seventh had been broken by the drive from the Roer to the Rhine
and the enveloping movements north of the Moselle. The First and
the remainder of the Seventh had been virtually destroyed in the
Saar and the Palatinate. In addition, the Nineteenth Army had
been severely mauled by the preceding operations of the French
Army which finally cleared Alsace. Since the initial attack by the
Canadian Army on February 8, the Allies had taken 233,000 prisoners
to bring their total to over 2 million since the invasion of Normandy.
The heart had been torn out of the German armies in the west, and

their doom was already sealed when the Allies launched their full-scale drive across the Rhine.

DOWNFALL OF THE REICH

The third week in March saw the swift massing of Allied forces for the main assault on the Rhine barrier. Two bridgeheads had already been secured by surprise thrusts at Remagen and Oppenheim, but their full exploitation awaited the launching of the major assault, which was to strike north of the Ruhr toward the Westphalian plain and the heart of Germany. The magnitude of this operation reduced the chances of surprise to a minimum. A 60-mile smoke-screen concealed Allied movements for three days before the attack, but gave further proof that the attack was in prospect. A week-long air offensive against airfields and communications showed a deliberate Allied effort to isolate the Ruhr area in preparation for the offensive. The Germans were fully aware of where the danger lay, and they massed their strongest available forces in an effort to avert it.

The task fell upon Kesselring, who had been called from Italy after the collapse in the Rhineland to succeed Rundstedt as commander in the west. He found himself burdened with an unhappy legacy. He had no fresh reserves to bolster the shattered and depleted armies which had been driven in retreat beyond the Rhine, and the forces that were left were stretched thin by the need to stand guard along the whole length of the Rhine. Covering the Ruhr itself were the Fifteenth and the Fifth Panzer Armies, with the First Parachute Army on their right along the vulnerable stretch between Wesel and Arnhem. But part of this force was drained away by the effort to contain the Remagen bridgehead, and the concentration of other formations on the right wing below Arnhem further weakened the defences at the point of actual attack.

The assault began at 9 P.M. on the night of March 23. The British Second Army, swiftly regrouped to include the bulk of the forces which had been attached to the First Canadian Army during the Rhineland offensive, struck at three points along a 10-mile stretch between Rees and Wesel, while the American Ninth Army attacked south of Wesel on the right flank. The operation was a magnificent co-ordination of all arms. The actual crossing of the Rhine was accomplished under the charge of British and American naval forces, trained to perfection for this amphibious operation 200 miles from the sea. The air forces blanketed German ground defences; and on the morning of the 24th, when the troops had gained secure footholds on the east bank, a fleet of 6000 planes and gliders swung into action and accomplished the landing of the 2 airborne divisions ahead of the ground troops. The neutralization of the German air and ground defences made the operation a complete success. The airborne forces cut off the German forward positions from the rear while infantry and armour crushed them frontally. By the first afternoon the ground and airborne forces had linked up, the initial footholds had been consolidated into a single bridgehead 30 miles long by 7 miles deep, and the engineers were already in process of throwing bridges across the Rhine to carry the tanks and guns and heavy equipment which would make possible a complete breakout.

Against this powerful pressure the Germans were unable to stabilize an effective line of defence. Driven from the east bank of the Rhine, and denied the use of the upper Ijssel in this area by the airborne troops who seized the bridges across that river, the defenders fell back 15 miles east of the Rhine to a line based on Bocholt and Dorsten. But British armoured forces were upon them before they could complete their preparations. Two days of fighting broke the new German positions. On March 28 the British took Dorsten and their powerful armoured spearheads shook clear in a sweep toward Muenster, while on their right the American Ninth Army kept pace in an advance which was rapidly outflanking the Ruhr.

The envelopment of the Ruhr was an integral part of the offensive plan which was now rapidly unfolding. As the main drive swept into the Westphalian plain, its right wing was to form the northern arm of the pincers, while the southern arm thrust up from the area of Frankfort-on-Main. The acquisition of the Remagen bridgehead was an unexpected asset to the latter operation, and one of incalculable value. While its threat brought a German concentration along the Sieg river to prevent a direct attack on the Ruhr from the south, the weight of the American strength in the bridgehead was expanded toward the south within reach of the Third Army; and the co-ordinated operations of these two forces in turn gave protection to the Seventh Army in its thrust across the Rhine farther south.

These plans developed with speed and precision. On March 25, with the foothold north of the Ruhr securely established, the American First Army struck out from the centre of the Remagen bridgehead in an expanding drive toward the east and southeast. Simultaneously the Third Army surged forward 27 miles, outflanking Frankfort on the south and reaching the Main at Aschaffenburg. Next day the Seventh Army effected a surprise crossing north of Mannheim and swung up on the right flank of the Third, which in its turn was expanding its corridor northward toward the First. By March 29 the northward swing of the Third had captured Frankfort and had linked with the eastward-thrusting First in the vicinity of Giessen. While the Third continued its drive northward toward Kassel, the First also wheeled to the north in a parallel thrust toward Paderborn. It was now drawing an arc around the Ruhr to the south and east while the Ninth Army outflanked that region to the north. On March 31 the Ninth broke through the German defences on the Lippe river near Hamm; and next day the First and Ninth came together near Lippstadt to complete the double envelopment of the Ruhr.

This was an irretrievable disaster for the Germans. The great industrial areas of Silesia and the Saar had already been overrun. The loss of the Ruhr and its resources was a fatal blow to German war production. Even more shattering to all prospects of a coherent defence was the loss in manpower. The Allies had thrown a net around virtually the whole of the Fifteenth and Fifth Panzer Armies, as well as part of the First Parachute Army. Out of approximately 60 divisions on the western front, 21 were trapped in the Ruhr. All attempts to break out eastward were repelled, and escape was rendered hopeless by the Allied advance far beyond the doomed pocket. Its reduction proceeded steadily at the hands of the American Fifteenth Army together with parts of the Ninth and First—a total of 17 divisions. By April 11, with the capture of Essen and Gelsen-kirchen, the pocket was down to half its original size and resistance had begun to collapse. Three days later it was split in two as forces from north and south joined near Hagen. The eastern portion was quickly mopped up. The remaining part was liquidated on April 19, bringing the total yield of prisoners to 325,000—double the original Allied estimate of the German forces involved.

The Ruhr had thus yielded an even greater toll than the encircle-ment of the Sixth German Army at Stalingrad, hitherto claimed as the largest double envelopment in the history of war. It meant that the whole German centre had been torn out, and that no solid defensive force stood between the Allies and Berlin. The First and Ninth Armies, leaving part of their forces to deal with the Ruhr, swept eastward against little more than local opposition, the speed and scope of their progress limited chiefly by the problem of supplies. The Ninth drove across the Weser on April 5, pressed on through Hanover and Brunswick, and on April 11 reached the Elbe in the vicinity of Magdeburg. One bridgehead across that river was wiped out a few days later by a desperate German counter-attack, but another and firmer foothold was established 15 miles southeast of Magdeburg, and that city itself was captured on April 18.

Farther south a similar curving sweep was meanwhile in progress, with the Third and First Armies driving eastward in close co-ordination. The closing of the Ruhr trap came when the northward thrust of the Third Army had reached the approaches to the vital junction of Kassel. In an abrupt change of direction, the Third swung its weight eastward on a broad front between Kassel and Fulda, assailing those two anchor points and driving through the outskirts of the Thuringian forest. Fulda was taken on April 3. Next day Kassel fell after bitter fighting, and Patton's armour swept beyond Eisenach to capture Gotha. The Third had crashed the

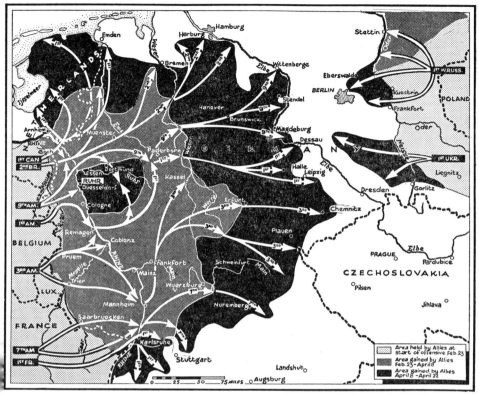

By permission of the New York *Times*

THE CLOSING PHASE IN GERMANY

barriers guarding the Thuringian plain; and while it rolled eastward with infantry closely following the tank spearheads, the First Army came up on its left flank south of the Harz mountains. On April 8 the First advanced 13 miles, crossing the Weser and capturing Goettingen. In two days its advance carried it to Nordhausen while the Third reached within striking distance of Erfurt and Weimar. By April 13 the First was battering its way into the outlying defences before Leipzig while the Third bypassed it on the south and drove across the Mulde toward Chemnitz. The First in its turn bypassed Leipzig on either side, drawing a siege arc about it and closing up to the Mulde, while its northern wing swept toward Dessau and the Elbe. On April 16 the First effected a junction with the Ninth a few miles west of Dessau at Kothen, pocketing the German forces in the Harz mountains whose liquidation during the following week yielded 56,000 prisoners. Meanwhile the ring was steadily tightened around Leipzig and the assault broke through the defences into the city itself. On April 19 the last resistance collapsed. Halle fell the same day, and from Magdeburg to besieged Chemnitz the Americans established full control of the Elbe-Mulde line on which they awaited an imminent junction with the Russians advancing from the east.

These drives, like those that were simultaneously in progress on either flank, were paced throughout by massed air power which was now virtually unchallenged. The month of April saw the death of the once mighty *Luftwaffe*. It died ignominiously, its remaining planes lying grounded and helpless for lack of fuel. The Allied air assault on oil and transportation had strangled German air power. Allied advances had captured refineries and storage depots and the bulk of German airfields. The fields from which German planes might still operate, and particularly those equipped with special runways for jet-propelled fighters, were mercilessly attacked during March and April. A last desperate effort by the Germans to give battle early in April was beaten down with heavy losses to the enemy. In four days up to April 10 the Allies attacked 50 airfields and destroyed 745 planes. That day saw a record effort by German jet-propelled fighters, which cost over 100 planes of all types destroyed in the air and nearly 300 on the ground. From then on the German air force was finished, and Allied fliers swept the airfields at will, demolishing the helpless planes that lay on the ground. Over 1000 were destroyed on April 16 to bring the total for the month to more than 3000. The disintegration of the German fighting forces on the ground was accompanied by their annihilation in the air.

While three armies in the centre drove into the heart of Germany against meagre opposition, four others were meeting stiffer resistance on either flank. Even with the bulk of their country overrun, the Germans still clung to the hope of prolonging resistance in the areas that remained. In the north they clung to the rocket coast and the ports of Holland and northwest Germany. In the south, where they envisaged the establishment of a national redoubt in the mountainous region centering on Berchtesgaden, they fought bitterly to protect the approaches to this last fortress and to gain time in which to consolidate for a final stand.

The three armies of the 21st Army Group which launched the main thrust across the Rhine had each a distinct task assigned to it. The first objective of the American Ninth Army on the right was to form the northern arm of the pincers against the Ruhr; and when the trap was closed, it was transferred back to the 12th Army Group for the drive to the Elbe. Meanwhile the British Second Army in the centre struck toward the North Sea and the ports of Bremen and Hamburg; and on the left the Canadian First Army fanned out in a dual movement designed to cut off Holland and to crush the German forces remaining in that country.

Following the breakthrough beyond Dorsten, the British drove swiftly northeast toward the last obstacles guarding the open Hanover plain. Their impetus carried them to Rheine and Muenster by April 2, and prevented the Germans from making a stand on the Dortmund-Ems canal. Beyond lay the wooded heights of the

Teutoburger Wald, stretching southeast below Osnabrueck; and here the Germans tried to establish a new line which would extend eastward across the corridor between the Ems and the Weser. But this was weakened by the British capture of Rheine, and by the advance of the Ninth Army toward Hanover which broke through the Teutoburger Wald around Bielefeld. By April 4 the whole barrier had collapsed. The British outflanked it at both ends and broke through with strong armoured forces into open country. Osnabrueck was captured, the Ems and the Weser crossed, and at a speed of as much as 60 miles in 24 hours the British drove northeast toward Bremen.

Their advance was checked a few miles below that port by desperate German resistance. The Germans rallied to defend their North Sea ports on a line covering Emden and Oldenburg and Bremen and extending along the Aller to Celle. On April 10, while one spearhead battled on the outskirts of Bremen, the expanding British right wing broke through north of Hanover to reach the Aller in a thrust which presented a growing threat to Hamburg. In two days of fighting they captured Celle and thrust a bridgehead across the Aller; but fierce German resistance together with extended supply lines temporarily halted their progress except for a further eastward extension of their right flank. On April 16 however their drive was renewed in force. Breaking out of their Aller bridgehead, they swept to the Elbe below Hamburg and closed rapidly toward that port. By April 21 they had fought into the suburbs of both Hamburg and Bremen, and had thrust a wedge between them which threatened to flank Bremen from the east and north.

The left flank of this advance was supported by the Canadian Army. In the initial stage after the crossing of the Rhine, some of the stiffest fighting was at the northern end of the bridgehead, where the Germans sought to consolidate the shoulders of the British penetration and contain its expansion. There was a two-day battle before the Germans were dislodged from Rees, and four more days were needed to drive them from Emmerich. But these gains, together with the progress of the main thrust north of the Ruhr, gradually secured elbow room. To the British and Canadian units which had been temporarily transferred from the Canadian First to the British Second Army, others were added as the flank expanded. By April 2 the Canadian First Army was once again in action as a separate formation, and had embarked on the liberation of Holland—a task which, according to Clement Attlee in the House of Commons, was now regarded as "an essential operation which cannot wait".

In the operations which followed, the area between Zutphen and Hengelo became the pivot for pressure in two main directions. One was toward the north to cut off the whole of Holland. The other was toward the Zuider Zee with the objective of splitting Holland itself. Driving across the Twente canal between Zutphen and Hengelo, the Canadians struck simultaneously toward the north and the west. At the same time other formations pressed toward the Ijssel below Zutphen, attacking the rear of the defences which the Germans had built on the east bank, while a concerted attack toward Arnhem from the south threatened to flank the old Dutch defence line on the west bank and to pinch out the whole southern part of the Ijssel line.

On April 5 a breakthrough beyond Hengelo allowed the armoured forces to shake free in a swift and powerful drive toward the North Sea. On an expanding front the Canadian forces, including a Polish armoured division, swung past the tangled waterways east of the Zuider Zee. One flank fanned out northwest across the Ems at Meppen. The other struck eastward to threaten the rail and highway centre of Meppel. On April 9, with the escape route through Meppel doomed, the Germans breached the dikes in that region, flooding the stretch of land between Meppel and Zwolle and reducing their land routes from western Holland to the causeway across the mouth of the Zuider Zee.

Meanwhile the drive toward the north was aided by the dropping of parachute troops in northeast Holland on the night of April 7. Two days later contact was established between these forces and the steadily advancing armour. East of the Ems the drive ran into stiff resistance along the Kuesten canal below Oldenburg, and by mid-April a hard struggle was in progress to hold and expand a bridgehead which had been thrust across that waterway. Farther west however there were fewer obstacles. When a knot of resistance was encountered at Groningen, it was bypassed to the east by columns which on April 15 reached the North Sea to complete the isolation of Holland. Groningen fell next day; and while one force fanned eastward along the coast, others proceeded swiftly with the task of clearing northeast Holland. By April 18, all that remained to the Germans in this sector were a few isolated pockets along the coast.

Farther south, meanwhile a bitter struggle was in progress. The experiences of the Canadian Army on the Scheldt and in the Hochwald were repeated in northwest Holland. The bridgeheads across the Twente canal were slowly expanded in hard fighting. A desperate German defence at Arnhem held the offensive from that direction in check for over a week. Between these two points there was bitter fighting along the Ijssel line. On April 11, however, the expulsion of the Germans from Deventer and the crossing of the Ijssel weakened the German position; and its collapse came on the 14th when the capture of Arnhem and the entry into Appeldoorn undermined what remained of the Ijssel line. The Germans fell back to the Grebbe line, flooding the area between Amsterdam and Utrecht. On April 18 the Canadian advance reached the southeast shore of the Zuider Zee; and the Germans, breaching the causeway which held back the waters of the North Sea, gathered themselves for a last-ditch defence of the cities of northwest Holland and the ports of Amsterdam and Rotterdam.

The tenacity of the enemy on the northwest flank had its parallel in the southeast. The crossing of the Rhine by the American Seventh Army was followed by a rapid swing to the Main to cover the flank of the Third, and then by an eastward thrust whose flank in turn was protected by the French First Army which crossed the Rhine between Mannheim and Karlsruhe on March 31. By that date the

Seventh had taken Mannheim and Heidelberg and was driving toward Wurzburg and Heilbronn. Both those towns offered a stubborn defence. Wurzburg was not cleared until April 6. Heilbronn held out until the 12th. But while these actions partially dammed the advance, they did not completely halt it. The towns were bypassed before they fell, and by April 14 the Seventh Army had driven through Schweinfurt to Bamberg and had covered one-third of the distance from Heilbronn to Nuremberg. Yet the gains were scored against stubborn and persistent opposition, and on the southern flank of the Seventh a spearhead which thrust from Heilbronn to Crailsheim was assailed by counter-attacks which forced it briefly to give ground. Still farther south the French, after capturing Karlsruhe on April 4, had plunged into the Black Forest and were being held to slow progress in that difficult region.

The latter half of April however saw a new surge forward. On April 16 the Seventh drove forward to Nuremberg, and in five days of hard fighting encircled and captured that Nazi shrine. By the 19th the French had broken through the Black Forest and were sweeping forward in a drive which carried them through Stuttgart on April 22 and on to the Swiss frontier, sealing off the remaining German garrisons in the Black Forest region. The Seventh swung southward, supporting the French thrust and sweeping toward the Danube on a broad front below Nuremberg; and a new shift of direction by the American Third Army also carried it southward toward the Danube and the fastnesses of Bavaria and Austria.

By the end of the third week in April the downfall of Germany was clearly in sight. The imminence of a junction between the Americans and the Russians which would split the Reich in two was tacitly acknowledged by the Germans in a division of command which placed Busch in charge in the north and entrusted Kesselring with the defence in the south. Germany was being battered into fragments, and would soon be reduced to isolated pockets of resistance. No useful military end could be served by further resistance. The Nazis still clung to the forlorn and desperate hope that dissensions between the Allies might be used to divide them in the very moment of victory, thus making possible negotiations which would mitigate the consequences of defeat and win a moderate peace for Germany. But a more far-reaching objective was implicit in the effort to avoid any formal surrender, and by a defiant resistance to lay the foundations on which a legend could be built for future use.

From that point of view the Germans were no longer fighting the existing war, but were engaged in the preliminary campaign of the next. Both the military clique and the Nazi party had hopes of evading responsibility for the military disaster which had over-whelmed the nation. Each could envisage a situation in which it would be possible to throw on the other the blame for Germany's military collapse. Each was now striving to enshrine itself as the embodiment of a heroic resistance which refused to accept defeat even when all was lost. In the creation of such a legend, two centres emerged as strategically paramount. One was Berlin; the other was the southern redoubt. But already the Russians were in Berlin, and the national redoubt was crumbling as the concerted power of the Allies closed on it from every point of the compass.

VIENNA AND BERLIN

How vital a place the idea of an Alpine redoubt occupied in German plans was shown by the desperate defence of its eastern approaches. The Russians inched forward only slowly along the arc which Konev and Petrov were pushing toward Moravska Ostrava. In central Slovakia the Russian drive toward the middle Hron encountered tenacious resistance, illustrated by the week-long battle which ended with the capture of Zvolen on March 14. Above the Danube the bridgehead which Malinovsky had thrust across the Hron to the outskirts of Komarno was wiped out by a German counter-drive during the third week in February. And in Hungary the Germans continued their desperate efforts to forestall a Russian drive toward Austria and to recover the ground that had been lost during the previous offensive.

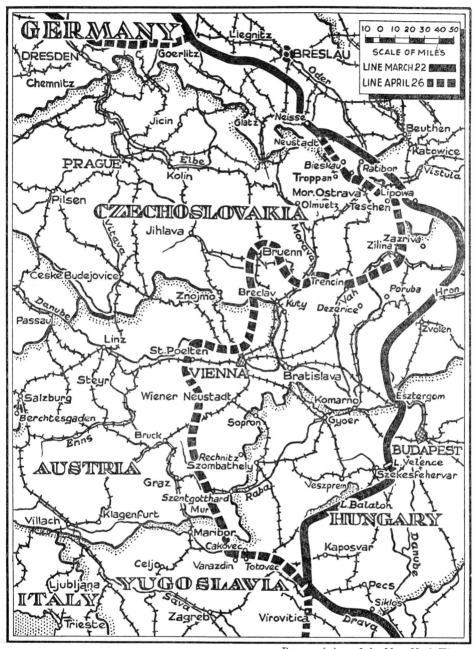

By permission of the New York *Times*

THE SOUTHEASTERN FRONT, SPRING 1945

The failure of the sustained German efforts to relieve Budapest in January, and the fall of that city on February 13, did not end the struggle for control of the Danube. In spite of the Russian sweep to the Oder and the gathering threat to Berlin, the single serious effort at a counter-offensive was mounted not in Germany but in Hungary. Massing strong forces which were spearheaded by 11 tank divisions, the Germans in the first week in March struck at the Russian positions on either side of Lake Balaton and along the Drava. The main blow fell on the sector north of Lake Balaton. Simultaneous attacks were launched south of the lake, and across the Drava at a point some 30 miles west of the Danube. The immediate objective of these concerted assaults was to cut off and regain the area between Lake Balaton and the Danube and to destroy the Russian forces below Budapest. The ultimate aim, according to Moscow, was to force the Danube itself and gain a bridgehead for a drive eastward toward Rumania. The outcome fell far short of these exaggerated hopes. In a fortnight of bitter fighting the Germans succeeded in gaining some ground but failed to capture any major strategic points. The Drava bridgehead was sealed off and assailed by strong Russian attacks. The penetrations on either side of Lake Balaton were achieved only at heavy cost. The Russians followed their accustomed tactics of absorbing the attacks, giving ground where necessary but exacting a mounting price from the enemy while they awaited an opportunity to regain the initiative against the exhausted foe.

In mid-March their moment came. By the 12th the Germans had forced a crossing of the Sarviz canal which runs southeast below Szekesfehervar, and were throwing the main weight of their attack into a furious effort to extend their gains on either side. The resulting shift of forces gradually weakened their left wing, and Tolbukhin seized his chance. On March 16 he struck with two columns which drove west and southwest in a converging attack toward Szekesfehervar. The Germans rushed tank reinforcements to the threatened sector, but they arrived too late to redress the situation. On the third day Tolbukhin threw in his armour to exploit the initial penetration; and by this time Malinovsky had swung his left wing south of the Danube and was driving north of the Vertes mountains toward Komarno and Gyoer.

Under the impact of this concerted offensive the whole German position crumbled. By March 25 the Russians had overwhelmed the defences between Lake Balaton and the Danube, and their combined armies were sweeping westward on an expanding front. Tolbukhin had regained Szekesfehervar and was driving through the Bakony mountains beyond Veszprem and Zirc. Malinovsky had retaken Esztergom and driven to within 6 miles of Komarno on the south, while his forces north of the Danube renewed their offensive across the Hron. Gyoer, a vital centre of defence and communications, fell to Malinovsky on March 28. Next day, in an advance of 20 miles, Tolbukhin took Szombathely and reached the border of Austria. Komarno fell on March 30; and on the same day Tolbukhin, whose forces had cleared the eastern shore of Lake Balaton in hard fighting and were now swinging down the western shore, opened a drive on his left wing against the German positions between Lake Balaton and the Drava which by April 4 completed the expulsion of the Germans from Hungarian soil.

By that date Vienna was in imminent peril. The direct approach to the city lay through the gap south of Bratislava between the Danube and the Neuseidler See, and here the Germans had gathered strong forces to bar the Russian passage. But the line was outflanked by the twin advances of Tolbukhin south of the Neuseidler See and Malinovsky north of the Danube. With both flanks turned, the defence collapsed under a frontal assault by Malinovsky's left wing. Tolbukhin's impetuous assault overran Sopron on April 1 and Wiener Neustadt on April 3 and wheeled up toward Vienna from the south. On April 5 the attack broke through three strongly fortified lines guarding the approaches to the city. A spearhead drove around the city to the west, and in two days fought its way through the Wiener Wald to reach the Danube northwest of Vienna. Astride the Danube,

Malinovsky's progress was equally rapid. On April 4 he captured the pivotal centre of Bratislava and drove through the Little Carpathians on a broad front toward the Morava valley. South of the Danube his forces broke the German lines along the Leitha on April 5, smashing the last defences of the Bratislava gap. On the same day his forces joined with those of Tolbukhin on the southern outskirts of Vienna, cutting off the remnants of the Sixth Panzer Army which had defended the city from the east. All efforts by the trapped Germans to break out toward Vienna were beaten back, and their liquidation proceeded remorselessly during the succeeding week which saw the simultaneous crushing of resistance in Vienna itself.

On April 7 Tolbukhin's attack from the south drove into the limits of Vienna proper. At the same time the forces which had swung round the city pressed toward it from the west and northwest, while Malinovsky cleared the banks of the Danube to the east and northeast. By April 10, after four days of bitter street fighting, Tolbukhin had captured the central district of the city and Malinovsky had cleared the northern suburbs. The remaining defenders were pressed into an area bounded by the Danube river and the canal which ran south of it, forming an island 3 miles long and barely half a mile wide.

Three more days brought an end to resistance. On April 13 the defence was crushed, and Vienna was completely in Russian hands. Tolbukhin's forces wheeled westward, and pressed forward against stubborn opposition along a broad front whose right wing was aimed at Linz while its left threatened the industrial city of Graz. By mid-April however this drive came to a temporary halt well short of these objectives. Below the Carpathians the chief weight of the Russian efforts was thrown into Malinovsky's thrust northward toward Bruenn (Brno) in conjunction with a new converging offensive toward Moravska Ostrava; while farther north on the main front along the Oder and Neisse the Russians launched their massive and long-expected drive toward Berlin.

While the Allies in the west were sweeping from the Rhine to the Elbe, the Russians on the Oder were massing the guns and armour which would make possible a crushing and decisive blow against the German capital. By mid-April their preparations had been completed, and their action would bring that "one good strong heave all together" which, as Churchill had said in March, was all that was needed to topple what was left of Nazi Germany. Preliminary probing attacks from the Oder bridgehead west of Kuestrin paved the way for a massive assault on the night of April 15. Backed by tremendous artillery support and covered by strong air forces, 4000 tanks crashed into the German lines. The Oder defences were broken; and on April 17 a powerful drive by Konev across the Neisse brought the full pattern of the offensive into operation.

The operations against Berlin, with their basic hammer-and-sickle design, had many features in common with the drive on Vienna. There was the assault on the left flank which swept around a natural defensive area to assail the city from the south, the closing of the pincers from the south and east which cut off large forces southeast of the city, the swing around the capital to the west to isolate it while resistance was reduced by a closing attack from all directions. The major difference was the weight of the frontal attack on Berlin from the east, where Zhukov's forces carried the brunt of the direct assault which broke the main German defences.

Zhukov's drive was launched on a 50-mile sector between Zehden and Fuerstenberg. He was already across the Oder in the centre of this stretch on either side of Kuestrin. Other crossings were effected during the initial stage of the drive on either side of the original footholds. Three main prongs emerged as the attack progressed. On the north a spearhead drove into the corridor between Berlin and the Hohenzollern canal with the aim of outflanking the capital. In the centre a direct frontal attack from the vicinity of Kuestrin struck at Berlin from the east. Still another prong thrust southeast from the original bridgehead in a second flanking threat to Berlin from the south.

The left prong of Zhukov's main drive was thus skirting the northern fringe of the region of lakes and forests lying southeast of Berlin. Simultaneously Konev was swinging around that region to the south and west. From his positions along the Neisse he struck with his main forces on the sector between Forst and Goerlitz. His right wing ran into strong opposition around Cottbus, where a heavy tank battle developed during the first two days. By April 19 however the German defences had been broken. Konev had thrust two bridgeheads across the Spree between Cottbus and Bautzen, smashing the last natural defence line east of the Elbe; and while one spearhead drove directly west in the direction of Dresden and Leipzig, another swung behind Cottbus and wheeled north toward Berlin.

The two jaws of the vise closed rapidly and inexorably on the doomed German capital. The weight of Zhukov's assault battered down the solid system of fortifications between the Oder and Berlin. By April 21 he had penetrated the city from the northeast, and his forces which had cut the motor highway around the outskirts were sweeping along it in two directions, extending their arc against Berlin itself and flanking the German artillery which was using the highway for gun positions. By this time Konev's rapid dash from the south had carried him almost to Berlin's outskirts, and his spearheads were fanning out westward in a threat of encirclement. Two days later, with one-third of Berlin already in Zhukov's hands, Konev entered the city from the south; and on April 24 his forces made a preliminary junction with Zhukov inside the city limits.

This contact of the two army groups completed the encirclement of the Germans in the Brandenburg lake country south of Berlin. A considerable part of the German Ninth Army was caught in the sack and assailed by a drive from the east which was now in progress, linking the two initial sectors of the offensive and liquidating the trapped German forces. Meanwhile an outer ring was closing around Berlin itself. The northern prong of Zhukov's drive, after hard fighting against the German fortified lines west of the Oder, broke through for spectacular gains. On April 23 a rapid surge carried it north of Berlin through Oranienburg and across the Havel river at Hennigsdorf. There it wheeled south to Nauen, cutting the roads and railways northwest of Berlin; and on April 25 Zhukov's continued advance below Nauen joined with the column which Konev had driven north past outflanked Potsdam to complete the encirclement of Berlin.

A bitter and relentless struggle was now in progress for the dying capital. From the outskirts the Russians drove down Berlin's broad avenues toward the heart of the city. The Germans had organized the defence into a series of zones, and fought from road blocks and fortified buildings and pillboxes at street intersections. Berlin's subways and sewers provided underground strongholds in which strong forces could lurk and passages from which they could make surprise sorties in the rear of their opponents. It was a grim and fantastic struggle that turned one of the world's great capitals into a nightmare battlefield where armed men stalked each other among ruins and through blackened tunnels in deadly personal combat.

By April 28 the end was close at hand. The Russians had made still another junction inside the city, cutting off the southwest section and reducing the main defence area to a pocket of 25 square miles. The focal points were the Tiergarten which had been turned into an underground fortress, and the Chancellery where Hitler was said to be directing a stand to the death. There was a growing strain of masochism in the reports of Nazi propagandists which glorified the horrors that Berlin was enduring and the determination of Hitler to go down with his capital in a flaming holocaust that would leave nothing surviving. But the last-ditch stand crumbled as Russian veterans of Stalingrad pressed the final assault. On May 2 the last defenders of Berlin surrendered, and the hope of creating a deathless legend came to an end. The Russians estimated that the fight for Berlin had cost the Germans over 500,000 in killed and captured, in addition to nearly 200,000 from the pocket southwest of Berlin which was liquidated on the same day.

THE DEFENCE DISINTEGRATES

The twelve days of the battle for Berlin saw a series of developments which brought swiftly nearer the final victory of the Allies. One was the splitting of Germany and the establishment of contact between the eastern and western Allies. While Konev's right wing swept north to Berlin, his left continued its drive westward to reach the Elbe below Torgau on April 23. Barely 25 miles now separated his forces from the American First Army on the Mulde, and no important enemy forces remained between the two armies. On April 25, Russian and American patrols met each other in the area west of Torgau to complete the disruption of Germany into two separate parts.

This historic event, which had been so eagerly anticipated, actually came as an anticlimax. From the military point of view the formal contact no longer held more than a casual significance. All chance that the Germans could maintain effective contact between north and south had long since been ended by the progressive disruption of their armies and the herding of their remaining forces toward the Baltic and the Danube. West of Berlin the steady widening of the Russian corridor brought Zhukov in his turn to the Elbe, where his forces made contact with the British on May 2 and with the Americans next day; and by that date an even more significant junction had been reached along the Baltic coast between Rokossovsky and Montgomery.

The unleashing of the offensive which carried Zhukov across the middle Oder was promptly followed by a drive by Rokossovsky along the lower reaches of the river. Striking on a front of 25 miles between Stettin and Schwedt, his forces battered against the stout German defences which confronted them. In several days of bitter fighting they secured a bridgehead on the sector below Stettin and gradually enlarged it against desperate German resistance. On April 26 the defence gave way. The Russians drove the enemy from both Stettin and Schwedt and swept 19 miles beyond the Oder for a complete breakthrough. Fanning out on a front of 80 miles, Rokossovsky drove west along a broad stretch of the Baltic coast. On April 29 his advance carried him into Mecklenburg and brought the capture of Anklam and Neubrandenburg. On May 1 he took Stralsund, and next day both Rostock and Warnemuende were in his hands and his spearheads were racing toward those of the advancing British.

By this time Montgomery had finally broken the deadlock below the North Sea ports. The expanding wedge that was driven between Hamburg and Bremen cut the last communications linking the two towns; and while one force pressed into Hamburg's suburbs, another closed around Bremen. At midnight on April 23 the decisive assault on the latter port was launched by 4 divisions, and on the 26th the town was in British hands and only scattered resistance in the port area remained to be mopped up.

This success was followed by renewed pressure on either flank. On April 28 the Canadians, who had been steadily developing their bridgehead over the Kuesten canal toward Oldenburg, lashed out in a new direction with a surprise crossing of the Ems at Leer to present a new threat to Emden. On the 29th the British, reinforced by an American corps, drove across the Elbe below Hamburg, capturing Lauenburg and establishing a bridgehead which by May 1 had been expanded to 20 miles in width and had reached a depth of 12 miles. Next day they burst from its confines to overwhelm the crumbling German defences. In a single surge they drove north to the Baltic, cutting off Denmark and capturing the port of Luebeck. On May 3 they drove into Hamburg, which the Germans hastily declared an open city; and while Allied fliers wreaked havoc among the ships in which the routed Germans were trying to escape to Denmark and Norway, the converging British and Russian forces effected a solid junction in the Wismar area between Luebeck and Rostock. The northern pocket was split. The capture of Oldenburg by the Canadians on May 2 foreshadowed the collapse of the western segment; while in the dwindling pocket gripped by the Russians and the British the disorganized Germans embarked on mass surrenders which were a prelude to complete capitulation.

By this time indeed the leaders of the Reich were frantically seeking some escape from the full consequences of national military disaster. By the latter part of April even the nominal remnants of direction and control had slipped from Hitler's hands. The resulting rivalries between military and party leaders, whose details remained obscure up to the time of writing, were sharpened by the need for prompt action if anything was to be saved from the wreckage. Even Himmler's authority was rapidly evaporating, and its last shreds vanished with the failure of his effort to divide the Allies by the offer of a separate peace.

The offer was conveyed through Count Folke Bernadotte, deputy chairman of the Swedish Red Cross, who was in Germany on Red Cross business. At Himmler's request the Count met with him at Luebeck in the early hours of April 24. Bernadotte was informed that Hitler was suffering from a brain hemorrhage and could not live more than two days, and was asked to request the Swedish government to arrange for Germany's unconditional capitulation to the Allies in the west in order that she might be free to throw all her remaining strength into the struggle against the Russians in the east. It was a proposal that never had the slightest chance of success. Britain and the United States at once informed Moscow of the overture and of their intention to reject it; and Bernadotte carried back the reply that only unconditional surrender to the three leading Allies on all fronts would be accepted.

This was a final blow to Himmler's ascendancy. A new group emerged to seize control of the shadowy claim to authority which was all that now remained to any German government. On May 1 the Hamburg radio, with every effort at solemn fanfare, announced that Hitler had met his death in Berlin, and that the new Fuehrer was Admiral Doenitz who claimed to have been appointed by Hitler as his successor on April 30.

The combined scepticism and indifference with which the Allies regarded this announcement was a vivid commentary on the hopelessness of Germany's situation. A few weeks previously the news that Hitler was dead would have been hailed as a major event which would drastically change the prospects of the war. By the end of April the situation was such that neither Hitler nor any other German leader could do anything which would affect the imminent outcome. The forces of disaster had escaped from human control as far as Germany was concerned. Whether Hitler was alive or dead, or who took over his nominal leadership, was no longer of serious account. The initial appeal by Doenitz himself was an implicit revelation of impotence. He could only plead for continued resistance to the Russians and hint that he was still prepared to deal with Britain and the United States. Such a course held only despair. All hope of securing a separate peace had vanished, and all prospects of prolonged resistance were ebbing as the surrender of the German armies in Italy began a swift process of piecemeal capitulation in the field.

The triumph in Italy was a hard-earned and gratifying reward after months of strain and frustration. Almost from the beginning the Italian front was the victim of fluctuating decisions on strategy. In the allotment of men and supplies the operations in the west had a paramount claim which on several occasions had to be satisfied at the expense of Italian operations. The offensive strength which made possible the successful drive on Rome was sapped during the summer by the diversion of the Seventh Army to the invasion of southern France. As a consequence, the assault on the Gothic Line was launched without the superiority of force that was necessary to offset the German advantage in terrain. The Allies were not strong enough to effect the proposed double envelopment which would destroy the German forces on the Adriatic flank and open the way for a sweep northward to the Alps and the shattering of the remaining forces in Italy. The Gothic Line was penetrated, but the Germans held firm on the approaches to Bologna and continued to bar the way toward the Po valley.

During the autumn and winter, in consequence, there was stalemate along almost the whole Italian front. Once more the Allied forces were condemned to dreary and rain-drenched months amid the peaks of the Apennines or in the muddy coastal plain. On the Fifth Army Front only a few local actions broke the monotony. The Eighth Army was more active during the early winter as it continued its efforts along the Adriatic flank. But it was still working against the grain of the country, and in its painful advance across the drenched countryside there was always one more river to cross—the Montone, the Lamone, the Senio. Dogged pressure during November and December resulted in an improvement of positions on this flank. Forli was taken on November 10, Ravenna on December 15, Faenza on December 17. A week later the Senio was reached on a broad front, and by the first week in January the Allies were in full control of its east bank. But the effort and the cost involved in these operations discouraged their continuance; the Eighth Army was weakened by the transfer of troops to handle the troubled situation in Greece; and during the remainder of the winter the Allies contented themselves with pinning down the German Tenth and Fourteenth Armies in Italy and preventing the diversion of good quality troops from that front to the Oder or the Rhine.

But if the Allied forces in Italy felt that they were the victims of neglect, the Germans facing them were far from happy about their own position. They too realized that they were committed to a secondary theatre and that their fate would be decided by operations on other fronts. As the Russians swept to the Oder and the Danube and the Allies battered their way toward the Rhine, German leaders in Italy became increasingly uneasy at the prospect that resistance would collapse in their rear. By February they were exploring the possibility of forestalling such a development, and German emissaries were approaching the Allies with suggestions of a surrender in Italy.

The moving spirit was General Karl Wolff, commander of the SS and police and German plenipotentiary in Italy. The secret and roundabout negotiations which he initiated led on March 19 to a personal interview in Switzerland between Wolff and two Allied representatives. Although the conversations were unsatisfactory as far as concrete and acceptable proposals were concerned, the Allies were prepared to continue the negotiations. But Himmler was suspicious of Wolff's trip to Switzerland and placed him under stricter control, and the recall of Kesselring from Italy made it uncertain that his successor as military commander, General Heinrich von Vietinghoff, would fall in with Wolff's plans. By the beginning of April it was clear that no further progress was likely and that the decision would have to be forced on the Germans by defeat in the field.

The final offensive in Italy opened on the night of April 9. Behind a heavy artillery barrage and an air bombardment by 1000 bombers, the rested and reinforced Eighth Army struck on a broad front along the Senio river. Flame-throwing tanks cleared the Germans from the diked banks of the 50-yard stream; a solid bridgehead was established in the face of opposition from 5 German divisions; and by April 11 the Allies had advanced 4 miles to the Santerno river and were driving along a 25-mile front astride the Rimini-Bologna highway and northward to Lake Comacchio.

This was a powerful wheeling movement to roll up the German flank and break through the last barriers guarding the Po valley. The Germans fought fiercely to hold the advance beyond the Santerno and through the Argenta gap west of Lake Comacchio; but though they slowed the Allied progress, they were unable to bring it to a halt. By April 15 the Allies had taken Imola and were pushing beyond the Sillario 10 miles past the Santerno in the face of persistent counter-attacks. Next day the offensive was broadened to its full scope when the Fifth Army, after a diversionary thrust along the west coast through Massa and Carrara, struck behind a massive air and artillery barrage in the centre south of Bologna. The whole German left flank was threatened with envelopment, and a major Allied breakthrough would spell the doom of the enemy armies in Italy.

On April 19 the break came. The right flank of the Eighth Army, after a week of battering against some of the most concentrated defences it had yet encountered, crashed through the Argenta gap and sent its armour sweeping into the Po valley. This was a decisive achievement. All the German reserves had now been engaged, and there were no forces for a major counter-attack such as alone could redress the situation. They still fought hard to bar the way to Ferrara, but their main purpose was now to withdraw their threatened forces from the Bologna area. On April 20 the Fifth Army drove forward 7 miles, cutting the highway northwest of Bologna. Next day that city fell to the combined forces of the two Allied armies. By the 23rd spearheads of both armies had reached the Po, bypassing Modena and fighting into the outskirts of Ferrara, while masses of Allied planes hammered relentlessly at the roads crowded with retreating German columns. The defence was completely shattered, and the only question remaining was whether any part of the German forces could make good a retreat to the Alps.

That question was answered by the speed of the Allied advance, which was powerfully aided by the activities of the Italian partisans. The Allied breakthrough was the signal for a concerted and carefully planned rising in the chief cities in northern Italy. Patriot forces drove the Germans from such centres as Milan, Turin, Genoa and Venice, seizing utilities and communications and harbour facilities and preserving them from destruction. The last relics of the Fascist régime, which had rested solely on German support, collapsed completely. Mussolini, fleeing with his mistress and a party of supporters, was captured near the Swiss frontier. A summary trial followed by a swift execution brought the Duce's career to a sordid end. The bodies of the dictator and his companions were taken to Milan and exposed there to the blows and execrations of those over whom he had once held absolute sway.

Meanwhile the Allies were plugging the escape route of the Germans in Italy. The right wing of the Fifth Army raced north toward the Brenner Pass. Mantua was bypassed and Verona taken on April 26. Brescia and Bergamo fell two days later. The historic quadrilateral which guarded the Alpine route running east of Lake Garda was thus overwhelmed before the Germans could organize a

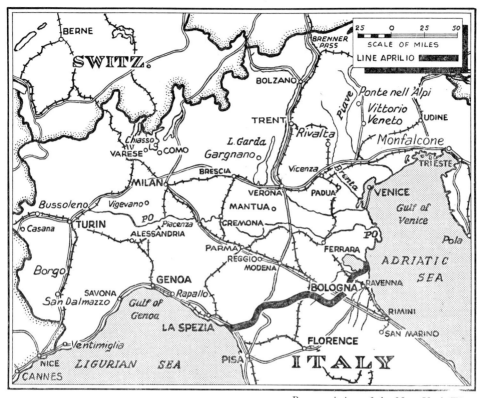

By permission of the New York *Times*

NORTHERN ITALY

stand to protect their retreat. Their armies were split and cut off from their main route of escape; and while the Eighth Army swung around the head of the Adriatic, capturing Venice and driving on toward the Yugoslav frontier, the Fifth swept over northwest Italy to capture Genoa and Milan and Turin, and a French force stabbed across the western border against the Fascist army in that region. By April 29 over 100,000 prisoners had been taken, the surrender of a whole division to Brazilian forces marked the beginning of mass capitulations, and negotiations for the surrender of the whole German army group had reached the final stage.

On April 19, the day of the definite Allied breakthrough, General Wolff had an interview with Hitler and Himmler near Berlin. He found Hitler still clinging to the illusion that "in two more months the break between the Anglo-Saxons and the Russians will come about and I shall join the party that approaches me first." The Fuehrer insisted that the armies must maintain their resistance during the interval. But Wolff knew that the game was lost, and von Vietinghoff agreed. New contacts were made with the Allies, and at Caserta on April 29 the envoys of Wolff and von Vietinghoff accepted unconditional surrender, to come into effect at noon on May 2. On the latter date the remnants of the two German armies in Italy laid down their arms. The Italian army in Liguria had surrendered the previous day. Across the border in Yugoslavia, Tito's forces trapped two German divisions above Fiume and obliged them to surrender; and while he drove on to enter Trieste, a New Zealand column dashed toward the border to receive the formal surrender of the garrison in that town and to occupy the port.

Two days after the capitulation in Italy, an even more dramatic surrender took place in northern Germany. Here as on most of the remaining fronts the burning desire of the German forces that remained was to avoid falling into the hands of the Russians. This was the object behind the overtures which were first made to Montgomery on May 2. On May 3 a mission headed by Admiral von Friedeburg, commander of the German navy, arrived with a proposal that remnants of three armies retreating before the Russians should surrender to the British.

In the interview which followed, Montgomery's sense of theatre was dramatically evident. To the initial German proposition he answered decisively: "No, certainly not. Those German armies are fighting the Russians . . . I have nothing to do with the happenings on my eastern front. You go surrender to the Soviet commander. The subject is closed." At once, however, he opened another and wider subject by asking if the Germans were prepared to surrender not only the forces mentioned, but all the others in the northwest including those in Holland and Denmark.

This was not an unreasonable bid. There were already signs that the Germans were reconciled to an early suppression of the remaining pockets in the north. In Denmark the Germans had virtually surrendered their authority and were preparing for withdrawal. In Holland, where hostilities were practically at a standstill, the Germans had consented to the dropping of food by Allied planes to the starving population, and later to the passage of food convoys through the battle lines. But the Germans rejected Montgomery's proposal, and put forward instead a proposal for a slow and protracted advance by the British by agreed stages.

Once more they were cut short. Montgomery refused to discuss what he would do in the future. But he proceeded to give the Germans a stunning revelation of what they might expect. In a dramatic gesture he produced his own operational map, showing the position at the moment and revealing to the Germans for the first time the extent of Allied progress in the west. They adjourned to lunch and to think it over; and the Admiral on leaving burst into tears and wept steadily throughout the meal. This tribute to his performance must have been supremely satisfying to the actor as well as to the soldier in Montgomery. He clinched it when conversations were resumed by demanding acceptance of his terms under threat of the continuation of hostilities and the annihilation of both German soldiers and civilians. There were further delays as the Germans departed to consult their superiors, but the issue had really been settled. Late in the afternoon on May 4, in a tent on Luneburg Heath, the Germans surrendered all their forces in the northwest except for their garrison in Norway.

All that remained was the wreck of the southern redoubt which was already falling apart. The German surrender in Italy applied not only to that country, but also to a considerable part of southwest Austria. It thus wiped out the barrier of the Alps on the south, while on the north the barrier of the Danube was being forced and the road opened to Austria from the west. The determination to crush the redoubt area before the Germans could organize a stand was indicated by the diversion of the American Third Army from the Chemnitz area southward into Bavaria. Driving across the tip of Czechoslovakia, where it nipped off the towns of Asch and Eger, the Third swung along the flank of the Seventh and took over part of its area, while the Seventh in its turn swerved toward the southeast. The right flank of the Third drove toward Regensburg, and the left flank skirted the southwest border of Czechoslovakia and pressed toward the Austrian border.

By April 28 the German collapse had begun. The line of the Danube had been completely broken after a week of stubborn fighting. The Seventh had broken through to capture Augsburg and was driving on Munich from that direction while its right wing swung southeast from Ulm toward the line of the Inn. The Third had taken Regensburg and Ingoldstadt and had driven a spearhead across the Austrian border northeast of Passau. Risings against the Nazis were reported in Munich and Salzburg as the Allied armies approached. Munich fell on April 30 after a sharp one-day fight. Next day, as the two American armies closed up to the Inn, the German surrender in Italy transformed the whole position. The Seventh drove down the Inn and through the Brenner Pass, capturing Innsbruck and linking up with the Fifth Army below the Alps. Salzburg and Berchtesgaden fell on the same day, and Patton drove to within a few miles of Linz, while Tolbukhin's armies renewed their pressure on Austria from the east. The heart of the redoubt had been pierced and its defenders shattered; and on May 5 the remnants of the German First and Nineteenth Armies agreed to surrender, effective the following day.

UNCONDITIONAL SURRENDER

By May 6 the area of organized resistance was reduced to Bohemia and Moravia. The forces that remained in Austria and Yugoslavia were rapidly being mopped up. The only resistance on German soil was maintained by the stubborn garrisons of Breslau and Dresden whose surrender came during the next two days. Only western Czechoslovakia remained, and its collapse was already imminent as Allied forces closed on it from all sides.

The Russian capture of Vienna was followed immediately by a concerted effort against the Germans in Czechoslovakia. Above the Danube, Malinovsky broadened his penetration of the Little Carpathians and swung his main weight up the Morava valley while a parallel spearhead farther west struck toward Bruenn. At the same time the armies of the Fourth Ukrainian front, whose command had been transferred from Petrov to Yeremenko, resumed their pressure toward the Moravian gap. With Malinovsky aiming at Olmuetz and Yeremenko's right wing hammering toward Troppau (Opava) the Germans were threatened with a pincers movement which would cut off the bulge extending eastward into Slovakia beyond Teschen and Zilina.

These thrusts made slow progress against bitter resistance. On April 16 Malinovsky tore a 12-mile breach in the German defences in Moravia and surged to within 18 miles of Bruenn. But the defence stiffened on the approaches, and it took until April 26 to drive the Germans from that arsenal city. There still stiff fighting as the Russians sought to broaden this salient eastward, where they reached the old battlefield of Austerlitz on April 29. Their advance up the Morava, though it made steady progress, took a fortnight to cover 25 miles above Hodonin after the capture of that town on April 13. During the same period Yeremenko ran into equally fierce opposition on the arc covering Moravska Ostrava. On April 22, however, he took Troppau whose fall weakened the flank of the German defences; and on April 30 Moravska Ostrava fell and the Moravian gap was at last in Russian hands. The capture of Zilina on the same day, followed by that of Teschen on May 3, marked the German withdrawal from the Slovakian bulge; and while the Germans threw in strong tank forces which held Malinovsky to slow and grinding progress below Olmuetz, their main forces withdrew across the border into Moravia.

The design was clearly to stabilize a new and more concentrated position in the area centering around Prague. Any hope of success, however, was fading as Allied forces thrust into Czechoslovakia from north and west and Czech patriots battled the Nazis in the capital itself. On May 1 a strike at the Skoda arms works in Prague touched off a general uprising. German tank forces, supported by the troops of the renegade Russian General Vlasov, were rushed to restore order; but they were only partially successful, and Vlasov shortly changed sides again and called on his men to aid the advancing Russians. From the west the United States Third Army drove a column across the border to take Pilsen on May 6 and advance toward Prague, and Marshal Konev sent a tank force racing south from the Berlin area and across the frontier below Dresden. With these powerful columns slashing across their rear from two directions, the Germans had little chance to consolidate on new lines, and their retreat from the east continued across Moravia and into Bohemia.

The last vestige of the southern redoubt was now on the verge of extinction. Except for Schroener's army group in Czechoslovakia, all organized resistance had already been ended by successive capitulations in the field. Germany lay completely at the mercy of the Allies, and the only question was whether the conquest would be achieved through piecemeal military surrender, or whether it would be crowned by a formal capitulation by the government which claimed nominal authority.

Doenitz and his associates decided on the second of these courses. A refusal to the end to acknowledge defeat might contribute to some future legend, but it would not save Germany from unchecked domination by the Allies. A formal surrender might be used to gain tacit Allied recognition of the Doenitz government as representing the German Reich, and might make possible its survival as the Allies became aware of the desirability of dealing through some effective German authority. A series of pronouncements indicated the hopes now cherished by Doenitz and his colleagues that they would be left in power in spite of their Nazi pasts. Albert Speer, Minister of Armaments and Production, coupled a public admission of inescapable defeat with an implied appeal to the Allies for a generous treatment of the heroic German nation. Doenitz asserted on May 5 that the struggle against the Western Powers had become senseless and that he was only trying to save his people from the Bolshevik invader. The new Foreign Minister, Count Lutz von Schwerin-Krosigk, harped on the same theme; and in his broadcast announcing that Doenitz had ordered the armed forces to give up the fight, in language which gave no hint that Germany had any cause for repentance, he appealed for a spirit of reconciliation on the part of the Allies and for "that freedom without which no nation can lead a bearable and dignified existence."

Yet it was only the military leaders that were formally accepted by the Allies as responsible agents. In the early hours of May 7, General Jodl as the representative of the High Command signed at Rheims the brief document which committed Germany to unconditional surrender, effective May 8 at 11.01 P.M. Central European time. On May 8 a second ceremony took place in battered and captured Berlin at which Keitel, Friedeburg and Stumpff as heads of the three German armed services put their names to the document which sealed the most complete defeat ever acknowledged by a modern Great Power. Even this did not immediately end all hostilities, for the German troops in Czechoslovakia continued to fight against the Russians while they withdrew westward in an effort to surrender to the Americans. But three Russian armies closed swiftly about these remnants, herding them into the region northeast of Prague and crushing the last organized resistance on May 13.

The Reich which Hitler had boasted would last a thousand years had fallen, and the Nazi party with all its arrogance and brutality had been dragged down with it. Death or captivity fell to the lot of the leading Nazis one after another. Goering and Rosenberg and Ribbentrop, as well as such figures as the odious Quisling and the drunkard Robert Ley and the vicious radio propagandist William Joyce, fell into Allied hands. The hated Himmler committed suicide after his capture. Goebbels and his family poisoned themselves. There was no reliable eyewitness to Hitler's fate, but all evidence pointed to his suicide in a Berlin bunker on the eve of the city's fall. The leading German generals were taken captive. After several days of confusion, during which the hopes of Doenitz and his colleagues for permanent authority seemed to be growing brighter, this dubious government was dissolved and its members placed under arrest. The sole authority remaining in Germany was that of the Allies, and on them fell the task of restoring normal life to the prostrate nation as well as to the lands it had ravaged, and of uprooting the evil forces which had brought such disaster on Germany and the world.

One great architect of victory had not lived to see the hour of triumph in Europe. On April 12, President Roosevelt died suddenly from a brain hemorrhage. His death came as a heart-felt shock to millions of people throughout the Allied world. So familiar had his voice and personality become through newsreels and the radio that men and women all over the globe had come to feel a personal acquaintance with him and were stricken with a sense of profound personal loss. These emotions were heightened by the sense of world tragedy resulting from the removal of the man to whom peoples in all lands had almost unconsciously looked as the champion of their hopes for a new and better world. More than any other Allied leader, Franklin Roosevelt had given voice to the ideals of individual freedom and social justice in a way that strengthened the faith and rallied the confidence of all who sought a renewed recognition of fundamental human values. Those ideals would not disappear with his death, nor would new champions be lacking. But the testing time was drawing near when their realization would be put to the issue. It was on Roosevelt that multitudes of men and women had relied to uphold them successfully in the shaping of the peace. Because he had helped to strengthen these ideals in the public consciousness, he had already contributed much toward their fulfilment. But the world was not so rich in leaders of courage and vision and sympathy that it could lightly afford the loss of this man before his full work was done.

3

JANUARY TO APRIL: THE FAR EAST

THE RECONQUEST OF BURMA

EVEN before the apocalyptic climax in Europe released the full power of the Allies for an overwhelming concentration against Japan, the situation in the Far East was undergoing a process of rapid and fundamental change. The westward thrust which carried American forces to the inner ring of Japan's island defences transformed the outlook not only in the Pacific, but also on the Asiatic mainland. If Japan still held the initiative in China, her grip on the outer fringes of her empire had been seriously weakened. Her imperial lifeline was constricted by Allied sea and air power. Air supremacy, applied in a new and expanding technique, provided Allied land forces with the power and the mobility they needed for a successful assault from the direction of India. The strategic concepts of a year previously could be drastically revised in the light of these new factors. In particular, the initial success in northern Burma took on a new perspective. A limited operation was expanded into a major campaign; and at the far perimeter of her conquests, Japan was thrown back in a crushing and decisive defeat.

In this theatre, where both combatants lay hundreds of miles distant from their main bases, everything hinged in the first instance on the vital question of supply. The three Japanese armies in Burma

—the Fifteenth, Twenty-eighth and Thirty-third—lay at the end of long sea communications which stretched through the South China Sea and into the Indian Ocean to feed an essential stream of men and material into the main supply port of Rangoon. These once secure arteries lay increasingly exposed to the closing grip of the Allies. From their bases in China, American fliers kept up a relentless harrying of Japanese shipping as it moved along the Chinese coast. In the latter part of 1944 the Japanese offensive against the coastal air bases forced the Fourteenth Air Force back into the interior; but by that time the westward advance through the Pacific had carried the Americans to the Philippines and had placed them virtually astride Japan's sea routes to the south. Japan's own waters, as well as her homeland, lay under the shadow of American air power based in the Marianas. Allied task forces were striking heavily at Formosa and carrying their blows to the coast of China. And American submarines, which had already taken a mounting toll of Japan's merchant marine, now operated with increasing effectiveness and impunity against the convoys which sought to slip through the closing ring.

While the supply line to Burma was thus being throttled almost at its source, it was also under attack at the other extremity. Throughout 1944 there was a steady movement of British naval power to the Far East. A strong fleet of battleships and carriers operated in the Indian Ocean. British submarines ranged from the Bay of Bengal to the Java Sea and harried Japanese shipping on the approaches to the Malacca straits. Allied fliers struck persistently at Rangoon and the surrounding waters and extended their attacks to the naval base of Singapore. The early part of 1945 found the Japanese forces in Burma threatened with almost complete isolation.

This was a primary element in the shift in the balance of forces that had taken place during the past year. The vital place which Burma occupied in Japanese strategy was indicated by the first-rate quality of the troops which originally composed the garrison, and which had been strongly reinforced at the beginning of 1944. With well over 100,000 combat troops, including a large proportion of veteran units, the Japanese had been able in March of that year to counter the Allied attacks with a strong and dangerous thrust into India. But the disaster which overtook the invaders on the Imphal plain marked the end of Japanese offensive efforts and the decisive passing of the initiative to the Allies. With a strangling grip closing on their lines of supply, the Japanese were unable to replace their losses and to maintain their strength relative to that of their adversaries. They could draw a certain number of replacements from their garrisons in Thailand and Malaya, and some raw recruits were rushed from Japan to be hastily trained in Burma. But these sources were limited, and were inadequate to compensate for the virtual destruction of the crack units which had launched the invasion of India, or to offset the mounting toll inflicted on the remaining defenders by the subsequent Allied advance.

To take advantage of this situation, however, the Allies themselves had to solve formidable difficulties. They too were operating at the far end of vast and extended supply lines. The tremendous demands of the invasion operations in Europe imposed a first claim on Allied war production. The needs of the rapidly expanding offensive in the Pacific ran a close second in priority. Allied forces in Burma had to be content with what could be spared from these two major theatres. Yet unless the Allies could mount and maintain a full-scale offensive in ever-increasing strength, the weakening of Japan's position in Burma would have only a limited significance. It might bring an end to any serious threat to India, but it would not in itself dislodge the Japanese grip on Burma—the bastion which barred the way to China and guarded the western flank of the Japanese conquests in the Indies.

The logical approach was from the sea. The decline of Japanese naval strength, and the restoration of British naval supremacy in the Indian Ocean, set the stage for a series of amphibious attacks on the Burma coast which would culminate in the capture of Rangoon, finally trapping the Japanese forces in Burma and exposing them to destruction at the hands of Allied forces advancing up the same natural river routes that the Japanese had followed in their conquest of the country. But standing in the way of such a campaign was one of the most persistent bottlenecks in Allied war production—the shortage of landing craft. On successive occasions the necessities of the European theatre frustrated the plans for Burma. Landing craft that had been despatched to the Far East were recalled for the Anzio operation. Preparations for the Normandy invasion called for all the equipment available; and this was succeeded by the invasion of southern France, which had itself been delayed until success in Normandy made possible the release of landing craft for use in the Mediterranean. It was not until the end of 1944 that it at last became possible to set on foot definite plans for an invasion of Burma from the sea.

The alternative to waiting on this event was an attempt to reconquer Burma by an overland invasion from India. Never in all history had such an enterprise been successfully undertaken. The grain of the country, running north and south, imposed forbidding barriers of high ridges thrusting down from the Himalayas, and fever-ridden jungles that were all but impenetrable. Even to build a road through this wild and inhospitable country had been regarded as impossible. No natural passageway existed from east to west. Communications between Calcutta and the frontier rested on a single railway, part of it narrow gauge and linked only by ferries at the crossing of the Brahmaputra. To mount and maintain an offensive in such a country, depending only on existing land supply routes, was virtually a hopeless task.

The answer lay in the new dimension that was made available by air power. General Wingate's daring concept had been to abandon dependence on land supply lines and to rely primarily on air transport. Troops could be flown over the obstacles of mountains and jungles and set down within striking distance of their objectives. Supplies could be landed on improvised air strips or dropped to the forward troops. There were limits to this procedure, which restricted the combat forces to relatively light equipment unless land transport could be provided for the heavier guns and tanks; but its effectiveness within these limits had already been shown. Air transport largely made possible the success of the advance on Myitkina, although the forces which closed on that northern base were so weakened and so hard to reinforce that the Japanese garrison withstood a siege of 11 weeks before it was eliminated. Air power had retrieved the situation in Arakan after the 7th Indian division was cut off and surrounded, and had enabled the encircled garrison at Imphal not only to maintain itself for over two months, but to inflict a shattering defeat on the Japanese Fifteenth Army. The new methods had proved themselves brilliantly and decisively, and their evolution made it possible to contemplate a full-scale and concerted effort to reconquer Burma from the north.

The possibility of a sustained and unhampered system of air supply was clinched by the virtual elimination of the Japanese air strength in Burma. In the earlier operations that strength was still great enough to offer serious threats to Allied plans. It had made possible the temporary Japanese success in Arakan, and had added to the hazards of the situation in northern Burma and Assam. But Allied ascendancy rapidly asserted itself over the actual battlefields, and ultimately over the whole of Burma. By August 1944, Japan's fighter force had been almost totally annihilated. In nine months, Allied fliers had destroyed 800 enemy planes in combat or on the ground, and no replacements could be spared from the desperate effort that Japan was making to beat off the closing attack in the Pacific and to gather a reserve against the prospective invasion of the home islands. The air was cleared for the transports, and Allied fighters and bombers could range almost unhampered over Burma, giving constant cover to the ground troops and striking relentlessly at enemy supply lines all the way to Bangkok and Rangoon and Singapore.

As a result, the difficult and vulnerable communications across the jungle floor were largely replaced by air communications that were immune from enemy interference. Air supply expanded to keep pace with the rapid expansion in the scale of ground operations. In the year ending in March 1945, a total of 550,000 tons of cargo was carried by air to the fighting fronts in Burma. Almost half of this was transported during the last three months, and the final month accounted for 98,000 tons. Jeeps and guns, bullocks and mules, troop reinforcements and supplies of all kinds, were carried in an uninterrupted flow and set down in the immediate battle zone. Without this vast and unimpeded system of air transport, only small-scale and laborious operations could have been undertaken along the frontier. With it, a powerful and crushing blow could be struck with the object of annihilating the Japanese forces in Burma.

THE LEDO ROAD

At the end of the monsoon in the autumn of 1944, Allied forces were disposed in four widely separated sectors around the rim of the central Burma plain that lies between the Chindwin and the Irrawaddy. To the west, in the coastal province of Arakan, lay the XV Indian Corps, composed of 2 West African and 2 Indian divisions. Nearly 200 miles to the north was the main body of the Fourteenth Army which had fanned out from the Imphal plain and was pressing toward the Chindwin along a front of 100 miles. This force embodied the IV and XXXIII Corps of British, Indian and African troops and an available strength of 10 divisions plus armoured and other special formations. In northern Burma, moving out from the area of captured Myitkina, were 4 Chinese divisions and the British 36th division under General Sultan as successor to General Stilwell; and to this body was attached an American brigade known as the Mars Task Force—the only American ground combat troops operating in Burma. Finally, along the Salween east of the border with China, a Chinese force faced the Japanese who had pushed across the border from Burma before the progress of the invaders was brought to a halt.

The operations in northern Burma had been the pivot of the preceding campaign in the early part of 1944. Their immediate objective had been to open a land route to China; and as the advance pushed forward and the gains were consolidated, the construction of the road from Ledo followed hard on the heels of the combat troops, paralleled by a pipeline whose construction was if anything more important than that of the road itself. The capture of Myitkina which crowned this phase of operations was only one stage toward the completion of the task. The assignment called for the extension of the Allied gains to Mongyu, where the Ledo road would link with the old Burma road, and hard fighting through appalling country lay ahead before this could be achieved. But in the process of pursuing this immediate objective, wider vistas were opened. In pushing southward with the object of protecting the road, Sultan's forces were gradually drawing an arc toward Mandalay from the north. Their advance, joined with the progress of the Fourteenth Army from the west, rapidly developed into a converging movement which threatened the Japanese hold, not only on the region around Mandalay, but on the whole of Burma. From a limited though still far-flung and difficult operation, the northern drive was expanding into an integral part of the bold plan for the reconquest of Burma by an invasion overland.

The initial springboards for this new phase were Myitkina, the pivotal base which was the northern terminus of the railway from Mandalay, and Mogaung on the railway 30 miles to the west. From the latter point the British 36th division struck out in a southwesterly direction along the railway corridor between two steep ranges. This drive, which threatened to dislodge the Japanese from one of their main communication routes, also helped to cover the flank of the Chinese offensive south from Myitkina. Striking along the general line of the upper Irrawaddy valley, this attack had as its first objective the town of Bhamo. This Japanese base on the Irrawaddy, the starting point for a spur which ran eastward into China to connect with the old Burma Road, was one of the main obstacles along the route which the Ledo Road must follow from Myitkina to its goal; and on the ability of the Chinese forces to carve their way through to a junction with other Chinese armies attacking on the Salween front depended the completion of the effort to reopen a land connection with China from the west.

The monsoon season of 1944 failed to halt the progress of military operations in northern Burma. The attack against Myitkina was pressed to a successful conclusion, and pressure was maintained beyond Myitkina and Mogaung through the remaining weeks of the monsoon. Progress was inevitably retarded by weather conditions, which seriously impeded the air operations on which so much depended, and which made for hard going through the sodden and steamy jungle. The dogged advance down the railway was maintained in spite of intense heat in the narrow rain-drenched valleys and in the face of stubborn Japanese rearguard opposition, and by mid-September the spearheads of the 36th division were some 60 miles below Mogaung. From Myitkina the Chinese were also probing south through difficult jungle country, and patrols fanning out to the westward even established a tenuous contact with the Chinese forces along the Salween. When in the latter part of September the Allied efforts temporarily subsided to patrol activity, extended footholds had been gained for the launching of the more serious operations that were in prospect.

The approaching end of the monsoon was signalized by the resumption of the offensive in strength on October 15. In the railway corridor the British still found themselves faced with stiffening resistance as they approached the outlet to the central plain. After a month of battering progress which resulted in an advance of some 50 miles, they were brought to a halt by a stubborn Japanese stand at the village of Pinwe, a few miles above the junction of the main railway with a spur leading to the important base of Katha on the Irrawaddy. In contrast, the Chinese thrust toward Bhamo met comparatively light opposition in its early stages. The enemy seemed content to accentuate the difficulties of an advance through the jungle by small-scale harassing activities, and to husband his limited forces for the defence of selected strategic points. It was only during the second week in November, as they approached within a few miles of Bhamo, that the Chinese encountered a stubborn Japanese effort to bar their further advance.

At this stage the offensive expanded into a converging operation whose multiple prongs and swift surprise thrusts were characteristic of the whole ensuing strategy in the Burma theatre. While one column of the Chinese First Army advanced down the Irrawaddy in a frontal threat to Bhamo, a second swung eastward into the jungle country in a flanking move against the Japanese base. Almost simultaneously a spearhead of the Chinese Sixth Army, which had struck out from Hopin on the Myitkina-Mandalay railway, completed a difficult and secret jungle march of 50 miles. Bursting out at the Irrawaddy where it winds in an easterly direction between Katha and Bhamo, this force struck halfway between the two towns. River craft with outboard motors that had been dropped from the air enabled it to plunge across the river and capture the town of Shwegu before the astonished garrison could rally for a determined defence. Fanning out along the south bank of the Irrawaddy, the victors thrust one prong south of Bhamo to meet the flanking column that converged from the east. By November 17 the town had been completely isolated, and the Japanese battalion which held it gathered itself behind strong defences for a suicide stand that lasted a month. By the time its last desperate charge was shattered and the town was occupied on December 15, the main advance had long since bypassed it and was engaged in the last stages of the battle for the Burma Road.

The continued southward advance in this area rested on two main prongs. From Shwegu, elements of the Chinese 22nd division supported by the Mars Task Force plunged 50 miles through the jungle to overwhelm a Japanese detachment at the village of Tonkwa and press on to the rugged region of the Shweli river. This column, whose flank was to some extent covered by the continued advance of the British 36th division to the west, offered similar cover in its turn to the Chinese 30th division which had bypassed Bhamo on the east. There was a stubborn battle by this last force for the village of

Namhkam; but when on January 15 the Japanese were dislodged from this position, the final objective in northern Burma was almost in sight.

It had been brought closer by the simultaneous operations which were in progress along the Salween. Here the task of the Chinese forces was to dislodge the Japanese from control of the stretch of the Burma Road east of Mongyu while the advance in Burma closed on that point from the west. It was a slow and arduous process of dislodging the enemy from one mountain bastion after another. From Tengueh, captured on September 14 after a protracted siege, the Chinese pressed slowly forward, clearing the Japanese from their controlling positions along the road. At Wanting, the last bastion before Mongyu, the enemy made a desperate stand. The Chinese claimed the town on January 3, but the Japanese struck back and regained it next day, and it was not until January 20 that they were finally dislodged. By that date the advance from the west beyond captured Namhkam had all but closed the gap. Although a few scattered pockets of Japanese remained to be mopped up, the Allied command felt able to announce officially on January 22 that the Ledo Road to China was open; and six days later the arrival of the first convoy at Wanting symbolized the new hopes that were dawning with the restoration of an overland connection between China and her allies.

THE ROAD TO MANDALAY

With the Ledo Road a reality, the northern combat area, the scene of so much toil and sacrifice by the men who built the road as well as by those who cleared the way, declined in importance as a separate operational sector. The troops who had pushed through that wild and remote region, however, remained very much in action. Below the road the Chinese continued their advance toward Lashio. Their flank was still covered by the parallel advance of the 36th division; but the importance of the latter movement was now subordinate to that of the advance of the Fourteenth Army from India, and to the wide concentric assault which was developing toward the central plain and the focal objective of Mandalay.

The success with which the northern combat group carried on operations in defiance of the monsoon was matched by that of the forces which fanned out from Imphal in pursuit of the remnants of the Japanese Fifteenth Army. Their unremitting advance through mud and ceaseless rain struck in two main columns toward the bases from which the enemy had launched his disastrous invasion of India. On the northern sector the capture of Tamu on August 4 dislodged the Japanese from an airstrip and supply junction; and while elements of the 11th East African division struck down the Kabaw valley, other forces thrust across the intervening ridges to the Chindwin river. At Sittaung a bridgehead was established on the east bank, and the northern spearhead was now in a position not only to fan out against such Japanese forces as remained west of the middle and upper Chindwin, but to continue the difficult drive across the grain of the country toward the Irrawaddy.

Simultaneously the main southern spearhead, with the 5th Indian division in the van, drove down the road from Imphal south toward Tiddim. Here the Japanese put up the same sort of persistent rear-guard resistance as they did in the railway corridor. The direct advance ran into successive road blocks which had to be turned by flanking columns striking in wide sweeps through the jungle. When in mid-September the Japanese made a stand in strong positions at the crossing of the Manipur river, the Indians threw a left hook around the obstacle. Swinging in an 88-mile detour through high jungle-covered hills, the flanking column struck behind the Manipur positions, dislodged the Japanese from their defences further on at the village of Tongzang, and cleared the way for an advance by the main force which carried it to within 16 miles of Tiddim.

It took almost four weeks to cover the remaining distance. The steep winding road to Tiddim—its assailants called it the Chocolate Staircase—proved an obstacle that had to be turned by another jungle march. The flanking column continued its drive to swing around Tiddim from the east, but the Japanese dug in for a determined stand which stalled further progress for a fortnight. At last the arrival of better weather made it possible to mount a strong air attack which shattered the defences; and on October 15 the Indians closed in from two directions to overwhelm what was left of the garrison.

From Tiddim the advance wheeled eastward toward the Chindwin, where the base of Kalewa guarded the strategic defile which was the gateway to Burma from the west. It meant 60 miles of hard going against an enemy who continued to make a stand wherever a defensible road block could be established, and to cling tenaciously to the many strategic features offered by the terrain. It took until November 7 to dislodge the Japanese from Kennedy Peak, a 9000-foot eminence dominating a single narrow trail. A short distance beyond, however, Fort White was captured after a sharp two-day struggle on November 9. The Indians were now approaching a junction with the East Africans who had been working their way down the rain-drenched Kabaw valley and had thrown a force eastward to conduct a parallel advance down the Chindwin. On November 16 they joined with the Indians to capture the village of Kalemyo and to press on along the last stretch of road toward Kalewa. There was stiff fighting for the ridges which covered the approaches to this stronghold; but the frontal advance from the east was strengthened by tank support, and the Africans with a strong force of artillery threatened the town from the north as they advanced along the Chindwin. On December 2 the Japanese were driven from Kalewa. All enemy resistance west of the Chindwin had now been virtually eliminated; and with the forcing of the river beyond Kalewa the way was opened for a drive to the central plain and the Irrawaddy.

By this time a parallel drive was in progress across country farther to the north. In the last week in November a thrust was launched by the 19th Indian division beyond the middle Chindwin from the vicinity of Sittaung. Almost at the same time the 36th

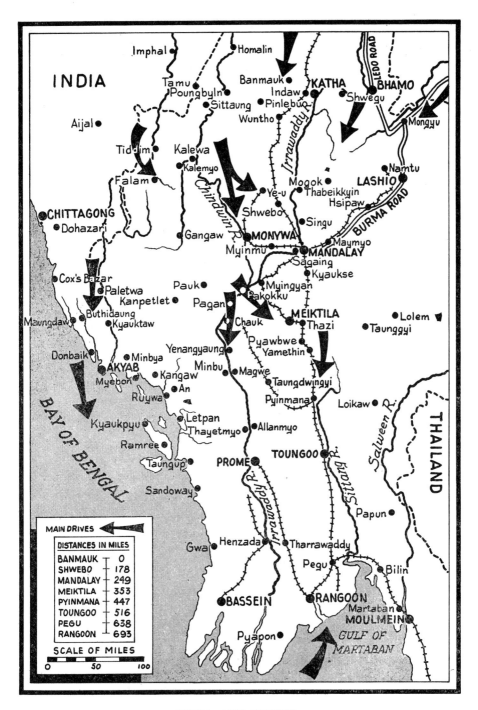

INDIA AND BURMA

division, which had been checked for three weeks by strong Japanese positions at Pinwe, launched a new attack which broke through on November 30. Their renewed advance down the railway carried them into Katha and the nearby town of Indaw on December 10; and six days later their patrols west of Indaw made contact with the spearheads of the force which had struck east from the Chindwin. The two sectors, so long and so widely separated, were now linked; and while the 36th advanced down the Irrawaddy from Katha, troops of the 19th division occupied the railway town of Wuntho after covering 150 miles in eight days and struck south in a parallel drive along the railway leading to Mandalay.

This was an unfolding of the basic pattern of the operations which were to result in the reconquest of Burma—a lateral thrust from the west to meet and speed up the advance from the north, a new swing southward from the positions this gained, a further lateral thrust below them repeating the process and forming the descending rungs of a ladder leading beyond Mandalay to Rangoon. And supplementing this main advance which formed the backbone of the offensive were others on either flank—the swing of the 36th division which threatened Mandalay from the east, the ladderlike amphibious descent of the west coast which culminated with a seaborne expedition against Rangoon from the south while the land advance swept down upon the port from the north.

Thus the success of the Japanese at the end of December in checking the northern column after a rapid advance which carried it 54 miles below Wuntho was nullified by the progress of the 2nd and 20th divisions driving east from Kalewa. Gathering speed as they approached easier country, they rolled over the enemy rearguard opposition, and on January 2 the 2nd division reached and captured Yeu at the head of a spur railway from Mandalay. The 20th division struck down the railway toward the road centre of Monywa and the bend of the Irrawaddy west of Mandalay. The 2nd division continued its eastward advance, driving on into the good tank country of the central plain. The town of Shwebo was taken on January 7;

and this success, placing the 2nd division astride the main railway, undermined the resistance of the Japanese farther to the north. The 19th division broke through and swept down to a junction with the captors of Shwebo; and while these drove south along the railway, the 19th division swung east toward the Irrawaddy. By January 20 it had established bridgeheads across the river at Singu, 46 miles above Mandalay, and at Thabeikkyin 20 miles farther north. The collapse of Japanese opposition west of the river was speeded by the 20th division, which captured Monywa on January 22 after a six-day siege; and from north and west strong forces were now in a position to close on Mandalay.

The enemy now concentrated his chief efforts on holding the line of the Irrawaddy and averting the threat from the north. The initial bridgeheads, held by the 19th Indian division, came under savage and persistent attack; and while the bend of the Irrawaddy west of Mandalay was largely cleared by the end of the first week in February, the Japanese clung to a foothold opposite the city itself in the hilly region around Sagaing. None of these activities prevented the steady sapping of their strategic position in central Burma. The Allied forces that had debouched into the central plain could now bring to bear their superior strength in tanks and artillery as well as in man-power; and while the tactical air force gave constant cover to the advance, providing added firepower to shatter Japanese ground defences and break up enemy counter-attacks, the strategic bombers struck at the whole system of communications on which the Japanese in Burma were dependent, and through which the Fifteenth Army in the Mandalay area had to be fed with munitions and supplies.

By the beginning of February the 19th division had begun to pass to the offensive and slowly to enlarge its bridgeheads against bitter resistance. Its increasing pressure from the north was shortly supplemented by a greatly increased threat to Mandalay from the west. On the night of February 12, advance elements of the 20th Indian division drove across the Irrawaddy near Myinmu, 30 miles west of Mandalay. Although initial opposition was comparatively light, the Japanese reacted promptly and vigorously. Violent and repeated attacks were thrown against this new foothold during the next ten days, and the air forces which had helped to make the crossing possible were called on to lend vital help in breaking up the enemy's armoured counter-assaults. But the bridgehead itself was strengthened by tank reinforcements, and the pressure was shortly eased by still another breach of the Irrawaddy line. On the left flank of the 20th, 5 miles to the east, the 2nd division forced a crossing on February 26 in the face of stiff opposition and under the handicap of defective equipment which plagued all the river operations in this phase. The two bridgeheads were quickly merged into a single broad foothold; and on the same day the forces in the two northern bridge-heads finally cleared the 20 miles which originally separated them and strengthened their position for an imminent breakout. The prongs for a converging drive from two directions were poised and pointed at Mandalay.

By this time a more spectacular stroke in an entirely new quarter had vastly widened the field of operations. While pressure by the XXXIII Corps in the western bridgehead focussed the enemy's attention on the frontal threat to Mandalay, the IV Corps had thrust a powerful force into the Chin Hills below Tiddim. Moving swiftly and secretly through the rough and roadless jungle country of the Gangaw valley, this force suddenly struck the Irrawaddy opposite Pagan, 92 miles southwest of Mandalay. On February 14 they launched an assault across the mile-wide swollen river. There were the usual difficulties with leaking boats and faulty outboard motors which failed in midstream, and the attack met a hot fire from the Japanese positions on the high eastern bank. But planes and artillery beat down the defences, and a solid bridgehead was established and held against the Japanese reserves which were rushed from the area below Mandalay and thrown into fierce counter-attacks in an attempt to wipe out this new threat.

With Japanese resources now almost completely engaged, the decisive stroke was launched. Near Pakokku, 20 miles above Pagan, another column began its crossing of the Irrawaddy on the night of February 19. Two days later the 17th division, with the most powerful mechanized force that had yet been thrown into the campaign, broke out of the bridgehead and struck toward the Japanese base of Meiktila on the main highway 75 miles south of Mandalay. Headed by a strong force of medium tanks which was supported by armoured cars and self-propelled guns and covered all the way by bomber and fighter planes, the column had a combination of firepower and mobility which carried everything before it. A dash of 82 miles carried it to the outskirts of Meiktila on February 27. The eight airfields surrounding the town were swiftly occupied; airborne forces were promptly flown in to strengthen and consolidate the attacking force; Meiktila itself was captured after a sharp struggle, and a force was thrown 10 miles farther east to assail Thazi on the railway below Mandalay. It was a bold and successful bid to choke off the supply routes and bar the main road of retreat, and it threatened not merely the Japanese defenders of Mandalay, but the whole Japanese force of some 30,000 in central Burma.

Mandalay itself had now been reduced to a secondary objective whose doom was already sealed. On March 1 the 19th division broke out of the northern bridgehead and drove southward along the Irrawaddy. Its frontal advance still encountered strong rearguard opposition which slowed its progress during the first few days. But an armoured column struck out on a flank march which turned the Japanese positions; and on March 8, after an all-night dash of nearly 18 miles through almost trackless country, the tanks thrust into Mandalay from the north. By the following day the main elements of the Japanese garrison were besieged in Fort Dufferin, whose stout defences withstood the battering of medium artillery and enabled the defenders to beat off the first assaults. But a slow process of reduction was pressed as a steadily tightening ring closed around the city. The 19th division sent flanking forces stabbing east of the town. One spearhead in a 50-mile dash over little-known trails captured Maymyo on the road to Lashio, and a detachment swinging east and south of Mandalay completed its encirclement by making contact with the 2nd division which had driven from the western bridgehead to cut the last escape route. With the final assault and capture of Fort Dufferin on March 20, the whole of Mandalay was in British hands.

This was a prize whose capture was highly gratifying from the point of view of prestige. In its strategic aspect, however, it was already overshadowed by the more significant prospect of the destruction of the Japanese XV Army. The remnants of this force, now reduced to about 30,000, comprised the last substantial enemy force in central Burma, and the net was rapidly closing about it as Allied forces planted themselves across the remaining routes of escape.

The chief route eastward lay along the main road which linked Mandalay with the terminus of the old Burma road at Lashio. Any chance that the Japanese might use this is an avenue of retreat was largely forestalled by the flanking column which seized the base of Maymyo, and finally eliminated by the continued advance of the northern combat group. Below the newly-opened Ledo Road, Sultan's forces thrust southward in several prongs which paralleled the main thrust down the Irrawaddy toward Mandalay and gave it added security. While the 36th division smashed across the Shweli river and drove forward in hard fighting to Mogok, Chinese columns closed on Lashio to capture it on March 8, and ten days later another Chinese force secured Hsipaw 45 miles to the west. By the time Mandalay fell, the key points in the road to Lashio were in Allied hands and the Japanese were being cleared from the intervening stretches. The two Chinese forces from Hsipaw and Lashio made contact on March 26. The 36th division fought its way through to the road and linked up with the Chinese on April 1. The task of the northern combat group was now virtually completed, and the campaign was about to enter its closing phase as the destruction of the remaining forces in central Burma set the stage for the drive on Rangoon.

Below Mandalay the pivot of the struggle was the Meiktila area. The seizure of this point by the 17th division after bitter fighting meant that a wedge was thrust between the Japanese in central Burma and those farther south, and the enemy rallied with desperate efforts to restore contact. For a full week the position was critical as the Japanese hurled strong and repeated counter-attacks against the perimeter defences of the airfields which were vital to the maintenance of the whole position. But the attacks were beaten off; and with the capture of Mandalay the Meiktila position became the anvil for the hammer which swung down from the north to shatter and disperse the Japanese divisions in the intervening area.

The main blow was delivered by the 20th division. Striking from the bridgehead area below Mandalay, a strong armoured spearhead backed by motorized infantry drove 60 miles in three days to reach a point less than 20 miles above Meiktila. While the struggle for the latter point continued to rage in full fury, the 20th division cut the main road and railway and swung north toward a junction with another prong which the division had thrust directly south from Mandalay. The Japanese pocket was split, and the pincers were rapidly closing around the remaining forces in central Burma. By desperate efforts the Japanese delayed the closing of the trap. They organized a strong stand in the vicinity of Kyaukse and held open a 20-mile gap through which the retreating forces sought to filter into the hill country to the east. Elements of three divisions eventually made good their escape, but at the price of severe casualties and the abandonment of their heavy equipment, and under constant harrying from the air. On March 30 the capture of Kyaukse, shortly followed by a link-up with the force holding Meiktila, marked the virtual elimination of the pocket; and the subsequent mopping-up process was crowned by the capture of Thazi on April 10. The Japanese XV Army had been shattered as an effective fighting force, its flying remnants seeking safety in the hills and jungles. Since the beginning of the year the British forces in central Burma had counted 17,000 enemy dead; the whole of the central plain was firmly in their hands, and the stage was set for the drive on Rangoon and the completion of the reconquest of Burma.

THE ROAD TO RANGOON

The advance through central Burma, and the progressive increase in the forces engaged, resulted in a serious and growing strain on supply lines, and particularly on air supply. The difficult and restricted overland routes could be used during the dry season for the transport of the heaviest type of equipment, but this almost exhausted their capacity; and although the use of the Chindwin and other waterways proved valuable as a supplement, the striking power of the Fourteenth Army continued to depend on air transport. Imphal was the main base during the initial stages of the drive; and when the advance to the area of Mandalay carried operations beyond convenient range, Chittagong replaced Imphal as the chief supply centre. Meiktila however was the most advanced point which could be effectively served from this point, and bases still farther south were needed to sustain the rapid thrust toward Rangoon which was now in prospect.

This was the paramount objective of the Arakan campaign which was in progress simultaneously with the operations around Mandalay. The amphibious resources of Southeast Asia Command, inadequate though they were for a major effort, still lent themselves to a series of seaborne landings which would carry the XV Corps down the west coast of Burma parallel with the advance farther inland. There were other objectives, secondary but still important, which these operations would serve. They held the prospect of eliminating the Japanese forces in Arakan, thus removing a potential threat from the flank of the main advance. The conquest of Arakan would release four divisions of the XV Corps for use in a final and concerted blow against Rangoon; and this added available strength, coupled with the securing of advanced bases to sustain the main offensive, heightened the possibility that the drive on Rangoon could be completed in the few weeks that remained before the coming of the monsoon.

The Arakan offensive was launched in mid-December. The 25th Indian division captured Buthidaung and struck down the Mayu peninsula, supported by the 82nd West African division advancing astride the Mayu range, while the 81st West Africans attacked down the Kaladan valley. The immediate objective was Akyab, the chief Japanese coastal base whose airfields were vital to the general advance. In contrast to the experience of the previous year, when Japanese resistance not only barred the road to Akyab but threatened to envelop and destroy the attacking force, the attack met with swift success. A fortnight's advance carried the Indians the length of the Mayu peninsula to a point overlooking Akyab. The Japanese made no serious effort to defend that base. When a triple amphibious attack was launched against Akyab on January 3, it was discovered that the enemy had withdrawn two days previously. Akyab was occupied without opposition, and a key port and air base was in British hands.

The next main objective was Taungup, 150 miles to the south. This small port, connected by road with Prome on the Irrawaddy, was a main trans-shipment point for supplies going north along the coast, and was the southern terminus of a coastal road running north to the lower Kaladan valley. In the latter region a stubborn Japanese force had concentrated to oppose the advance of the West Africans; and as part of the preliminary moves toward Taungup, the isolation of this force and the blocking of its routes of supply and retreat became one of the immediate tasks of the XV Corps.

The noose was flung with a landing on the Myebon peninsula 32 miles below Akyab on January 12. Under cover of naval and air bombardment, the troops made good their foothold in the face of strong opposition from Japanese forces that had retreated from Akyab. A little over a week later their position was strengthened by a further landing some 20 miles down the coast in the vicinity of Kangaw. Here a road block was thrown up and consolidated against strong and persistent Japanese attacks backed by a heavy concentration of artillery; and with the enemy's supply route thus effectively choked off, his forces in the lower Kaladan region were relentlessly compressed between the Indians who had landed in the south and the Africans driving down from the north.

Meanwhile a longer amphibious hop had carried the XV Corps to the immediate approaches to Taungup. On January 21 the 26th Indian division, which had hitherto been held in reserve, landed on the northern tip of Ramree island. This island, which offered potentialities as an air base, guarded the western sea approaches to Taungup and offered a preliminary foothold for a direct attack on that port. The Japanese garrison fought stubbornly, and for the remainder of the month confined the British advance to the northern part of the island. But on January 26 a force of Royal Marines drove ashore on Cheduba island south of Ramree and gained a base from which the defenders of Ramree could be threatened from the rear. On February 4 a landing on the southern tip of Ramree itself brought the end within sight. Caught between two forces, the Japanese defenders were overcome during the next few days, and by February 10 all major resistance had been overcome and only scattered parties remained to be mopped up.

By this time the Japanese concentrations along the lower Kaladan had been annihilated or dispersed, and the Africans were driving toward a junction with the forces that were still stubbornly engaged around Kangaw. The Japanese turned from their efforts to regain the latter position and concentrated on an attempt to prevent a junction. But they were menaced by still another coastal landing below Kangaw which captured Ruywa, again cutting the coastal road and seizing the terminus of a track leading eastward through the mountains toward the Irrawaddy. The new blow virtually brought an end to the struggle around Kangaw. On February 20 the forces there made contact with the advancing Africans, clearing the Kangaw area of what remained of a garrison of 2700; and the whole of Arakan north of that point was under British control.

The Japanese apparently expected a direct attack on Taungup and prepared to resist strongly. The next blow, however, fell over 40 miles up the coast, where a landing was made at Letpan on March 13. Air power helped to break the infantry resistance that was encountered and to reduce the strong points in the coastal defences, and the British from their new foothold pressed down toward Taungup from the north. They were opposed by stiff resistance as the Japanese sought to extricate their forces, and it took them over a month to attain their goal. Although the town was reached on April 4, it was only on the 16th that the Japanese were driven from Taungup. The last important port on Burma's west coast was in British hands; its garrison was harried by air power as it strove to retreat along the road to Prome; the remnants of 2 divisions in Arakan were cut off or in flight; and the British had secured the coastal bases from which they could support the vigorous and decisive drive which was now launched against Rangoon.

Their success came not a moment too soon. The monsoon was barely a month away, and Rangoon lay 300 miles south of the main attacking force in the Meiktila area. Barring the way were the Japanese Twenty-eighth and Thirty-third Armies with a strength of approximately 50,000. It was a race with the weather in which speed was vital, and speed could only be attained by a crushing concentration of strength which would smash through Japanese resistance and allow the armoured and motorized forces to sweep down at full speed on Rangoon.

This situation called for daring thrusts in which the spearheads would virtually ignore the risks to their flanks and their communications. The victory in Arakan, and the wiping out of effective Japanese opposition or even reconnaissance activities in the air, gave assurance that the offensive would enjoy the continued support of adequate air supply. The decision was taken to contain the most threatening Japanese concentrations, to bypass others and leave them to be dealt with by supporting forces, and to drive with twin prongs toward Rangoon down the two main routes along the valleys of the Irrawaddy and the Sittang.

The western thrust was launched by the XXXIII Corps. Its prospect of a swift advance southward was compromised by the fact that it faced the preliminary necessity of dealing with a strong Japanese force concentrated in the oilfield region around Chauk and Yenangyaung. This pocket was first split by a pincers movement from the Pakokku area. While one force struck south down the Irrawaddy, another swung around Chauk from the east and south; and on the opposite bank of the river still another force was already waiting to deal with any enemy attempt to escape to the west. Chauk was taken on April 18, and a linkup of forces established a firm line between that point and Meiktila. Meanwhile an outer ring was being forged by a column which slashed south and west to take Magwe and then swung north toward the spearhead driving down the Irrawaddy toward Yenangyaung. With the fall of that centre on April 22, the Japanese pocket was virtually eliminated, and the XXXIII Corps could throw its main weight into the drive toward Rangoon.

By this time it was being outpaced by the parallel drive farther east. The operations in the oilfield region, and the continued resistance beyond that area, restricted the speed of the advance. When Rangoon actually fell, the western spearhead was still fighting at Prome 180 miles to the north. But its success in containing and liquidating the Japanese in the oilfield area had freed the IV Corps from the chief danger on its flank, and left it free to thrust with all possible strength down the road and railway leading from Meiktila to Rangoon.

The drive started at the beginning of April. In the first stages it encountered stiff opposition. The Japanese too were fighting for time, and they tried to check the advance wherever a strong natural position offered a chance for an effective stand. There was a stubborn three-day battle for the supply and headquarters centre of Pyawbwe before it was captured on April 11. Some 15 miles farther south another stand was attempted, and still another was organized where the road ran through a narrow defile 20 miles farther along. But the armoured spearheads of the IV Corps, aided by guerillas of the Burmese National Army operating ahead and on the flanks, bypassed and overwhelmed these positions and gathered speed as they rolled forward. The last serious attempt at organized resistance above Pegu was at Pyinmana; and when this was brushed aside on April 21, the IV Corps was unleashed in a dash which swept through the main centres before the Japanese could organize their defence. At Toungoo the British came upon the strongest defences yet encountered, but so unexpected was their appearance that the fortifications were captured without a fight, and the leading tanks even ran down a Japanese policeman directing traffic at a crossroads. Behind the ground forces came special crews which rapidly put captured airfields into service-able condition, including the three important fields at Toungoo, and enabled the supply services to the forward troops to be maintained without interruption. By the end of April Pegu, the last major obstacle, had been bypassed, and the IV Corps was within striking distance of Rangoon.

Against that port other forces had gathered for a decisive blow. The amphibious resources of Southeast Asia Command were too straitened for the main invasion to be launched by sea, but they were adequate for a supporting operation which would give insurance against a last-minute check to the land advance and make certain the attainment of its goal before the monsoon. Forces of the XV Corps, released by the victory in Arakan, were available for a new seaborne operation. The powerful East Indies fleet swept the sea approaches and gave support to the landing. Paratroops of the Indian Airborne division were dropped south of Rangoon on May 1 to neutralize the coastal defences; and on May 2 the main force went ashore on either side of the muddy Rangoon estuary 20 miles below the port.

The blow met virtually no opposition. The advance of the IV Corps had already doomed Rangoon, and the Japanese had abandoned the city rather than risk further irreplaceable losses by a suicidal stand. The seaborne troops drove swiftly into the town, and on May 3 the capture of Rangoon was officially announced. The victors fanned out to meet the columns closing in from the north. Pegu had already fallen on May 1, and on May 6 the IV Corps, which had been abruptly slowed by bad weather, made contact with the forces pushing out from Rangoon. Meanwhile the western spearhead had taken Prome on May 2; and when this force in its turn made contact with the XV Corps 60 miles above Rangoon on May 17, it closed the major phase of a campaign which in five months had seen an advance of over 600 miles through wild and difficult country without adequate land communications—a campaign which, obscured though it was by greater and more decisive events elsewhere, had by its unprecedented character set a landmark in the evolution of military operations.

New and arduous campaigns still seemed in prospect before the Japanese were expelled from southeast Asia. With the pivotal base of Rangoon in British hands, Singapore appeared as the next major goal; and the invasion of Malaya was to be paralleled by a simultaneous offensive toward Thailand. The new situation brought a redistribution of the forces engaged in the Burma campaign. The Chinese and American forces in the north were flown to China to bolster resistance there. The Malayan attack, which was set for September 9, was to be launched by 7 divisions of the Fourteenth Army. Other units of that veteran force were regrouped in a new formation, the Twelfth Army, with a strength of 6 divisions and 5 independent brigades; and these were assigned the double task of pressing eastward toward the border of Thailand and of cleaning out the enemy pockets that had been bypassed during the drive on Rangoon.

Once again the monsoon brought no halt in the fighting, in spite of the difficulties imposed on ground operations and the interruption of air supply. The bulk of the Japanese forces, with a strength of between 40,000 and 50,000, now lay east of the Sittang except for a foothold within the bend of the river near its mouth. If their supply position was poor, the wild country was easily defensible, and the

British thrusts were confined to mired tracks and were held to slow progress. East of Thazi the drive into the Shan States encountered a series of road blocks, and it was not until July 25 that the capture of the main centre of Taunggyi was announced. There was even stiffer resistance to the column pushing out from Toungoo, which took nearly three months to advance 35 miles; and the effort to clear the railway from Pegu to Moulmein made only minor progress. The accomplishments of the Twelfth Army were to be measured less in ground gained than in the casualties inflicted on the enemy, and particularly on the trapped forces trying to escape across the Sittang.

The advance to Rangoon had cut off some 20,000 Japanese in southwest Burma. Part of these were in the lower Irrawaddy valley, and were largely liquidated during the next two months; but the larger portion lay in the Pegu range between the Sittang and the Irrawaddy. Compressed from all sides, and with the IV Corps planted across the main exits from the hills toward the east, the besieged Japanese forces gathered their strength for a concerted effort to break out. They were grouped in five parties which on July 20 made a determined and simultaneous attempt to strike across the Sittang at selected spots. The British forces, lying in wait for just such an event, inflicted fearful losses. In a week of battle the remnants of the Japanese Twenty-eighth Army were virtually wiped out, losing over 10,000 dead and 1000 prisoners. It was the last major engagement the British were called upon to fight; and though it was relatively small in scale, it was one of the most crushing and one-sided defeats ever suffered by the land forces of Japan. With this triumph added to the capture of Rangoon, the bitter memories of earlier British disasters in Burma were at least partially assuaged.

Setback in China

The completion of the Ledo road and the reopening of a land connection with China came at a time when the fortunes of that long-suffering country were at their lowest ebb. Four years of blockade, added to the loss of her richest provinces and the disruption of her economic life, had resulted in a virtual paralysis of China's military effort. Chinese forces had played a major part in restoring a land connection with the outside world; but if her strength was to be invigorated sufficiently to allow her to regain the initiative against the enemy forces whose new offensives had split her territory in two, China needed both a drastic internal reorganization and a flood of material aid from her allies.

Hitherto the trickle of supplies that had reached China from outside had been flown in "over the hump" from India. In the latter part of 1944 there was a substantial increase in the cargo transported over this difficult and dangerous route. Monthly tonnage reached over 20,000 tons in October, and by the following January it had risen to over 46,000 tons. But the greater part of this consisted of the fuel that was vitally necessary to supply the 14th American Air Force which operated in the Chinese theatre, and to provision the Superfortresses which were striking from Chinese bases. Little remained for the ground forces, and even that little was bitterly grudged by the advocates of air power as the decisive weapon which could beat back the Japanese if it were employed to the full. The Ledo road, with its projected capacity of 40,000 tons a month, could not by itself overcome these difficulties. It would supplement the air supply route and ease the burden in the matter of heavier cargo, and the pipeline which accompanied the road would transform the situation as far as fuel supply was concerned; but a far greater volume of traffic was needed if Chinese armies were to be effectively equipped for a large-scale offensive role.

Equally serious were the difficulties to be overcome within China itself. A tangled political situation complicated the desperate economic and military problems faced by Free China. Within the government a group of reactionary ministers clung to power in the face of opposition at home and mounting criticism abroad. There were charges that officials in high places were more concerned with retaining office and advancing their personal fortunes than with effective prosecution of the war. Their implacable hostility to

Communism, which was apparently shared by Chiang Kai-shek, contributed to an internal rift that barely stopped short of civil war. Some of the best divisions in the national army were diverted from the front to blockade the Communist areas, thus helping to immobilize both factions as far as an effective struggle against the Japanese was concerned. This paramount political division made it harder to keep other factions under control, and particularly to assert effectively the authority of the central government over the local war lords or to exercise any real control over the provincial forces. National conscription had largely broken down. The armies were badly organized, badly equipped and badly led. If the Chinese criticized the Americans for failing to carry out their projected plans for training and equipping new forces, the Americans complained that the Chinese had failed to provide either the number or the quality of recruits that had been promised. Incompetence and corruption were blamed not only for military inefficiency, but for the inflation and black market activities and barely concealed traffic with the Japanese which marked China's disorganized economic life. Beset by internal ills and external pressure, China's will to resist seemed almost at the last gasp.

This situation, with all its cross-currents and inherent dangers, was symbolized by the recall of General Stilwell in October 1944. Stilwell had been Chief of Staff to Chiang Kai-shek and commander of the American forces in the China-Burma-India theatre. His dual capacity, and the fact that he had a considerable body of Chinese troops under his command, involved the most intimate relations with Chiang. Yet almost from the outset the two men found themselves at odds in both ideas and temperament. Stilwell pressed for a degree of authority which Chiang was reluctant to concede. His insistence that lend-lease supplies should be shared with the Communists was stubbornly opposed by Chiang's conservative advisers. His plans to train and utilize substantial bodies of Chinese troops, in whose fighting qualities he had a profound and affectionate faith, met with persistent obstruction. The climax came when an American mission, sent out to advise on measures to revive China's military effectiveness.

pressed for unity between the central government and the Communists
and for the entrusting of active command over all forces to an
American general. These were hard conditions to impose on the
head of a state; and while Chiang agreed to both in principle, his
refusal to accept Stilwell as the American commander led to the
recall of that general from the task to which he had given so much
devotion and energy. His retirement, however, was followed by a
reorganization of the Chinese government which made it somewhat
more liberal in tone, and by steps to eliminate the worst defects in
the organization of the army and to seek a basis of accord with the
Communists. By the beginning of the year there were signs of
Chinese military rejuvenation, in spite of the serious situation that
had by this time developed as a result of the new Japanese advance.

Until 1944 the Japanese had made few serious efforts to extend
their conquests to southern China. Even in the provinces they had
overrun north of the Yangtse their effective control was largely confined to the main cities and transport routes. Great stretches of the
countryside were dominated by Chinese guerillas, whose activities
compelled the Japanese to launch repeated large-scale expeditions
against them. With over 30 divisions pinned down in occupied China,
and with the task of guarding the northern frontier against Russia
added to the burden of occupying and defending her newly-conquered
empire against mounting Allied pressure, Japan was reluctant to
embark on the extensive task of completing the conquest of even a
tragically weakened China. She had seized the chief ports on the
southeast coast to reinforce the blockade, and south of the Yangtse
she launched occasional thrusts into the "rice bowl" area around
Tungting Lake; but her main reliance seemed to be on economic and
political pressure to neutralize China as an active adversary and if
possible to force her to make peace.

The spring of 1944 brought a drastic change in this attitude.
The sea routes connecting Japan with her conquests in Burma and
Malaya and the Indies were now in growing jeopardy. They were
under attack not only by Allied naval forces, but also by the 14th

Air Force striking from its bases in China. By May, American fliers were claiming a toll of Japanese shipping in the vicinity of 20,000 tons a month. Construction of airfields was being pressed forward with the avowed purpose of preparing for a bombing campaign which would subject the Japanese homeland to an ordeal similar to that which Germany was enduring. An earnest of this intention was soon to be forthcoming with the appearance of the Superfortresses operating from Chinese bases. Meanwhile, in the face of manifold difficulties, the reorganizing and rearming of Chinese ground forces was under way, and 35 divisions were being trained and equipped under Stilwell's direction at bases in Yunnan. A revitalized Chinese army backed by powerful American air strength might emerge to pave the way for an Allied landing on the Chinese mainland as a prelude to a concentric assault on Japan itself.

There were thus impelling motives for the Japanese to abandon their holding tactics and to strike out in a serious and sustained offensive south of the Yangtse. The first aim of the resulting operations was to seize the chief bases of the 14th Air Force and thrust it back out of range of the coast. Other advantages would accompany success in this primary aim. A corridor would be driven through the heart of south China along the general line of the Canton-Hankow railway; and this achievement, following the recent clearing of the line from Hankow to Peiping, would pave the way for a continuous land route to the borders of Indo-China. It was true that most of the rails along the Canton-Hankow line had long since been removed by the Chinese, and a 300-mile gap separated the branch line at Liuchow from the border terminus of the Indo-China rail line toward which it offered the most direct approach. But a roadbed existed along both these routes; and if the Japanese could find and lay the necessary rails, their whole system of imperial communications would be transformed. They would be freed from dependence on vulnerable sea routes and would have a continuous land supply line, not only through the whole length of China, but by way of the railways of Indo-China and Thailand to Burma and

Singapore. In addition, the corridor would sever the coastal area of southeast China from the main regions to the west, and thus seal off the sector in which Allied landings might most reasonably be anticipated.

JAPAN STRIKES SOUTH

The Japanese drive was launched in the latter part of May 1944. Striking south from the region around Tungting Lake, it closed on Changsha, the main centre which had previously beaten back three Japanese thrusts. This time it served as only a brief impediment to the advance. It was bypassed and encircled; and while its defenders withstood a siege of three weeks before the defence was broken on June 20, the advancing Japanese spearheads thrust on to close around Hengyang.

This was an objective of major importance. The airfield at Hengyang was one of the chief bases from which attacks were directed against Japanese coastal shipping. The town stood at the junction of the two main railway lines leading to Canton and Liuchow, and its fall would open both these routes to a further Japanese advance.

The Chinese, still shaken by the costly defeat at Changsha, strove to rally for the defence of Hengyang. They were unable to halt the Japanese on the approaches to the city, or to check the progress of an outflanking movement which closed the ring around Hengyang in the last week in June. But inside the town a garrison of 16,000 put up a stubborn defence, and relief forces battered at the Japanese lines. In spite of their weakness in heavy weapons the Chinese on two occasions succeeded in breaking the encirclement, but the Japanese succeeded in closing the gap and restoring their grip on Hengyang. On August 8, after a siege of 47 days, the last resistance was crushed. A final desperate counter-attack by the Chinese in an effort to retake the city was beaten back, and this pivotal strategic position remained firmly in Japanese hands.

The campaign now unfolded in a broader pattern. After a preliminary thrust south of Hengyang, the Japanese threw their main

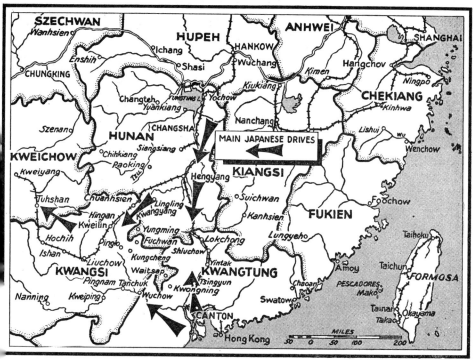

MAIN JAPANESE DRIVES

By permission of the New York *Times*

INTERIOR CHINA

strength into a thrust southwest down the railway toward the next main objective of Kweilin. At the same time freshly reinforced Japanese columns fanned out from Canton toward the west, and another force which had established itself on the Liuchow peninsula opposite Hainan island struck north in a converging drive. The objective appeared to be to pinch off a broad foothold on the coastal area west of Canton, to expel the American air force from its bases at Wuchow and Tanchuk, and to thrust one main prong toward Liuchow while the other from Hengyang moved down through Kweilin.

The operations proceeded slowly and deliberately. Given the exhausted state of the Chinese armies, and the extensive superiority of the Japanese in firepower and mobility, their progress during the next few weeks was not impressive in its speed. It was none the less inexorable in the final outcome. Its pace was to a large extent determined by the need to organize communications and supply services behind the advance. American fliers contributed to these difficulties by harrying supply lines and striking at troop concentrations. But while Chinese ground forces were able to impose occasional checks on advanced spearheads, they were outmatched by Japanese strength in tanks and artillery and motorized transport, and their efforts at Changsha and Hengyang had for the moment exhausted a large part of their vigour and rendered them incapable of a successful stand.

Thus although the Japanese took most of the autumn to attain their immediate objectives, a series of lunges carried them forward against dwindling opposition. The fall of Hengyang was followed by a relative lull while the Japanese consolidated their grip on the surrounding area, improving their lines of communication and gathering the necessary forces and supplies for a new advance. At the end of August they fanned out along a broad arc west and south of Hengyang. One column striking directly west, after a fortnight of relatively easy progress, ran into unexpectedly sharp resistance at Paoking; but this obstacle was bypassed and surrounded, and its garrison was subdued by October 4. With this thrust protecting the northern flank, the main drive rolled forward in three main columns along the railway toward Kweilin and through the area east of that line. The air base at Lingling was captured early in September. An attempt to halt the frontal advance at the border of Kwangsi province, 90 miles above Kweilin, collapsed about the same time. On September 12 the Americans began the evacuation and partial destruction of the great base at Kweilin, their main centre of operations in south China; and by the latter part of September the Japanese forces were less than 30 miles north of the city and were threatening to flank it from the east and south.

West of Canton the other main arm of the offensive was also rolling forward. Its converging prongs drove into southern Kwangsi province and forced the Americans to abandon a fourth major base at Tanchuk on October 1. Beyond this point the impetus of the advance ebbed temporarily; but the Japanese still retained the initiative, and while the main forces gathered their strength for a new surge, the spearheads stabbed out along a broad front whose right flank wheeled northwest toward Liuchow and whose left was thrusting forward toward Nanning.

The final week in October found Japanese preparations at last completed for a new and concerted effort. The assault broke through the Chinese positions guarding the approaches to Kweilin; and while one main column drove toward it astride the railway, a second launched a flank attack from the east, and still another swung down to the southeast to threaten the city with encirclement. This time their movement was rapid and decisive. In the week beginning November 27 the spearheads gained from 70 to 100 miles. Kweilin was bypassed and cut off; and while the trapped garrison rallied for a final stand, the Japanese offensive swept down the railway toward Liuchow.

These new disasters were almost fatal in their results. China's dwindling hope of checking the Japanese advance had been pinned to an effective stand at Kweilin. This was to be the Chinese Stalingrad whose unyielding defence would turn the tide of invasion.

There was in fact a stubborn effort to hold the town itself, and it was only after a week of street fighting that a Japanese assault on November 9 broke the last defences and resulted in the complete reduction of the town on the following day. But this was a brief resistance compared to the protracted struggle at Hengyang, and it did little to impede the main Japanese advance. With the sweeping aside of the field defences on the approaches to Kweilin, virtually all organized Chinese resistance was for the moment at an end. On the same day that Kweilin fell, the Japanese claimed the capture of the air base and communication centre of Liuchow. West of that town the southern force, which had launched a simultaneous and converging offensive, made contact with the northern arm to complete the corridor severing Free China; and along a front which stretched some 200 miles the Japanese continued their westward sweep with nothing to bar their way.

The outlook in China was now at its bleakest. The loss of Liuchow was followed by the fall of still another air base at Nanning a fort-night later. The main centre of American air activities was virtually forced back 400 miles to Kunming in the remote interior, and even here there was no assurance of permanence. The Japanese drive rolled unimpeded along the railway west of Liuchow, capturing Ishan and Hochih and overrunning almost the whole of Kwangsi province. By the first week in December it had taken Tuhshan, well inside the borders of Kweichow province, and its forward spearheads were barely 50 miles from the provincial capital Kweiyang.

This thrust held fresh and alarming prospects. Kweiyang was a centre from which good roads led west to Kunming and north to Chungking. These points lay 300 and 200 miles away; but in view of the recent speed of the Japanese advance and the poverty of Chinese defensive resources, distance could no longer be relied on for anything but a temporary respite. If the enemy established a firm grip on Kweiyang, the heart of Free China would be menaced. A drive to Kunming would cut communications with the west and neutralize the Ledo Road whose completion was now in sight. A drive to Chungking would be significant from the aspect of prestige rather than of strategy, but the political effects of Chungking's fall would be serious if not actually fatal for Free China.

In the event such prizes proved to be beyond the Japanese grasp. Their westward advance had now reached its limits. Supply difficulties were making themselves felt once more, and the spearheads that had stabbed into Kweichow province had outrun effective support and were vulnerable to any vigorous counter-attack. The 14th Air Force, though it had lost its major bases, had dispersed its strength at previously prepared fields in the interior and was striking with unabated energy at Japanese forces and communications. Fresh troops were flown down from the north, and counter-attacks were thrown in against the light Japanese forces that had reached Tuhshan. In danger of being cut off, and with their provisions exhausted, the Japanese fell back rapidly beyond the border of Kweichow province, and Chinese pursuit was only checked by stiffening resistance in the area of Hochih.

The Japanese were content for the present to accept the limits thus imposed on their westward gains, and to thicken the corridor by completing their control over the main Canton-Hankow railway. Their gains below Hengyang, which had hitherto served as a broad base for their westward drive, were now used as a springboard for a southward thrust to meet a new offensive north from Canton, while other columns expanded the eastern side of the existing corridor and pushed toward the Canton-Hankow line. On January 28, with the fall of the town of Kukong after two days of street fighting, the last remaining gap was closed, and the Japanese were in full control of the main railway and had broadened their corridor to more than 300 miles.

East of this corridor serious efforts were now in progress to eliminate the air bases that had been cut off in the coastal region and to strengthen the Japanese grip on the coast itself. In August, while the main drive was under way, a thrust into Chekiang province had captured the airfield town of Lishui, and early in September the

Japanese had secured the port of Wenchow. Late in September a coastal landing led to the capture of Foochow. There was little further activity in this region during the remainder of 1944; but early in the following year a general campaign was launched against the remaining ports and airfields. On February 7 it was announced that the last of the American air bases in south China had been abandoned. At the same time Japanese forces were spreading along the coast from Swatow; and their apparent determination to consolidate their position was shown on March 10 when they expelled the French from their last vestige of authority in Indo-China and seized full control over all important positions and facilities.

By the spring of 1945 the Japanese were ready to resume their westward advance. Following a series of thrusts north of the Yangtse in March which drove the Americans from Laohokow, one of their easternmost airfields, a strong triple-pronged drive was launched from captured Paoking toward the important air base of Chihkiang. By the beginning of May the Japanese spearheads were within little more than 50 miles of the town. But the few months that had passed since the subsidence of the earlier offensive had brought major changes in China's defensive position. Veteran Chinese divisions, released by the completion of operations in northern Burma, had been flown in. Supplies were flowing in by land and air, and American air strength was being shifted from Burma and India to the Chinese theatre. The training programme was beginning to bear its first fruits in new divisions ready for combat. The Japanese ran into stiffening resistance as they approached their goal. Their advance bogged down; and then, while devastating blows hit them from the air, two strong Chinese columns closed a pincers movement behind the main Japanese force, trapping part of it and driving the rest back in flight. It was a decisive check which marked the turn of the tide and the end of Japan's hope for further victories on the Asiatic mainland.

Even the victories of the past year were now seen to be barren. Their strategic value had been undermined by Allied mastery in the western Pacific and the invasion of the Philippines and Okinawa.

The drawing of these larger land areas into the theatre of combat imposed increasing demands on Japanese military strength. The prospect of an assault on Japan itself was drawing inexorably closer, and called for a concentration of Japan's defensive resources. The capture of American air bases on the mainland had not preserved Japan from bombing attacks nor checked the slow strangulation of her sea communications. A land route to Japan's outlying conquests lost most of its value when there were no resources available to use and exploit it. Burma was lost, and there was little hope of saving Malaya. The cutting of China's newly restored communications, which in the previous autumn had seemed a real possibility, was now beyond the power of the forces which Japan could afford to devote to such an effort. Even the achievement of splitting China in two and isolating the southeast coastal region was of limited significance. The corridor was still a barrier to the establishment of a firm Allied grip on the coast by an offensive from the inland provinces, but the barrier was a slender one. The forces that would be necessary to hold it in strength were more urgently needed in other quarters. It was vulnerable to any assault that could be launched in real strength; and Japan, thrown back on the defensive in this area, was forced into a reversal of the whole strategic policy that lay behind the drive into south China, and compelled to abandon the gains which had been won by the only victories she could count to her credit during this year of war.

THE PHILIPPINES AND IWO

The crushing of the desperate Japanese resistance on Leyte, and the accompanying disasters to Japanese naval and air power, represented a major landmark in the Pacific advance. American forces were now squarely planted within the main bulwarks guarding the approaches to Japan. Their next task was to enlarge their foothold in a way that would allow them to deploy their strength in preparation for the prospective blow against Japan itself. From Leyte they were in a position to expand their conquests to the rest of the Philippines and to seize other island footholds still closer to the Japanese homeland. Their possession of the initiative allowed them to choose the time and place for each successive blow. Their overwhelming margin of strength made it certain that they could batter down the most stubborn Japanese opposition. Formidable obstacles still lay between them and the final goal, but the most that Japan could hope was to fight a delaying action in the few outlying positions that remained to her, and to husband her main strength for a last desperate stand on her own shores.

Even before the mastery of Leyte was completed, plans were in train for the next step. In a regrouping of forces, command of the Leyte operation was passed to the Eighth Army, while the Sixth, which retained a number of veteran divisions that had been involved in the Leyte campaign, made ready for the invasion of Luzon. It was on this main island that the bulk of the Japanese strength in the Philippines was concentrated, and the possession of Luzon's harbours and airfields was a prime necessity for the operations that were to follow.

While the external threat was gathering, the Japanese found themselves assailed from within. All through the period of occupation, Filipino resistance remained alive in the remote and mountainous sections of the islands. Guerilla forces had created effective local organizations and had succeeded in making contact with American military authorities. By the end of 1944 these bands were under direction from MacArthur's headquarters and were in many cases under the leadership of American officers. They were now called into full action to harry and confuse the Japanese, to attack communications and blow up bridges in order to impede troop movements, and to disrupt military dispositions in preparation for the invasion of Luzon.

Particular efforts were made to draw Japanese strength to the southern part of the island. The guerillas were especially active in that region, and feint operations by transports and small naval craft drew Japanese attention toward the southern coast. Dummies were even dropped from planes to give the impression of paratroop landings. To heighten Japanese concern, the blow at Luzon was preceded by an invasion of the nearby island of Mindoro. With an audacity which testified to the completeness of American naval and air ascendancy, a convoy from Leyte sailed through the heart of the archipelago and past the Japanese-held islands in the southern Visayan group. During the three days it took for its 600-mile voyage it was several times attacked by small forces of Japanese planes; but the threat was beaten off, and early on December 19 a force of 2 regiments landed on the southwest coast of Mindoro.

Opposition was almost non-existent. There was no resistance on the beaches and only the feeblest attempt by ground forces to check the invaders. There were sharp air attacks after they were established ashore, but the Americans seized Mindoro's chief airfield at the outset and soon had it in operation for both defensive and offensive purposes. Here was a base on the western rim of the archipelago, where the climate was better and the rains less persistent than on water-bogged Leyte. The urgency of Japanese concern was shown by the fact that a naval force was risked in an attempt to cut off and destroy the landing force. On the night of December 26 a force reportedly composed of a battleship, a cruiser and 6 destroyers opened a bombardment of the beachhead. The ships were so promptly and so hotly attacked from the air that their fire was haphazard and ineffective. Three destroyers were sunk, and hits were claimed on both the battleship and the cruiser. The surviving ships fled, and thenceforth the foothold on Mindoro was secure and American fighter planes were within range of Luzon's air bases. At the beginning of January, new landings extended the American grip on the west coast and gave them a foothold on the east coast; and on January 3 an unopposed landing on Marinduque, between Mindoro and Luzon, seemed further confirmation of the approaching threat to Luzon from the south.

All through this period, American naval and air forces were engaged in an intensive effort to soften up Luzon's defences and to batter down Japanese air power. The Third Fleet continued its

far-ranging activities which had been in progress ever since the
previous summer. Three days of carrier attacks covered the Mindoro
landing, blanketing Luzon's airfields and ravaging shipping along the
coast. Through the rest of December and early January the planes
kept up their merciless pounding, striking repeatedly at Clark Field
north of Manila and taking a mounting toll of coastal shipping;
and the carrier task forces, after two days of heavy raids on Formosa
and Okinawa, extended their range by sending reconnaissance planes
over the coast of China, and then swung back to join in the bombardment of Luzon that covered the invasion.

As at Leyte, the landing itself was under the protection of the
Seventh Fleet which shepherded the convoy on the long voyage from
its assembly point east of Leyte to its destination in Lingayen gulf,
and which sent its heavy units inshore to reduce the enemy's coastal
defences. For three days, beginning on January 6, the ships hammered
at Japanese shore positions in the face of answering fire from coastal
batteries and of repeated air attacks. In spite of the damage to their
airfields and the loss of over 1000 planes during the preceding month,
the Japanese were able to launch persistent bombing attacks from
their bases on Luzon; but these were too light to do more than minor
damage, and the blanketing of Formosa and Okinawa by the Third
Fleet struck at possible sources of air reinforcements. The shore
defences were battered down. The landing forces, covered by cruisers
and destroyers, moved in on January 9 along a 15-mile stretch from
Lingayen to San Fabian. By nightfall 68,000 troops had been poured
ashore, four initial beachheads had been linked into one continuous
foothold, and the invading spearheads had penetrated inland as much
as 4 miles.

The Japanese were caught completely unprepared. Only a single
division guarded the broad central plain, the classic route of invasion,
which stretched southward to Manila. Last-minute efforts by the
Japanese to readjust their dispositions were hampered by damage
to communications and the continued harrying activities of Filipino
guerillas and American fliers. The covering activities of the Third

Fleet, whose carriers located and virtually destroyed four convoys off the coast of Indo-China and followed up with heavy blows at shipping in Chinese ports, forestalled the possibility of a relief expedition. The Japanese were reduced to committing their forces piecemeal as they could be brought into action, and to holding the mountainous sectors north and east of the Luzon plain until they had gathered sufficient strength for a counter-blow.

The American assault force consisted of 4 divisions, with 4 others in reserve. While the XIV Corps on the right struck south from Lingayen toward Manila, the task of the I Corps was to protect the advance by pushing back the Japanese in the hills to the north and east and cutting the two main highways leading north from Manila. This latter operation was as arduous as it was vital. Out of a Japanese strength on Luzon approximating 10 divisions, roughly one-third was in the north. So long as communications were unimpaired, reinforcements could be shifted toward Manila to strengthen the defences or toward the north to mass for a counter-assault which would threaten the XIV Corps from the rear.

Immediately on landing, therefore, the I Corps struck out against the Japanese hill positions on the northern flank, and fanned out on a steadily broadening front toward the main road from Manila to Baguio. The Japanese offered bitter resistance, with the brunt falling on their 2nd Armoured division. A three-week struggle raged around the village of Rosario, and by January 14 the Japanese were striking back with counter-attacks in defence of the highway. The bitterness of the fighting in this sector was shown by the fact that, although the direct advance toward Manila encountered no serious opposition until the last week in January, American casualties as announced on January 30 totalled 4254, and it was claimed that the Japanese had lost over 25,000 men and 103 tanks. By January 18, however, the eastward advance had driven the Japanese from the main highway along a 37-mile stretch. A second highway along the eastern edge of the Luzon plain remained in enemy hands, but by the end of the month a wedge had been driven to this road as well, and continuous pressure had kept the Japanese on the defensive and safeguarded the columns thrusting south toward the capital.

THE LIBERATION OF MANILA

The Japanese, caught off balance, showed little desire to challenge the Americans on the open Luzon plain. Opposition had been expected at the Agno river which offered a natural defence line; but although the Japanese had constructed fortified positions at this point, no serious attempt was made to hold them. Even so, the deliberate pace of the advance was shown by the fact that it took 10 days to cover the 50 miles from the Lingayen beachhead to the important road and rail junction of Tarlac. South of this town another river defence line was abandoned by the Japanese, and on January 25 the Americans seized Clark Field and gained possession of the main air base on the island. Japanese opposition now began to stiffen. Mortar and artillery fire from the hills southwest of Clark Field harassed the advance for a brief period, and there was a sharp clash at the village of Angeles before it was taken with its four airfields on January 27. But these efforts did little to slow the advance, which by the end of January had driven through the bottleneck of swamps above Manila bay and was moving rapidly toward Manila itself.

An enveloping movement against the city now developed as new forces came into action. On January 29 the 38th division and elements of the 24th—the assault forces of the XI Corps drawn from the Eighth Army—landed near San Narciso on the west coast of Luzon, and launched a rapid drive across the base of the Bataan peninsula to link up with the XIV Corps and prevent a Japanese withdrawal to Bataan. Two days later still another landing took place, this time by the 11th Airborne division at Nasugbu southwest of Manila; and the advance of this force was speeded by the dropping of parachute troops on February 3 to capture Tagaytay ridge and clear the way for an assault on Manila from the south. Meanwhile the threat from the north was broadened when the 1st Cavalry division was thrown

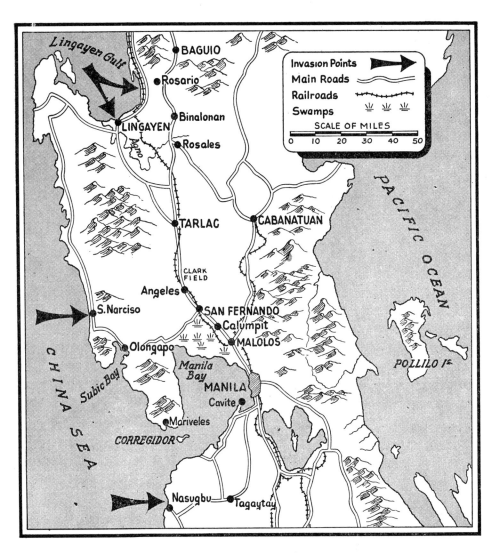

LUZON

out on the left flank of the XIV Corps to cut the second main highway leading north from Manila and advance down it parallel with the thrust of the 37th division along the other highway farther west.

In the face of these converging movements, Manila's fall seemed imminent. On the evening of February 3 a wide sweep carried the 1st Cavalry into the city from the east. A few hours later the 37th drove in from the north. Sporadic resistance in the northern half of the city was quickly crushed; and on the morning of February 6, with American forces now on the southern outskirts, MacArthur announced that Manila was in American hands.

The claim was decidedly premature. Although the Japanese realized that Manila itself was lost, they were determined to deny the use of Manila bay to the Americans as long as possible. South of the city the 11th Airborne division ran into hard fighting around Nichols Field and the naval base of Cavite, which held out until February 11. Inside Manila the Japanese, setting the torch to the main business district, withdrew in house-to-house fighting and concentrated their forces within the old walled city adjoining the harbour. Here walls 40 feet thick provided stout defences which had to be gradually battered down by artillery in the course of a fortnight's siege. At last on February 23 a breach was effected and American assault forces swept into the Intramuros district; and even then the remnants of the Japanese garrison, barricaded in three fortified buildings, maintained a last-ditch stand until March 4. It was a tragically devastated city that remained after the fierce and prolonged fighting that had been necessary to subdue the final resistance and complete the liberation of the Philippine capital.

During this period other operations directed toward the clearing of Manila bay were moving steadily forward. Troops of the XI Corps, pushing east from their initial beachhead, seized the naval station of Olongapo on Subic bay and drove along the road cutting across the base of the Bataan peninsula. On February 6 it was announced that they had linked up with the 6th division advancing from the east, cutting off the Japanese forces on Bataan, and spearheads were pushing down either coast of the peninsula. Stiff initial resistance by the Japanese was broken during the next week; and on February 15 a seaborne landing on the southeast tip of the peninsula followed by a swift linkup with troops advancing down the east coast brought the whole area under effective American control.

Bataan now became the springboard for an assault on Corregidor, the fortress guarding the entrance to Manila bay. A sustained aerial bombardment which began on January 23 had showered the garrison with over 3000 tons of bombs. Now the Seventh Fleet moved in to shell the defences, while the air forces joined in a co-ordinated attack which was the immediate prelude to assault. On February 16 a parachute landing on Corregidor took the defenders in the rear; and while they were rallying from this surprise, other invasion forces struck across the narrow channel from Bataan to establish a foothold and link up with the airborne troops.

Although the success of this well-planned operation, with its precision of execution, sealed the fate of Corregidor, it was another fortnight before resistance was finally subdued. The garrison took refuge in caves and in the elaborate tunnel system of the fortress itself, fighting bitterly and tenaciously in a suicidal stand, and blowing up the fortified positions along with their remaining defenders when further resistance became impossible. Gradually the survivors were rooted out or sealed up in the tunnels and caves. The effort to delay the fall of Corregidor cost the Japanese 4215 known dead and an unknown number blown up in the various explosions. By the beginning of March the last pocket had been mopped up, and Manila bay was at last open for use by Allied shipping.

There remained the task of clearing Luzon of the strong enemy forces which still remained there. With the fall of Manila, pressure was brought along a wide perimeter against the Japanese positions in the hills that rimmed the central plain. Below Manila a drive was launched into the southern part of the island, and this was supplemented on April 1 by the landing of a combat team at Legaspi on the southern tip of Luzon and a dual advance which crushed resistance in the south during the next 10 days. In other sectors the going was harder. West of Clark Field there was slow progress against relatively small Japanese forces that had taken refuge in the hills. On the eastern side of the central plain the Japanese had organized strong positions known as the Shimbu Line which barred the way to the coast. It took the greater part of March to dislodge the enemy from these defences, and a series of ridges still remained to be mastered before the coast was reached. On the northern flank the struggle continued with undiminished bitterness as the Japanese fought hard to check the American spearheads that were thrusting toward the administrative centre of Baguio and attacking Balete pass which guarded the entrance to the Cagayan valley. The relatively rapid subjugation of central and southern Luzon was followed by months of hard grinding effort to gain the remainder of the island.

In the interval American control was extended over the other main islands of the archipelago. An unopposed landing on Palawan on February 28 was followed during March by the securing of footholds on Panay and Cebu and Negros, all with relative ease. A landing on Mindanao on March 10 led to the speedy capture of Zamboanga on the western peninsula; but opposition stiffened as the advancing forces pushed toward the main part of the island, and fresh landings and hard fighting were needed at a later stage before resistance was overcome.

Complete mastery of the Philippines was thus a protracted task. On all the islands, and particularly on Luzon and Mindanao, the Japanese tactics of avoiding battle on the beachheads or in open country but fighting back savagely in the hills meant that substantial American forces remained occupied in the effort to wipe out these troublesome and far from negligible garrisons which still retained strong positions circumscribing the actual area of conquest. But while this situation pinned down a number of American divisions and restricted full freedom of movement, its strategic significance was of minor importance. For all essential purposes the Philippines were back under American control. Their main harbours were open to full use by warships and supply and transport shipping. Their airfields provided increased facilities for the steady expansion of air power and extended its range still more effectively over Formosa and the coast of China. The land area that had been secured gave a substantial base for the massing of the forces and supplies that would soon be needed for the projected invasion of Japan; and the prospective launching of this hazardous enterprise drew nearer with the seizure of new outposts which advanced American striking power a long stage closer to the ultimate goal.

THE BATTLE FOR IWO

The perimeter which the Pacific advance had now established from the Marianas to the Philippines, and the springboards which had thus been gained for the direct assault on Japan, still lay 1500 miles from that objective. Apart from the mainland of China, no other land area suitable for a major base existed in the intervening region with the possible exception of Formosa, and major operations against either China or Formosa had now been ruled out by the decision to strike directly at Japan without the delay that such operations would impose. These plans however made necessary the securing of intermediate bases, not merely as staging points for the invasion effort, but to bring Allied air power within more effective reach of the Japanese mainland. The preliminary phases of the air offensive were already under way, but to develop it to the full extent needed to weaken Japan's power of resistance a more intensive campaign from within a much shorter radius was regarded as essential.

This project called for a deep thrust into at least one of the island chains—the Kuriles, the Bonin-Volcano group, or the Ryukyus—which radiate from Japan like the spokes of a wheel. For practical purposes, only the Ryukyus offered a choice which would serve the primary needs of Allied strategy. The island of Okinawa in the Ryukyus, with an area of 485 square miles, was large enough to accommodate a substantial number of airfields and to serve as a concentration point for ground forces, and it possessed half a dozen or more harbours that could be used as supply ports or naval anchorages. Of the other two island groups, the Kuriles could virtually be ruled out for strategic purposes. They lay far off the main course of the Pacific advance; and while the air and naval base of Paramushiru was a frequent target for bombers and was occasionally hit by naval forces, it was neither important nor valuable enough to be marked as an objective for invasion.

The Bonins and Volcanos held an intermediate position, both geographically and strategically. Their islands, relatively small in area, offered few of the advantages of Okinawa. They had almost no harbours, and there was little prospect that they could be used for large scale operations by any substantial forces of heavy bombers. None the less they were of real significance to the air strategy against Japan. By the end of 1944 the Marianas had become the main base for the offensive operations of the B-29's. This meant that the big bombers were operating at the formidable distance of 1500 miles from their main target. Not only did this reduce their operational bomb load; it meant also that they were deprived of fighter protection on their missions over enemy territory. For offensive purposes, an intermediate base within fighter range of Tokyo would be of the utmost value. Defensively there were considerations of almost equal weight. The islands lay along the direct air route from the Marianas to Tokyo. They provided Japanese planes with bases for both interception and counter-blows. From Iwo a number of damaging raids were launched against the B-29 bases on Guam. Japanese radar stations picked up approaching American bombers and gave warning to the home defences, and Japanese fighters attacked the heavy bombers on their way to and from the target. The expulsion of the enemy from these positions, and their acquisition by American forces, promised greater efficiency in the bombing of Japan at a greatly reduced cost.

In theory there were three possible objectives whose seizure would serve the desired purpose. In reality the choice was virtually limited to Iwo. Hachijo in the Izu group could be made to serve as a fighter base, but it was only 150 miles from Tokyo, and its capture hardly seemed worth the hazards that would be involved. Chichi Jima (Peel Island) in the Bonins had a sheltered harbour, but its shores were precipitous and it could accommodate only a single airfield. Iwo Jima (Sulphur Island) in the Volcanos had no harbour, but there was a narrow beach on which landing would be easier than on Chichi, and it was already the site of two Japanese airfields with a third under construction. Lying halfway between Guam and Tokyo, it would when captured place American planes within 750 miles of Japan's capital, and remove the Japanese planes which at present were within similar striking distance of the Marianas.

A number of air and sea attacks had already been directed against Iwo, first to neutralize it in preparation for the invasion of the Marianas and later to damage the fields from which Japanese planes were raiding Guam and Saipan. On December 7, however, a combined naval and air attack opened a period of sustained preparation for invasion. For more than two months the 8 square miles of the island were subjected to daily attacks by heavy bombers interspersed with bombardments from surface warships. In 10 weeks of bombing Iwo was hit with nearly 6000 tons, in addition to the weight of the shells from five raids by cruisers and destroyers.

The pre-invasion bombardment concentrated an even greater weight of explosives into a period of 3 days. The command team of the Fifth Fleet, which had taken over naval operations at the end of January, was in charge of the new series of operations initiated by the invasion of Iwo. While a covering force of carriers and battleships struck a long-contemplated blow at the Tokyo area, the main bombardment force attacked Iwo on February 16. Half a dozen of the oldest battleships afloat, whose heavy armour more than made up for their lack of speed in an operation of this sort, stood close inshore and raked the island with heavy shells with negligible response from the Japanese defences. Behind them gathered the invasion armada of 800 craft of all kinds; and on the morning of February 19 the V Amphibious Corps, composed of 2 Marine assault divisions with a third in reserve, drove ashore on the southeast coast of the island.

The landing spot was a narrow beach about two miles long. A few yards inland the ground rose in several terraces to the low ridge that formed a saddle in this sector. On the left, almost at the southern tip of the island, was the dormant volcanic cone of 550-foot Mount Suribachi. On the right, and occupying most of the area of the island, was a volcanic plateau rising nearly 400 feet on which the Japanese airfields were situated.

In the first moments after the landing the absence of serious resistance gave the impression that the Japanese defences had been demolished by the bombardment and that progress would be relatively easy. Nothing could have been more misleading. The island had been skilfully fortified and was held by a determined garrison of over 20,000 under an able commander. The low ridge along the saddle was fortified with a system of blockhouses and pillboxes connected by a network of trenches. The high ground on either side offered excellent positions for guns and mortars, many of them in stout emplacements which had not been knocked out or in caves which were virtually impregnable to bombardment. From Mount Suribachi on the south and the plateau on the north the whole of the beachhead could be brought under direct fire by guns which had been carefully registered on every yard of the low ground on which alone the troops and equipment could be landed. Many of these positions had been undetected by American reconnaissance, and the guns had held their fire so as not to reveal their positions during the bombardment. In spite of the tremendous pounding, the Japanese defences had largely withstood the shock. Gunfire proved incapable of demolishing them, and Iwo had to be taken by the men who were thrown ashore in the face of the most murderous fire that any landing force had yet encountered in the Pacific.

An hour after the landing, when the first wave had crossed the beach and the landing area was crowded with supporting forces and equipment, the Japanese laid down a sudden and terrible barrage,

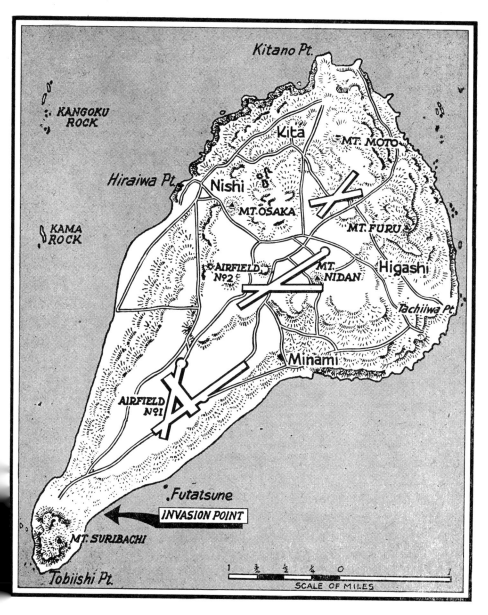

IWO JIMA

isolating and almost wiping out the leading troops and creating deadly havoc on the beaches. The Marines succeeded in advancing across the narrow and low-lying saddle, but they were pinned down by fire from the dominating heights on either side, and a number of supporting units were driven back in their attempt to land. The critical situation was saved partly by the fact that some artillery and a number of tanks had been got ashore, and these gave invaluable support against Japanese positions which the shells from the warships had been unable to reach effectively. Landings continued in the face of intense fire, and by February 21 the third division of Marines had come into action and 60,000 men had been put ashore. Yet in spite of their superiority of three to one in manpower over the defenders, the American position was critical. By dusk on February 21 they had suffered over 5300 casualties, and their attempts to advance against the high ground on either flank had been held to gains of a few hundred yards.

None the less a firm foothold had been established, and the tactical gains already made provided ground for further advances. The first of Iwo's three airfields had been captured, and Mount Suribachi was isolated and under closing assault. On February 23 a decisive effort dislodged the Japanese from the crest of Mount Suribachi; and although numerous parties in caves and blockhouses remained to be liquidated, this dominant height now ceased to be an obstacle and became a vantage point for the American attack as it concentrated against the Japanese on the plateau to the north.

Here there were several days of bitter uphill fighting. It took two days to advance 700 yards and reach the edge of the second airfield, and five more days of intense battling before this was captured on February 28. But by that date the first airfield had been put into operation and the general position had improved in favour of the Americans. They were now securely planted on the main plateau. They had fought their way out of the narrow and constricting neck of the lower part of the island and could deploy their full strength across its broader part. The 3rd Marine division had come fully into line between the 5th on its left and the 4th on its right, and steadily increasing pressure was forcing the Japanese toward the northern end of the island and threatening to split them in two.

It was still a costly and gruelling effort. Numerous ridges and almost innumerable caves provided the Japanese with positions from which they could oppose a heavy fire to the attempts to dislodge them. Intense bombardment by shore and naval guns followed by infantry assaults seldom brought the Marines more than a gain of a few hundred yards. Individual Japanese positions in caves and pillboxes had to be reduced by dynamite or flame-throwers when direct artillery fire proved ineffective, and the close-knit nature of the defences reduced the advance to a crawl while these small knots of resistance were wiped out one by one. At last on March 11 the advance of the 3rd division in the centre carried it through to the sea, splitting off a pocket on the right which was mopped up during the next few days, and pressing the bulk of the remaining Japanese garrison into a small area on the northern tip of the island. The last brief suicidal resistance ended on February 26 when this remnant was crushed or dispersed; yet even then there were still parties to be dealt with in the caves and crevices of the island, and the deadly and dangerous work of mopping-up had to be completed before the conquerors could enjoy complete safety on Iwo.

The island's 8 square miles had been dearly bought. Apart from the naval losses, which included the escort carrier *Bismarck Sea* as well as damage to the *Saratoga* and a number of other ships, the Marines had suffered heavily. Casualties as announced on March 16 totalled 19,938, or just under one-third of the forces engaged; and of these 4,360 were listed as killed or missing. A campaign which had been expected to take 5 days had lasted for 26; an enemy garrison whose resistance was to have been broken by intensive air and naval bombardment had survived to conduct a resistance that was skilful as well as fanatical; and even the death of over 20,000 Japanese (for as usual there were barely a thousand prisoners) was small solace for the price that had been paid in American lives.

Given the necessity of capturing Iwo, that price was unavoidable. It was true that the strength of the Japanese defences had been miscalculated; but even if that error had been remedied, there were few practical steps that could have been taken as a result. There was no chance of surprise at Iwo and no scope for manoeuvre. Once it was clear that the defences could not be shattered by bombardment alone, nothing remained but to launch a frontal assault over the naked ground, and to overcome the defenders by sending against him men whose bodies took the shock of concentrated firepower and pressed on through it to victory.

The only question at issue was the strategic need for taking Iwo at all. Its whole value lay in its contribution to the air assault on Japan; and the capture of Okinawa, on which Iwo had little or no bearing, provided a much more substantial base for air operations. But while Okinawa was only some 360 miles from the Japanese mainland, its airfields were 900 miles from Tokyo—a distance over which it would have been impossible to provide adequate fighter protection; and by the time Okinawa was secure, Iwo had been in American hands for three months and had been playing its part in the mounting air campaign. While it could have been bypassed, it is doubtful whether it could have been effectively neutralized without capture, and it would have remained a thorn in the side of the American strategic bombing forces. It was not in the number of planes and fliers saved, substantial as they were, that the cost of Iwo's conquest was justified. It was rather in the scope and weight which it added to an air campaign which at this stage was looked on as the vitally essential prelude to the invasion of Japan. These are factors which can hardly be computed with accuracy and finality; but in view of the formidable tasks which seemed to lie ahead, Allied planners could hardly afford to neglect any element which might increase the chances of success in the final and decisive effort.

4

MAY TO SEPTEMBER 1945

THE DOWNFALL OF JAPAN

THE final collapse of Germany at the beginning of May found Japan already standing at bay and summoning all her remaining strength to repel the massive assault which was in preparation against her. The desperate plight to which she had been reduced was all the more striking in view of the relatively small inroads which had as yet been made on either her territorial possessions or her military strength. She had been driven from Burma and dislodged from a series of strategic positions in the islands of the central and southwest Pacific, but she retained her grip on the Indies and on a large part of China, including Manchuria with its important resources and war industries. The land campaigns in Burma and the Philippines—the largest that had as yet been undertaken against her by the Allies—had been disastrous for the Japanese forces engaged, but these outlying garrisons represented only a fraction of her armed strength. The bulk of her armies stood in the home islands and on the Chinese mainland and had not yet been involved on any serious scale. None the less, Japan was already beaten; and although she was still in a position to prolong the conflict and make her adversaries pay dearly for their victory, she no longer had any hope of averting ultimate defeat.

This was the triumphant outcome of Allied strategy in the western Pacific. Its foundation was the mounting superiority of American naval and air strength, used in close co-ordination to drive a direct path to the very threshold of Japan. The very nature of the island campaign deprived the Japanese of any real opportunity to make full use of their land forces in defence of the approaches to their homeland. Not until the Philippines were reached was there any serious possibility of Japanese reinforcements reaching the imperilled garrisons in the face of Allied command of the sea; and not until that stage, when a substantial land base was needed in preparation for the assault on Japan itself, were the Allies obliged to invade an island area on which relatively large Japanese forces could be massed in readiness for the attack. And when this stage had been reached, the combination of air and naval power by which it had been attained was in a position to isolate Japan itself from the conquered lands overseas, and to batter the resources and defences of the home islands in preparation for a direct assault. Formidable and costly though such an enterprise might be, its success held good prospects of bringing the collapse of Japanese power on the Asiatic mainland without the need of engaging in a prolonged struggle with the remaining enemy forces in that region.

This situation placed Japan in an insoluble dilemma. With her sea power shattered and her air power outmatched, her greatest remaining resource was her relatively untouched strength in ground forces. But the direction of the Allied approach prevented the full employment of that strength at the real point of danger. It was even impossible to concentrate all available troops in Japan proper in the hope that they might repel the invasion. Withdrawal from China and Manchuria would mean the abandonment of vitally important resources, and would present the Allies with still greater facilities for massed air attacks and large-scale military preparations. Yet the retention of large forces on the continent offered no real prospect of salvation. Allied command of the air and the sea lanes subjected Japan to mounting bombardment and an ever-tightening blockade. With her supply lines to the mainland cut and her industries battered and devastated, it profited her little to retain control in China, and her armies there stood a good chance of being bypassed and neutralized as smaller garrisons had been in the course of the Pacific campaign. Whatever course Japan chose, she was under the shadow of inevitable doom.

At sea the Japanese had met with catastrophes that were irretrievable. American naval control extended to the very shores of Japan, and a fleet which could. challenge that control with any hope of success no longer existed. In the battle of Leyte Gulf the Japanese had committed the whole of their remaining battleship strength in a supreme effort to turn the tide, and had failed disastrously. The battered forces that remained after the engagement had been reduced to half a dozen battleships and a handful of aircraft carriers in varying stages of disrepair, and during the next six months the continued attrition of this surviving strength virtually eliminated the Japanese navy as a fighting force.

The ships that fled from Leyte Gulf found no safety in the waters they had once controlled, or even in their own home naval bases. The ubiquitous *Kongo*, located near Foochow in the latter part of November 1944, was sent to the bottom as the result of a bold attack by an American submarine. In March 1945, in the course of the carrier sweeps preliminary to the attack on Okinawa, American planes ranged over the Inland Sea and inflicted fresh damage on the warships that had taken refuge at Kure and Kobe. On April 6 a major prize fell into their grasp when the battleship *Yamato*, which had been damaged in several previous air attacks, was located with a covering force of lighter ships off the southwest coast of Kyushu. The chance to destroy the last modern battleship that Japan possessed was promptly seized upon, and urgency was added by the possibility that her sortie, instead of being merely an attempt to find a safer refuge than Kure, might presage a desperate blow at the American forces off Okinawa. On the morning of April 7 the carrier planes of Task Force 58 launched a concentrated attack on the Japanese flotilla. The *Yamato*, their main target, absorbed terrific punishment from bombs and torpedoes; but shortly after noon she was hit in a vital spot and sank after a tremendous explosion. Of the escorting ships, a light cruiser and 4 destroyers were sunk, 2 other destroyers were set on fire, and only 3 destroyers managed to escape undamaged.

This success finally sealed the doom of the Japanese fleet as a striking force. Out of an original 12 battleships, only 4 were left afloat, and these had been damaged in varying degrees. Out of 26 aircraft carriers, including one that had not as yet been put in commission, 7 were left; out of 18 heavy cruisers, 6 remained, and at least 2 of these were under repair. The remnants of the Japanese navy were driven into the protection of ports and dockyards, there to await the attack from the air which caught the chief surviving units at Kure in July and sent most of them to the bottom.

With Japan's sea defences shattered, an added burden fell on her hard-pressed air forces. The last faint hope of crippling the American fleet and thus averting or even delaying the approaching invasion lay in the use of air power. Japan's carrier strength had been virtually wiped out, but by April the advance of the Americans had brought them within reach of Japan's own land bases, and the main weight of Japanese air power could be thrown against the American ships off Okinawa and the fast carrier forces covering the operation. But the formidable and costly effort which this involved had to be undertaken at a time when the Japanese homeland was undergoing the first fury of massed bombing attacks. Japanese air strength was inadequate for the dual task of challenging American sea power and defending Japanese cities. Mounting plane losses were accompanied by damaging blows at plane production; and while output still remained above losses, the dwindling margin made it increasingly difficult for Japan to mount a campaign on a scale large enough to check the American amphibious advance, and at the same time to accumulate adequate air reserves for the final test when invasion would be launched against Japan itself.

The experimental phase of the strategic bombing campaign against Japan entered a new stage in the autumn of 1944. The first blows had been struck by the 20th Bomber Command of the Twentieth Air Force from bases in western China. They had shown that they could reach targets in southern Japan, as well as Japanese establishments on the mainland over a wide arc from Singapore to Mukden. But to conduct a sustained campaign on any substantial scale from existing Chinese bases involved supply problems of the most formidable kind, as well as the hazards attending long flights over enemy-occupied territory. If Japanese resistance was to be shattered from the air, as some of the planners continued to hope, bases more accessible and if possible closer to the main objective were virtually indispensable.

One of the vitally important results of the conquest of the Marianas was to make such bases available. Although distances from these islands to the main Japanese centres were still great, they were well within the capacity of the Superfortresses. With the sea routes secure, supplies could be poured into the Marianas in a volume that was impossible in the case of China, and their land area was extensive enough to provide the bases necessary for large-scale and sustained operations. Even before the conquest was completed, work was begun on an airbase on Saipan from which the 21st Bomber Command was to launch its first operations. By the beginning of 1945, other bases had been developed on Guam and Tinian; and while the China-based B-29's continued their attacks against targets on the Asiatic mainland, the forces from the Marianas took up the main air assault against Japan.

The new operations were initiated with a daylight raid on Tokyo by 111 Superfortresses on November 24. The Japanese capital, hitherto untouched except for the Doolittle raid in 1942, had lost the immunity which distance had so long conferred on it. Few developments were more aptly symbolic of the changing strategic picture than the fact that Tokyo could now be subjected to a methodical campaign of destruction from the air. The city was hit by three

further raids during the nine days that followed. In mid-December
the bombers turned their attention to Nagoya, which was attacked
three times within eight days; and on December 27 Tokyo was hit
again for the first time since December 3.

The main objective in these attacks was Japanese aircraft production. The China-based bombers had already directed damaging
blows at aircraft factories on Formosa and Kyushu, and throughout
this period they continued to attack these objectives. The raids
from the Marianas had as their chief targets two aircraft-engine
plants in the Tokyo area and two at Nagoya. There was necessarily
a good deal that was tentative and experimental about the initial
attacks. High-level daylight bombing of specific aircraft factories
was varied by attacks on the waterfront industrial areas of Tokyo
and Nagoya, and by a night raid on Tokyo on November 29. Except
for the first raid on Tokyo, fewer than 100 planes were employed in
each expedition; and while considerable damage was inflicted on the
selected targets, none of them could be regarded as conclusively
destroyed. The strategic bombers were feeling their way toward
most effective tactics in the midst of many difficulties and uncer-
tainties. Attacks on targets 1500 miles distant involved serious
navigational problems. An ocean flight meant less danger from enemy
action than a flight over hostile territory, but it also offered fewer
landmarks; and even more serious than the problem of locating the
assigned target was that of tracing a direct and accurate course back
to relatively small island bases. The strength of Japanese air defences
and the efficiency of Japanese firefighting and repair organizations
were unknown factors at the outset. Iwo Jima was still in Japanese
hands, a station which could warn the homeland of an approaching
raid and could send up fighters to intercept the raiders both going
and returning. Not least important, weather information was of the
scantiest, and experience from both raids and reconnaissance expeditions had to be gained before this disadvantage could be to some
extent offset.

During the first six weeks of 1945, in consequence, operations from the Marianas continued on a relatively modest scale. Six raids were launched during January and three in the first half of February with forces of from 60 to 80 planes. Tokyo and Nagoya continued to be the main targets, but the attack was extended to aircraft industries in the Kobe area. Meanwhile the raids provided material for a close study of tactical lessons and their application, and a period of accumulation of resources and intensive training of personnel laid the groundwork for a new phase of the campaign. In the two-week period from February 19 to March 4 there were only three major raids, all of them against Tokyo; but these showed an increase in strength to as many as 200 planes, and heralded the opening of a new series marked not only by a sudden increase in both size and frequency, but also by radically new tactics.

The decision had now been taken to launch a maximum offensive against Japan's leading cities, with fire as the basic weapon. The greatly increased use of fire bombs in the air offensive over Germany testified to their effectiveness against concentrated industrial areas. Circumstances made this weapon even more appropriate against Japan. There were comparatively few centres of war production on a large scale; but in these centres the manufacture of aircraft parts and other war materials was scattered throughout a multitude of small shops spread over a wide urban area. Bombing might knock out a large assembly plant or a key unit such as an engine factory; but to bring production to a standstill the chief Japanese cities had to be virtually demolished, and this could not readily be done by high level precision bombing with high explosive. Fire, on the other hand, would be even more effective than against European cities. The inflammable nature of Japanese cities may have been exaggerated in the public mind, but it remained true that they were more vulnerable than their European counterparts. New types of fire bombs, employing a jellied gasoline that spread rapidly and was hard to extinguish, offered particularly deadly weapons against the huddled wooden buildings of the factory and working class districts, and the relative inefficiency of Japanese firefighting organizations was a further element which favoured this type of attack.

For maximum efficiency it was determined to adopt completely new tactics. Instead of high-level daylight raids, the bombers were to be sent in at night at around 5000 feet. In view of the fact that the strength of Japanese anti-aircraft defences had not yet been established with certainty, this was a gamble which might conceivably result in disastrous losses, but the possible rewards seemed to outweigh the calculable risks. Night bombing essentially meant area bombing; but a low level attack combined with pathfinder technique would allow the introduction of an element of precision into the operation. A relatively restricted area could be selected for saturation by incendiary bombs whose fires, starting close to each other and concentrated in a space of a few square miles, would rapidly merge into a single conflagration before they could be brought under control. It was a technique which, if successful, opened up the prospect of a methodical and almost complete devastation of the leading cities of Japan.

The first blow was struck against Tokyo on March 10. During the succeeding week the other three leading cities of Japan—Nagoya, Osaka and Kobe—were hit in turn, and a second raid struck Nagoya on March 19. Each attack was delivered by between 300 and 400 planes whose bomb load averaged around 6 tons. All the fears that had been entertained concerning heavy losses were completely dissipated. Two planes were lost in the first raid over Tokyo; the four raids that followed were conducted without the loss of a single bomber. In terms of destruction the results showed considerable variation. The attack on Tokyo, directed against an area of 10 square miles, set raging fires which actually devastated 17 square miles. In Nagoya, on the other hand, the fires set in the first raid were quickly brought under control, and even the second attack was only moderately successful; whereas Osaka and Kobe, less well prepared or more inflammable, suffered damage over areas of from 7 to 12 square miles.

These fire raids, although basic to the new tactics, were not adopted as the exclusive method of attack. Following the second raid on Nagoya the bombers shifted to raids with high explosive on specific objectives. There was a low-level night raid on Nagoya on March 24, followed by attacks on Omura and Tokyo; and by the first week in April the bombers, using smaller forces than in the night fire attacks, had returned to daylight raids against specific objectives. They were vastly aided by the conquest of Iwo Jima and the establishment of a fighter base on that island; and on April 7 a new stage in the campaign was marked when long-range Mustangs escorted the B-29's on a dual expedition in daylight against Tokyo and Nagoya. Tokyo and Koriyama were hit on April 12; then on April 14 and 16 the night raiders returned with two devastating fire attacks on the capital. As a result of three fire raids, 35 square miles of Tokyo had been laid in ruins; its population was reduced from 7 to 4 million; and in Japan's four leading cities the destruction of homes and factories and the dislocation of essential services had reached the scale of a major disaster. Although the heavy bombers were diverted during the next four weeks to attacks on airfields in support of the Okinawa operations, the respite held little real hope that Japan could long survive the trial by fire which this initial series of raids forecast on a greater scale to come.

With the war thus brought home to Japan itself, the government found that political difficulties were added to its other troubles. Periodic boasts of heavy losses inflicted on the American forces, and repeated prophecies of the imminent destruction of the advance invading troops, failed to conceal the fact that the advance was continuing unchecked. When such boasts were alternated with urgent warnings about the increasing gravity of the situation, these only served to accentuate the complete failure of the government to check the tide of defeat. Any serious popular discontent or any widespread peace talk could be kept under effective control by the inquisitorial police system, but patriotic clamour for more stringent measures of national defence was harder to suppress. The extremist elements which advocated a full totalitarian system grew louder in their criticisms, and by the beginning of the year there was a rising campaign for drastic changes in both the structure and the composition of the government.

All attempts by General Koiso to satisfy these demands proved unavailing. He had come into office as premier when the American conquest of Saipan brought the fall of the Tojo cabinet. He had survived the conquest of the remaining Marianas and New Guinea, the invasion of the Philippines, the naval disaster of Leyte Gulf, the fall of Manila and the capture of Iwo Jima. But this long succession of disasters resulted in an increasing restiveness at the complete incapacity of the government to halt the steady and rapid deterioration of Japan's position. The inadequacy of measures to step up war production was tacitly acknowledged in March when a cabinet shakeup eliminated the ministers chiefly responsible for this aspect of the war effort. The shortcomings of Japan's air defences were made brutally apparent by the devastating fire raids on her leading cities. A new political organization, the Political Association of Greater Japan, was formally constituted at the end of March under the leadership of the extreme militarist, General Minami. It absorbed the Imperial Rule Association which had hitherto been one of the foremost embodiments of Fascist principles, and its avowed object was to press for more vigorous war measures, outside of and if necessary in opposition to the government itself. With the invasion of Okinawa the last blow was struck at Koiso's tottering regime. The cabinet resigned on April 5, to be succeeded by a ministry under Admiral Suzuki in which General Minami was included as a minister without portfolio.

The new cabinet showed little more promise of strength than its predecessor, and its legacy of defeat was increased by a new and ominous development. On the very day that Koiso fell, the Soviet Union denounced its neutrality pact with Japan. This treaty, concluded in 1941, had eased the danger on Russia's Asiatic flank and made it possible for her to throw her main strength into the

European struggle. It had also assured Japan against attack in Manchuria and freed her for the southward march of aggression on which she embarked at Pearl Harbour. Now, however, with the war in Europe drawing to a close, its main purpose had been served as far as Russia was concerned. Technically the denunciation of the pact left it with still another year to run, but the language in which the Soviet Union communicated its decision strongly suggested that the treaty was already regarded as void. Japan was accused of aiding Germany as her ally in the war against Russia, and of waging war on the allies of the Soviet Union. "In such a situation", the note asserted, "the pact of neutrality between Japan and the U.S.S.R. has lost its meaning and the continuance of this pact has become impossible." It was a formal step by Russia to free her hands for the fulfilment of her still secret Yalta pledge of ultimate entry into the war against Japan.

Faced with these growing perils, the new government could do little more than continue and broaden the measures already inaugurated by its predecessors. Preliminary steps had been taken in March to provide for a fuller mobilization of manpower and resources. Schools had been closed for a year to increase the labour supply for war industries. The Home Guard of trained reservists was now expanded to include men between 15 and 60 and women between 17 and 40, organized as the People's Volunteer Corps for work on military installations and for local defence in case of invasion. The final collapse of Germany in May, which left Japan struggling in isolation against the might of the United Nations, gave new urgency to the effort to mobilize all available resources in preparation for the supreme test. A special session of the Diet was called in June to express formal national approval of the dictatorial powers over persons and property which the premier had in any case a right to assume under the emergency clause of the constitution. It was indicative of the continued critical spirit toward the government that the Diet hesitated to approve such unchecked authority and insisted that a committee of its own members must be given a consultative position; but for all practical purposes the full resources of the nation were now at the disposal of the government for the purposes of total war.

It was only too apparent, however, that these resources were inadequate to stave off the approaching danger. It was true that in spite of the interruption of her sea communications, Japan still had considerable reserves of both munitions and raw materials, and could count on prolonging the struggle in spite of the closing blockade. A large part of her industrial system remained intact even after the first series of fire raids, and efforts were already under way to remove the more vulnerable industries to Manchuria where they would be in somewhat less danger from air attacks. On the other hand, the advantage to Japan of industries in Manchuria was growing steadily more dubious as a result of the progressive strangulation of sea communications between Japan and the mainland; and though there were frequent references to the possibility of continuing the struggle in Manchuria, such plans offered little hope of salvation to Japan proper. No steps that could now be taken could hold off the approach of the invasion. All that could be envisaged was a desperate and suicidal struggle which would defeat the invading forces after they had landed, and the relentless pressure of blockade and air assault made even this prospect less likely with every week that passed. Although Suzuki held out to the Diet the possibility that the Allies might be repulsed on Japan's own soil, the bleakness of the outlook was only too apparent, and there was a grim desperation in his assertion that "there is no alternative but to fight it out."

THE INVASION OF OKINAWA

Before the full weight of American invasion power could be thrown against the enemy homeland, one more preliminary step was needed. Air cover, so vital to the success of amphibious operations, had of necessity been provided hitherto by carrier-based planes. Their effectiveness was demonstrated by the successful landings in the Marianas and the Philippines; but they also had their limitations, and the disadvantages of depending on the fleet for support to land operations over any long period were soon to be demonstrated in even more striking fashion. The invasion of Japan, like that of Normandy, would call for sustained air support until adequate bases were secured on enemy soil. It was geographically impossible to secure a land base comparable to Britain in the extent of its facilities and its closeness to the invasion area, but that made it all the more urgent to gain command of the most suitable base that could be acquired within striking distance of Japan.

Once the mainland of Asia was ruled out, the choice narrowed down to the Ryukyus. The Philippines were too far away. Iwo, which was at extreme fighter range, was too small to serve as a main base. Even Okinawa was some 360 miles from the southern tip of Japan. But that was only half the distance between Japan and Iwo, and Okinawa's area and terrain made it the best choice available as the main advanced air base and staging point. Once control had been established on both Iwo and Luzon, Okinawa almost inevitably became the next objective on the road to Tokyo.

The subjugation of Iwo was immediately followed by preparatory operations against this new point of attack. Once again the fleet was charged with the dual task of softening the island's defences and isolating it from support by sea and air. The limited success achieved in the first of these aims repeated an experience that had become familiar from Tarawa to Iwo. Once more the invaders were to encounter ground defences which had stood up to bombardment from sea and air, and fortified positions which could only be carried in close combat after intense and costly efforts. The struggle for air domination, on the other hand, was marked by relatively new features indicative of the way in which the approach to the final objective brought fresh factors into play. Already the invasion of the Philippines had shown how difficult it was for naval air power to destroy an enemy air force which had relatively numerous land bases at its disposal and which was within reach of reinforcements. The new operations brought Japan itself within the air combat area, and the American fleet in its covering activities was committed, at least potentially, to joining battle with the main Japanese air force.

At the heart of this situation lay the need to neutralize the air bases in southern Japan as a prelude to the attack on Okinawa. The initial blow was struck by Task Force 58, whose strength had now risen to some 15 carriers and a dozen fast modern battleships. On March 18 and 19, in a foray which carried the warships to within 40 miles of the Japanese coast, the planes from the carriers swept over the airfields on Kyushu and struck at Japanese warships and shipping in the Inland Sea. It was an arrogant challenge to Japanese air power which did not pass unscathed. The carrier *Franklin*, hit by two bombs, was rent by fires and explosions; and although heroic measures by the crew and by supporting ships enabled the carrier eventually to make port under her own power, it was at the expense of fearful damage and the loss of nearly half her crew. The carrier *Yorktown* and several other ships received lighter damage, and Japanese planes pursued the force for two days as it moved away from Japanese waters toward Okinawa. In addition to ship casualties, 116 planes were lost in the course of these four days; but 528 Japanese planes were destroyed in the air or on the ground, besides further damage to planes and installations. It was a blow from which the Japanese took over two weeks to recover, and which prevented any serious air interference with the landing on Okinawa or the operations during the first few days.

The softening up of Okinawa began on March 23 with a sweep by carrier planes over the island and the smaller adjacent islands which were subsidiary objectives. On March 24 the battleships moved in to shell the southeast coast which offered one possible landing area; and on the same date the minesweepers began their methodical task of clearing away the minefields which protected the approaches to the island. On the 26th, while the battleships began a systematic bombardment of the defences along the west coast, the operations were broadened by two simultaneous blows. A strong British task force, headed by the battleship *King George V* and including four modern carriers, began a sustained pounding of the Sakashima group of islands southwest of Okinawa. For the next two months, apart from a fortnight's interval at the end of April, this force—attached for operational purposes to the American fleet as Task Force 57—concentrated on neutralizing the Sakashima airfields and preventing support from this quarter to the defenders of Okinawa. And on the same day the Kerama group, 20 miles west of Okinawa's southern tip, was invaded by American troops.

The Keramas formed an important stepping stone toward the main objective. The purpose of their seizure was to establish a seaplane base from which patrols could be maintained over the waters around Okinawa, and a repair station where emergency aid would be quickly available to ships damaged in the invasion operations. As it turned out, airfields were secured on Okinawa itself within a few hours of the landing, but there was no certainty beforehand that this would be the case, and the occupation of the Keramas was looked on as so essential that a full division, the 77th, was assigned to the task. The small Japanese garrison was quickly overwhelmed; and although part of it escaped into the hills, the islands for all practical purposes were fully under American control by March 28. The small island of Keise was also seized, and American heavy artillery was set up within range of Okinawa itself.

The invasion of Okinawa was launched on the morning of April 1. While a demonstration threatened a landing on the southeast coast in order to divert the Japanese garrison, an assault force of 2 Marine and 2 Army divisions drove ashore on the west coast in Hagushi bay, near which lay two of Okinawa's principal airfields. This was the spearhead of the newly organized Tenth Army composed of the XXIV Army Corps and the III Marine Corps. The 6th and 1st Marine divisions were on the left, the 7th and 96th Army divisions on the right. In the course of the subsequent campaign the 27th and 77th divisions came into action with the XXIV Corps, and the Marines were strengthened by a combat team from the 2nd division which was being held in reserve. The problems imposed by distance and by supply needs were illustrated by the fact that the invasion armada of some 1400 ships exceeded in numbers the maritime force employed in the invasion of North Africa; and included in the total were over 300 combat ships, among them the heavy older battleships which lent their weight to the intense naval and air bombardment that covered the landing.

The plan of invasion called for a thrust across the island by the two divisions in the centre, while those on either flank pivoted outward to north and south to form the sides of the corridor. It was expected by this means to split the defending forces, which could then be rolled up by simultaneous drives toward the northern and southern ends of the island. The drive across the island was completed with unexpected speed, but its tactical purpose was to a considerable extent frustrated by the fact that the Japanese commander had virtually abandoned the northern and central parts of Okinawa and had concentrated his forces at the southern end.

The Japanese garrison numbered approximately 120,000—nearly double the strength that had been estimated by American intelligence, and numerically almost twice as strong as the initial landing force. Massed in an area whose natural defensive advantages were further strengthened by skilful fortifications, and plentifully equipped with mortars and artillery which provided a formidable volume of fire power, this force stood a better chance of making a decisive stand than if it had been dispersed over a larger area. Whether or not the Japanese commander was deceived by the threat of a landing on the southeast coast, it was still understandable that he should concentrate his strength in the most favourable positions available.

What was less explicable was his failure to take advantage of the opportunities presented to him in the initial stages of the landing. Without dividing his forces, he could have mounted a strong rear-guard resistance inland from the beaches, where even the nine-day preliminary bombardment from sea and air could hardly have eliminated all the blockhouses and emplacements in that sector. Yet the invaders were allowed to land with virtually no opposition. So

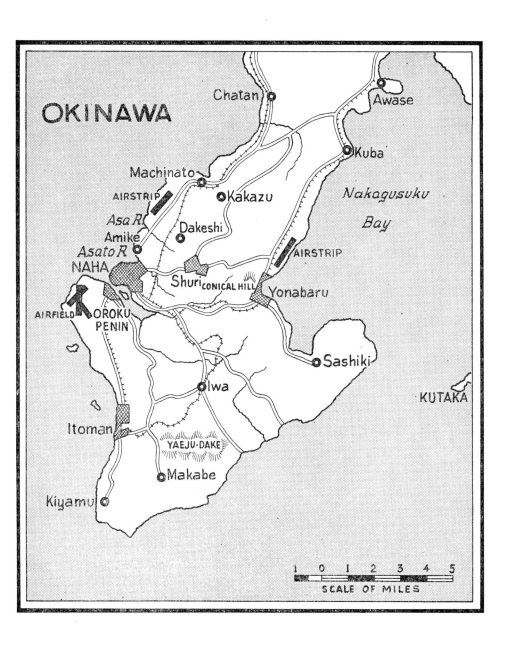

OKINAWA

Chatan

Awase

Kuba

Machinato

Nakagusuku
Bay

AIRSTRIP

Kakazu

Asa R

Dakeshi

Amike

Asato R

AIRSTRIP

NAHA

Shuri CONICAL HILL

Yonabaru

AIRFIELD OROKU
PENIN

Sashiki

KUTAKA

Iwa

Itoman

YAEJU-DAKE

Makabe

Kiyamu

1 0 1 2 3 4 5
SCALE OF MILES

concerned were the Japanese to consolidate their main positions that they gave up the two chief airfields without a struggle and allowed these vital objectives to be secured during the first three hours. No effort was made to lay down a barrage on the beaches, though these were within artillery range; and in contrast to the devastating curtain of fire which fell behind the first wave on Iwo Jima, there was an almost complete lack of interference with the supplies and reinforcements which poured ashore to make the initial foothold solid and secure.

In consequence, the advance across the 8-mile waist of the island, which had been expected to take as much as two weeks, was completed in little more than two days. The Marines turned northward into the more scantily populated section of the island, whose rugged and wooded terrain made progress slow even without serious enemy opposition. A strong knot of resistance was encountered on Motobu peninsula, two-thirds of the way up the west coast; but while the task of crushing and mopping up the Japanese in this position went slowly forward, the main advance rolled on. By April 22 all serious organized resistance in the northern part of the island was at an end, though scattered Japanese detachments remained to be rounded up; the little island of Ie off the west coast, with its three airfields, had been seized; and the Marines were freed to add their weight to the offensive against the southern sector where a struggle of the bitterest intensity was now in progress.

The southern peninsula was the most populous and cultivated section of Okinawa. It contained the only towns of any size, as well as the chief farming area. By falling back into this sector, the Japanese secured advantages which included not only the island's chief facilities for transport and supply, but also the main source of both food and civilian labour. The available labour supply was augmented by rounding up all the able-bodied males in the northern and central parts of the island and herding them into the southern redoubt. Above all, the broken nature of the country offered natural advantages for defence. Just south of the landing beaches a succession of ridges ran across the island, forming a series of highly defensible positions. The steep cliffs were honeycombed with a multitude of caves in which machine-guns and mortars and artillery were impregnable against anything except a direct hit on the opening. These were supplemented by man-made caves and blockhouses, by trenches which added to the defences in depth and linked the various strong points, and by minefields and barbed wire. Southern Okinawa was a fortress manned by a strong garrison, plentifully supplied with munitions and equipped not only with heavy mortars and artillery, but with large-calibre rockets fitted with aerial bombs.

The main defence line was anchored at three points—Naha on the west coast, Shuri in the centre of the island, and Yonabaru on the eastern flank. North of this, however, a series of positions in depth extended to a point about 4 miles above Naha, where Kakazu ridge formed the western flank of the first line of defence stretching straight across the island. By April 4 the divisions which had turned south had run into strong rearguard resistance which abruptly slowed their progress and brought them to a halt within the next few days. The 96th division on the right flank failed in repeated efforts to carry Kakazu ridge. The 27th, which took over the western sector while the 96th shifted to the centre, had no more success. The Japanese line held against both bombardment and assault. The defenders not only returned a heavy volume of fire, but also struck repeatedly in raids which included airborne suicide attacks and small scale seaborne landings behind the American lines. As the deadlock was protracted, it became clear that sustained and arduous efforts would be needed to dislodge the Japanese from the positions in which they were so firmly consolidated.

The prospects implicit in this situation, grave as they were from the point of view of the ground forces, were even more serious for the fleet. The invading forces had secured two airfields on Okinawa, and had been able to land their own artillery; but their resources were still inadequate to reduce the Japanese fortified positions by bombardment or to cover the operation against enemy air attack.

They still needed the support of the heavy guns of the fleet and the protection of carrier-based planes. The fleet thus found itself committed to a unique and extremely hazardous enterprise. The bombardment warships, instead of regaining their mobility once the foothold on Okinawa was established, were pinned down to a static role as floating artillery emplacements in support of ground operations. The fast carrier forces were called on to cover both the forces on land and the naval forces offshore, and in addition to maintain their efforts to neutralize the Japanese air bases from which the chief danger was now to be apprehended.

For although it was unprecedented for warships to remain for so long in continuous action off a hostile coast, there was relatively little danger from the coast artillery defences. Even the danger of a major attack by enemy naval forces, which had been so real at Leyte, had been dissipated by the victory of Leyte Gulf. There was none the less a real threat from small suicide craft carrying powerful charges of explosives and launching sudden surprise attacks against the immobilized American ships, and even from Japanese swimmers bent on self-sacrificing but destructive missions. Above all, however, there was the threat from air attack under conditions which offered suicide tactics a maximum chance of success.

In the course of the Philippine campaign, the increasing number of *kamikaze* or "Divine Wind" fliers taking part in air attacks on American shipping gave evidence that the Japanese were assiduously developing this branch of the Special Attack Corps. The Okinawa operations saw their appearance in force against targets which were particularly inviting to pilots whose consecrated purpose was "sure hit, sure death". In practice, death was a much surer outcome than damage. The anti-aircraft armament of American warships had been progressively strengthened, enabling them to throw up a heavy curtain of fire which it was not easy for the attacking planes to penetrate, and the Japanese flier who dived his plane straight for his objective was an easier mark than a skilful bomber pilot who hoped to save himself and his plane to fight another day. Yet some *kamikaze* fliers did get through, to crash with their bomb load and inflict serious damage on their chosen target. In addition, Okinawa saw the appearance of a weapon which combined the main features of the *kamikaze* weapon and the German rocket bomb. This was the *baka* bomb—a small plane with a 16-foot wing spread which was launched from a larger plane on approaching the target. It was virtually a flying torpedo guided by a pilot who accepted certain death in the hope of hitting his mark. The craft carried over a ton of explosive, and was equipped with a racing engine whose speed was augmented by rockets to carry it down in its dive at the rate of some 500 miles an hour. The difficulty of hitting so small and fast a target was partly offset by the fact that its speed made it hard to control with any real accuracy. Its use involved a high cost in pilots for a small percentage of hits on American ships; but its relatively simple construction made mass production easy, and the Japanese counted heavily on this feature—and no doubt on an unlimited supply of pilots ready to join their ancestors—to make the *baka* bomb their most effective weapon of defence against the approaching invasion. The landing on Okinawa came before it was ready for large-scale use, but the protracted nature of the operations allowed it to be brought into action on a considerable scale in the course of the struggle.

The first large-scale air effort was launched by the Japanese on April 6. It was succeeded by almost weekly assaults on a substantial scale throughout the Okinawa campaign, interspersed by attacks of varying size which gave little or no respite to the forces engaged in the invasion. It was a prolonged ordeal during which the covering naval forces had not only to protect themselves as well as the supply ships and ground forces against attack, but to try to intercept the enemy planes short of their objective and to neutralize the bases from which they came. A force of small picket boats, spread out through an arc as much as 60 miles distant from the beachhead, did valiant work in protecting the anchorage against Japanese suicide surface craft and in giving warning of the approach of hostile planes. The cover provided by the carrier planes was augmented by land-based fighters as the captured airstrips were put into operation. Fighters from the carriers broke up Japanese raiding forces on their way to Okinawa and disrupted raid preparations by sweeps over Japanese airfields. A succession of carrier strikes against air bases on Kyushu, in the face of savage Japanese retaliation, was supplemented by a series of Superfortress raids against these same objectives. The background to the land operations on Okinawa was a tense and sustained struggle at sea and in the air, ranging all the way from the southern tip of the Ryukyus to the homeland of Japan.

These efforts were costly to both sides. In the course of three months beginning on March 18, the Americans claimed the destruction of over 4000 Japanese planes. More than 2300 of these were destroyed by the fast carrier forces in the air or on the ground, for a loss of 557 of their own aircraft. Against this there had to be set a steadily rising toll of American ships crippled or destroyed, largely as a result of suicide attacks. Out of 250 ships hit during the Okinawa campaign, only 34 were acknowledged as sunk, and none of these was larger than a destroyer; but a number of major units were damaged off Okinawa itself, and the supporting task forces sustained severe damage to at least 4 carriers in addition to the *Franklin*. The Japanese paid a high price in plane losses for the small number that got through to their targets, but they had some reason for feeling that the results, which could hardly have been achieved in any other way, fully justified the cost.

On land meanwhile the Americans faced a problem which was not very different in its essentials from that encountered on Iwo. They had been able to establish substantial forces ashore, including tanks and artillery; and so long as the Japanese were unable to destroy or drive off the covering fleet, the only threat to the supply system lay in the damage that the enemy might inflict on the ships waiting to unload their cargoes. Yet the fact remained that an assault had to be launched on a Japanese stronghold which was virtually self-contained and whose defences offered little prospect of a swift breakthrough. The heaviest bombardment failed to crush the Japanese fortifications or to silence their artillery and mortar fire. A relatively narrow front restricted the weight of the offensive which could be mounted. Its rugged and defensible nature presented no vulnerable spots through which a breach could be driven, and no opportunities for turning either flank. There were repeated discussions of the possibility of a landing on the southeast coast which might take the garrison in the rear; but the beaches here were small and protected by reefs, and there was little prospect that the Japanese could be taken by surprise. The force that could be put ashore would not be large enough to overcome the defences or to force the diversion of any substantial forces from the main Japanese line, while the enterprise would create new and serious supply problems and would draw off part of the fleet to cover the attack. The rejection of this project left no alternative but a frontal attack against the main line, which would involve the same deadly hand-to-hand struggle against individual Japanese positions as had been necessary on Iwo. "It is going to be really tough," General Hodge reported. "There are 65,000 to 70,000 fighting Japs holed up in the south end of the island, and I see no way to get them out except blast them out yard by yard."

It was Hodge's XXIV Corps which launched the first concerted offensive on April 19. Covered by an intense bombardment from every available gun on land and in the fleet, three divisions drove forward against the Japanese line. The first shock dislodged the Japanese from their forward positions; but even so the initial gains were limited to a few hundred yards, and the Japanese soon struck back with savage counter-attacks. The fighting was exceptionally bitter on the western flank, where the Japanese were determined to bar the road to Naha, and where a desperate struggle raged for Kakazu ridge. For five days its possession was uncertain; but during this period steady pressure in the centre and on the eastern flank gradually brought gains which threatened the stability of the Japanese line. On the night of April 24 the Japanese withdrew from their more exposed positions; but the occupation of the ground thus surrendered only brought the Americans up against the main Naha-Shuri-Yonabaru line, and by the beginning of May the situation had once more reached a deadlock.

The hard-won gains of the Americans had carried them to a line which ran roughly a mile or so north of the three main Japanese anchor points; and against these positions a new and still more powerful assault was launched during the second week in May. By the beginning of the month the 96th and 27th divisions had been replaced by the relatively fresh troops of the 77th and the 1st Marine divisions. The 6th Marines were now added on the western flank, and after a brief rest the 96th took over from the 7th division on the left. With 4 divisions in line, the Tenth Army on May 11 renewed its full-scale efforts against the Japanese defences.

The going was even harder than during the earlier drive. The most intensive bombardment could do little more than drive the Japanese into hiding while it continued. It was of little effect against the deep caves in which they took shelter; and as soon as the barrage lifted to allow the infantry to advance, the enemy emerged to pour a devastating fire on the attackers. They had to be cleared out with grenades and explosives and flame-throwing tanks equipped with long flexible hoses; and even after a few hundred yards of ground had been won, the gains were often insecure against the counter-attacks which the Japanese were able to mount from sheltered and fortified positions just beyond.

In this situation, a number of small strategic features assumed a critical importance. On the west coast the Marines in bitter fighting pushed almost to the outskirts of Naha, and even sent small patrols into the town itself. A full-scale assault on the town, however, was impossible so long as the Japanese held Sugar Loaf Hill which commanded Naha and the approaches to it across the Asato river. A Marine battalion which reached the top was assailed by Japanese counter-attacks from positions on the reverse slope which were sheltered from direct fire. In six days it lost three-quarters of its effectives and had to be replaced, and control of the small but important eminence changed hands a score of times before it was at last secured by the Marines on May 19.

On the eastern flank there was an equally bitter struggle for an even more vital height. This was Conical Hill north of Yonabaru—a 485-foot rise which not only covered that town and the airstrip above it, but also protected Shuri from the east and added to the difficulty of reducing that pivotal stronghold. Here too the attackers fought their way up the slopes but were unable for many days to dislodge the Japanese from the crest or from their positions on the reverse side. It took until May 21 for the 96th division to complete this arduous task; and when it was finally accomplished, the weary troops were reinforced by the 7th division which was in better shape after a period of rest to exploit the breach which now seemed in prospect.

The capture of Conical Hill threatened to undermine the whole Japanese line. Not only did it eliminate the chief obstacle barring an advance down the east coast; it also opened the way for a flanking move against Shuri. At this point too there had been bitter fighting for limited gains. A small hill known as the Chocolate Drop held up the advance for five days, and secure possession was only gained on May 16. Beyond it loomed the heights crowned by the ancient Shuri Castle which commanded the surrounding ridges. This was the key point of the whole Japanese defence system, and the assault toward it made painfully slow progress. But with the eastern flank giving way after the fall of Conical Hill, and with the way cleared for an assault on the western anchor point of Naha, the possibility of holding Shuri indefinitely began to fade. An encircling movement by the Marines on the west and the 96th division on the east threatened to cut off the garrison and brought a Japanese decision to withdraw to new lines. Leaving rearguard detachments to impede American progress, the Japanese commander pulled back the bulk of his forces during the last week in May. When on May 29 a Marine company scaled the precipitous slopes and assailed Shuri Castle, they found only a handful of defenders. Two days later the flanking forces made contact south of Shuri; and by this time the entry of the Marines into Naha and the advance of the 7th division down the east coast meant that the whole of the Shuri line had at last been overrun.

The end, however, was not yet in sight. The secrecy with which the Japanese carried out their retirement gave them time to regroup their forces in new defensive positions. They were further aided by a drastic break in the weather during the latter part of May, when heavy rains turned the primitive roads into seas of mud and made the use of wheeled transport almost impossible. Even after the rains let up, the mud remained an obstacle, and forward troops found themselves dependent for a time on airborne supplies and on planes to evacuate the wounded. Under cover of these conditions the Japanese were able to concentrate their remaining forces, now reduced to half their original strength, on the escarpment which rose to a height of from 300 to 500 feet at the southern end of the island; and here the American advance was once more checked at the end of the first week in June.

This again was a natural defensive position which could only be taken by direct assault. It lacked however the formidable fortifications which had strengthened the Shuri line; and although the attacking troops were battle-weary, their margin of superiority in strength over the battered Japanese was now far greater than at the beginning of the campaign when numbers had been almost equal, and they had been reinforced by the fresh troops of a Marine combat team. Japanese strength was further reduced by the trapping of a rearguard force on the Oroku peninsula, where they had sought to defend the last remaining airfield against the Marines who crossed from Naha to the southern shore of the harbour. They were cut off by a drive of the 1st Marine division across the base of the peninsula on June 7, and were liquidated by the 6th Marines in bitter fighting during the following week.

The main assault on the escarpment was launched by 3 divisions on June 10. The Japanese ignored a demand for honourable surrender which was dropped from American planes next day, after the first wedges had been driven into the defences, and the attack was pressed relentlessly to its conclusion. In surprise advances under cover of darkness the Americans scaled the cliffs confronting them, using ropes and scaling ladders, and secured a foothold on the plateau. While the 96th pinned down the defenders frontally, the 7th and the 1st Marine divisions drove back the flanks, and the assault was strengthened not only by the Marine combat team, but also by the 6th Marines who came into line after crushing the Oroku pocket. By June 20 the Marines had cut behind the escarpment to reach the southern tip of the island, and the remaining defenders had been split into isolated pockets which were rapidly being compressed and liquidated. On June 21 all organized resistance was declared to be at an end, and there remained only the customary tedious and dangerous job of liquidating the fanatical detachments which had been bypassed during the operations. It was the end of the most prolonged and costliest effort which the Americans had yet undertaken in the Pacific. In 82 days of land fighting, and in the covering air and sea operations, nearly 120,000 Japanese had been eliminated, including some 8000 taken prisoner, at the price of 79,500 American casualties. Although the American figure included over 30,000 classed as "non-battle casualties", the high number of cases of shock and fatigue bore striking testimony to the arduous and intense nature of the campaign; and the 9721 battle casualties suffered by the navy during a period of three months was equally a measure of the ordeal to which the fleet had been subjected. Yet the reward was a major strategic victory, and the price was hardly excessive for the securing of the final foothold that was needed as a prelude to the invasion of Japan.

THE BREACH WIDENS

All during the bitter struggle for Okinawa, secondary but still significant operations were in progress in other quarters. The breach which had been thrust into Japan's imperial defences by the invasion of the Philippines was consolidated and broadened. The smaller islands in the archipelago were brought under American control. The arduous work of crushing the substantial garrisons on Luzon and Mindanao was pushed relentlessly to a successful conclusion. A series of landings on Borneo widened the area of penetration and advanced the Allied spearheads toward both Malaya and the Netherlands East Indies. On the mainland of Asia there were simultaneous offensive moves as invigorated Chinese forces pressed upon the retreating Japanese and regained much of the ground that had been lost in the previous year. The last tenuous links between Japan and her conquered empire were severed, and Japan's main forces in China and the homeland drew together for a desperate stand within the last redoubts.

With the capture of Manila the chief task that confronted the Americans on Luzon was the elimination of the elements of the Japanese Fourteenth Army which were concentrated in the mountainous northern section of the island. From the beginning of the invasion there had been stubborn fighting as the troops of the I Corps strove to push into the hills overlooking the central plain. The Japanese clung tenaciously to fortified positions and strong natural defences, and American gains in three months of fighting were limited to a few thousand yards.

The two focal objectives in this sector were Baguio, the summer capital and military headquarters which barred the way to the western slopes of the main watershed, and Balete pass, through which ran the main road leading to the northern tip of the island by way of the Cagayan valley. The middle of April saw two divisions, after weeks of slow uphill fighting, stalled within barely 3 miles of the first of these goals. While the 37th pressed toward Baguio from the south, the 33rd was gradually working its way around the town to the west and north. It took a fortnight of dogged and grinding effort to break the deadlock; but by the final week in April the 33rd had penetrated to the highway above Baguio and was driving down it from the northwest. The Japanese defences were at last undermined. A concerted assault from two directions crushed the remnants of the garrison, originally estimated at 20,000, and captured the town on April 27; and the 33rd division, fanning out east and south, probed into the enemy hill positions beyond.

The 37th division, released by the fall of Baguio, now added its weight to the drive on Balete pass in which the 25th and 32nd were already engaged. Here Japanese resistance was even more stubborn and successful than around Baguio. Although the 25th division was reported on April 22 to have worked its way to within 2 miles of the pass from the south, it was stalled there during the remainder of the month, while the efforts of the 32nd to outflank the pass from the west along the Villa Verde trail made little more progress. By the beginning of May, sustained efforts were under way to soften up the Japanese positions by bombing defences and communications; and this was followed by a new effort to carry the heights on either side of the 75-foot cleft through which the road penetrated. At last elements of the 25th division, reinforced by a regiment from the 37th, succeeded in scaling the cliffs on May 13 and gaining control of the summit; and while the process went on of clearing the Japanese from caves and pill-boxes in the pass area, the main forces pushed down the northern slopes toward the village of Santa Fe.

It took another two weeks to cover the bare 4 miles which lay between the American columns and this objective. The converging columns of the 25th on the main road and the 32nd on the trail to the west were held up by stubborn defences which barred their progress and prevented a junction of the two forces. It was only after elements of the 25th had succeeded in working their way around the obstacle and outflanking Santa Fe from the north that the village fell on May 27, and the way was cleared for a link-up between the two main columns a few miles beyond.

Progress now became more rapid. The main Cagayan valley still lay 75 miles ahead, and the road wound through narrow river valleys dominated by hills on either side. But there were no such formidable defiles as Balete pass in which the enemy could rally for a protracted stand, and the 37th division which now took over the advance moved steadily forward. On June 10 the road junction of Bagabag was firmly in American hands; and while the 6th division entered into action and thrust northwest into the hills, the 37th launched an attack on the pass to the northeast which was the gateway to the Cagayan valley. By June 14 it had smashed its way through to the broad valley floor which stretched northward for 150 miles toward the port of Aparri.

In this open and level country the advance gathered momentum. The consistency with which the Japanese avoided any full-scale action in exposed positions was once more evident in their tactics in this sector. Their main forces took refuge in the mountainous country west of the Cagayan valley, leaving only small rearguards to impede the American advance. These remnants of garrisons in the chief towns presented few obstacles, and the 37th division rolled forward at a pace of over 10 miles a day.

Final mastery of the Cagayan valley was speeded by a swift concerted operation north of the main advance. Throughout the period when the slow work of dislodging the Japanese from their mountain bastions was going on, strong guerilla forces had been in operation behind the enemy lines. By the latter part of May they had cleared the northwest part of the island and were stabbing at Japanese positions and communications in the northern part of the Cagayan valley. On June 21 they struck with vigorous and decisive blows at two key points. In the centre of the valley they seized the town of Tuguegarao and held it during the next few days against Japanese counter-attacks. On the northern coast, where the way had been paved by the shelling of Japanese positions by light naval units, a party of American Rangers joined with the guerillas to seize the port of Aparri. Two days later, elements of the 11th Airborne division landed near Aparri to reinforce the captors. The northern exit from the valley was effectively blocked, and from north and south the main columns swiftly converged. The 37th division entered guerilla-held Tuguegarao on June 25, and two days later its spearhead made contact with that of the 11th division. The junction completed effective American control of northern Luzon. The remaining

THE CAMPAIGN IN NORTHERN LUZON

Japanese troops had been driven into the mountains and split into three pockets, and the largest of these northwest of Bagabag was under converging pressure from 3 divisions. Although the reduction of these enemy forces still promised to be a protracted affair, they were no longer in a position to impede the full use of Luzon as a base against Japan.

Resistance on the remainder of the island had meanwhile been reduced to equally negligible proportions. Even after the fall of Manila the Japanese remained planted in the Marikina watershed a few miles east and northeast of the city, where strong mountain defences were garrisoned by two special formations in divisional strength, and where the Japanese retained control of the main sources of Manila's water supply. Here, as in the north, it took dogged and sustained fighting to root out the enemy. The initial defence line was carried after a wedge had been driven into it in the middle of March, but the next six weeks saw progress measured in yards as the work went on of driving the Japanese from one individual hill position after another. By the middle of May, however, the main defences of the Shimbu line were crumbling. An eastward thrust by the 1st Cavalry division penetrated to the sea-coast below Infanta on May 13 and rolled up the coast, circling behind the Japanese forces in the Marikina hills. A pincers movement by the 43rd division, launched on March 10, succeeded after a week of fighting in capturing the Ipo dam some 20 miles northeast of Manila. Farther to the south the Wawa dam, the chief reservoir still in Japanese hands, was taken by the 38th division on May 28. The last sector of the Shimbu line had now been overrun, and the Japanese were pressed into steadily dwindling pockets in the mountainous and roadless country to the east. Meanwhile the southern part of Luzon had been cleared of all but a few stragglers; and with mastery in the north achieved by the end of June, the six months' struggle for Luzon was virtually at an end and only secondary operations against isolated pockets remained to be completed.

The campaign on Luzon was paralleled by the simultaneous effort to secure full control of Mindanao. The central islands of the Philippine archipelago were occupied with relative ease, their small garrisons wiped out or driven into the hills. Mindanao however was a more substantial land area on which the Japanese had half a dozen important airfields and a garrison of some 45,000. An initial landing in March gave the Americans a foothold on the Zamboanga peninsula, and guerilla forces were active in the northern part of the island, but efforts on a larger scale were needed before Mindanao could be brought completely into American hands.

On April 17 a full-scale campaign was initiated with landings on the west coast at two points above Cotabato. Comparatively light resistance was encountered at the outset. The main Japanese forces were concentrated in the west around Davao, where strong defences had been constructed against invasion. The two divisions of the American assault force penetrated swiftly into the interior. The 24th division, striking westward across the base of the island, reached the east coast at Digos after a ten-day advance and drove toward Davao 25 miles to the north. On the left flank meanwhile the 31st division wheeled up the centre of the island along the Pulangi valley. On May 9 a new landing on the north coast by a regimental combat team from the 40th division, shortly reinforced by elements of the Americal division, gave a fresh foothold in an area already under guerilla control; and these forces thrust south toward a junction with the column of the 31st division which at that stage was some 60 miles away.

By this time Japanese resistance had stiffened. The 24th division drove into Davao and captured it after house to house fighting on May 4; but north and west of the city they ran into strong prepared positions which imposed an abrupt check on their progress. The enemy, fortified in caves and pillboxes and strongly supported by artillery, struck back with repeated counter-attacks and with infiltration tactics which made American gains slow and often precarious. In the interior the threat of stronger opposition was undermined by the landings in the north, but the Japanese fought to prevent the junction of the converging forces in spite of having been caught off balance, and it was not until May 23 that the northern and southern columns at last made contact. When that happened, however, the decisive phase of the Mindanao campaign had been completed. The main body of the Japanese garrison was caught between the 24th division which extended its grip along the coast and the forces farther inland which barred the routes of escape into the interior. Elsewhere only scattered forces which had taken refuge in the hills remained to be mopped up. There was still stiff fighting as the effort went on to compress and destroy the main Japanese pocket; but by May 24 the last of Mindanao's airfields and the whole of the road network were in American hands, and during the succeeding month the slow pressure of American forces from east and west reduced the remnants of the Japanese garrison to an estimated 12,000 men.

On July 5, MacArthur's headquarters announced that the whole of the Philippines had been effectively liberated. In a campaign which saw the destruction or capture of 325,000 Japanese at a price of slightly over 60,000 American casualties of all kinds, it was claimed that Japanese forces totalling 23 divisions had been beaten and largely destroyed at the hands of 17 American divisions in the eight and a half months since the landing on Leyte. The 40,000 Japanese troops that remained in the Philippines were scattered in the hills or surrounded in widely dispersed pockets which were under relentless pressure; and from the secure bases on the archipelago the Allies were already striking out on the road toward the Indies.

Stretching southwest from the main Philippine group, two island chains offered parallel routes for this further advance. In the northern one the long island of Palawan pointed like a slender finger at the northern tip of Borneo. Farther south lay the Sulu islands, with the Tawitawi group at their extremity. Palawan was occupied with little resistance on February 28, Tawitawi on April 2. The sea passage between the Philippines and Borneo was thus brought under Allied control at both ends, and forces were planted barely 40 miles from

Borneo which was now singled out by repeated air attacks as a prospective invasion objective.

The conquest of the limited footholds which Japan had seized on the rim of that large and primitive island offered strategic and logistic advantages out of all proportion to the effort involved. The shoulders of the breach which the invasion of the Philippines had thrust into the Japanese inner zone, and which were being expanded in one direction by the assault on Okinawa, would be pushed out far to the southward on the other side. An advance along the north-west coast would carry the Allies far on the road to Singapore. A thrust into Macassar strait would place them within one of the main gateways leading to the Netherlands Indies. They would acquire naval and air bases commanding the whole of the South China Sea from which they could sever the last frayed communications between Japan and her conquered empire. Not least important, vital oil resources would pass from Japanese to Allied hands. Already Japan was being starved of outside oil supplies by the tightening blockade, and her home production faced methodical destruction from the air. By seizing some of the richest sources in the Far East, the Allies would not only decisively deny them to the enemy, but would greatly ease their own tremendous and mounting supply problem in one of its most essential aspects.

The first blow fell on the island of Tarakan off the northeast coast of Borneo. Here was a major oilfield whose product was so pure that it could be used for fuel without refining, and a position on which an advanced air base could be established to cover subsequent oper-ations. On May 1, after four days of preliminary bombardment by cruisers and destroyers, a brigade of the 9th Australian division landed on the western shore under covering fire from the warships. The Japanese garrison of 3000, initially taken off balance, rallied behind the fixed defences which covered Tarakan city and offered a brief but fierce resistance in the town itself. By May 6, however, they had been driven from this position, and the Australians fanned out to overrun the main oilfields and to secure command of the southern part of the island, aided by a Dutch force which landed on the southeast tip in mid-May. The remaining Japanese were herded into the hilly country to the north; and although the work of mopping-up went on until the latter part of June, all essential objectives had been secured by the end of May.

On June 10, after 10 days of air preparation, the 9th Australian division struck at the mainland of Borneo. The landing was made in the Brunei bay area on the northwest coast where there was an anchorage suitable for a forward naval base, and from which operations could be directed against another important oil-producing area. The invaders secured a foothold on Labuan island commanding the entrance, and established themselves at two points on the shores of the bay itself in the face of relatively light resistance. The town of Brunei and its surrounding airfields were captured during the first week, and the advance was pushed westward toward the oilfields around Seria and Miri. On June 20 an amphibious thrust to Lutong in Sarawak, over 60 miles west of Brunei, placed the Australians on the edge of the Miri field which was overrun during the next four days, and the simultaneous capture of Seria virtually ended this aspect of the campaign.

There remained Balik Papan, the key to the third of Borneo's major oilfields and a position of even greater strategic significance than those already acquired. Planted on the western shore of Macassar strait, it represented the chief obstacle to Allied command of that essential route toward the Indies. The entry of Allied naval forces into the strait for the first time since 1942 was a fresh landmark in the advance toward complete sea supremacy; but until Balik Papan itself was taken, the free use of the strait would still be denied to Allied shipping.

For months past, the oil refineries and airfields around Balik Papan and the shipping in its harbour had been periodic targets for Allied bombers. The Tarakan operation had been covered by repeated strikes during May; and by the beginning of June an intensified air assault was launched to neutralize the air bases and destroy defence

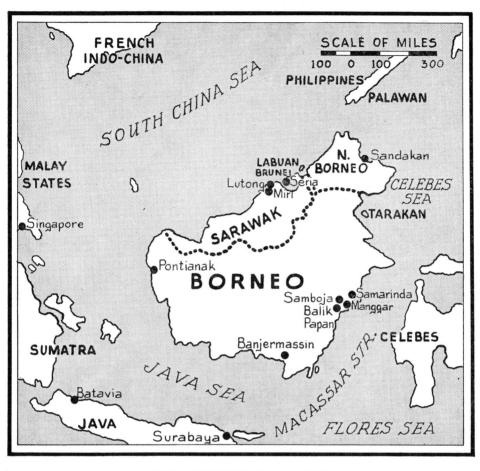

THE INVASION OF BORNEO

installations and facilities. On June 16 a force from the Seventh
United States Fleet, reinforced by Australian units, drove into the
straits, and under their covering fire the minesweepers began clearing
the way for the coming invasion.

For the next two weeks a sustained duel raged between the naval
forces and the Japanese shore defences. The cruisers and destroyers
forming the bombardment force were accompanied by a small group
of escort carriers whose planes gave effective cover against Japanese
air attacks. But the strong Japanese coastal defences kept up a
heavy fire against the ships offshore and impeded the work of clearing
the heavily mined approaches in Balik Papan bay. For a time it
was touch and go whether the work would be finished in time for the
scheduled landing; but at last in the final week in June it became
possible to send destroyers close enough inshore for their fire to batter
down the coastal defences and force the Japanese garrisons back
from their fortified positions covering the beaches.

On July 1 the assault troops of the 7th Australian division,
covered by a strong rocket barrage, effected a landing at Balik Papan
against relatively light initial opposition. As they pushed inland,
however, they ran into stiffening resistance. The town itself was
taken on July 4, together with the Manggar airfield a few miles up
the coast, and next day an amphibious crossing extended control to
the south shore of Balik Papan bay. The week that followed, however, saw hard fighting to expand these gains. The narrow coastal
plain extending above Balik Papan to the oilfield regions of Samboja
and Samarinda was hemmed in by mountains and jungle, and the
Japanese clung stubbornly to hill positions a few miles inland.
Above Manggar airfield, strong Japanese positions on a 200-foot
ridge commanded the routes along the swampy coastal plain, and it
took until July 11 for a column with the support of naval bombardment to bypass this obstacle and break through along the coast.
Their advance was again checked on the edge of the Samboja
oilfields some 15 miles farther north, but on July 18 the Japanese
defences collapsed and this major objective was secured by the

Australians. This success marked the end of the main phase of the invasion. The forces involved, which now included Dutch units, were occupied during the next few weeks in wiping out the remaining nests of Japanese resistance and gradually extending the perimeter against enemy hill positions. The main Balik Papan area, with one of the two chief adjacent oilfields, was under secure control, and the Allies were in command of the sea gateway to the Indies.

These unremitting blows in the Pacific, shattering Japan's outlying bastions along a 1500-miles front from Okinawa to Borneo, had repercussions which were felt on the Asiatic mainland. With their sea routes severed and their conquests in the Indies isolated from the main islands of Japan, the Japanese abandoned their effort to create a substitute land route which would maintain their links with Indo-China and Malaya. Leaving the garrisons in these outlying possessions to maintain themselves with their own resources, the Japanese embarked on a policy of concentrating their main forces for the defence of the homeland and of the projected mainland redoubt in north China and Manchuria.

Signs of this were clearly apparent at the beginning of May. With the defeat of their thrust toward Chihkiang in April, the Japanese began to move substantial forces northward out of the corridor which their earlier offensives had carved out. They made no serious effort to withdraw their strong forces in southeast Asia, which like those in the Indies were left to divert such Allied strength as they could from the main operations. In southern China, however, their decision was to leave only holding forces in selected areas, and to concentrate the bulk of their strength north of the Yangtse river.

In consequence, the Chinese were able during the summer of 1945 to regain a number of important centres that had been lost during the previous year. They were still however too weak to exploit to the full Japan's surrender of the initiative. American air power, strengthened by the transfer to China of the air forces that had been based in India, harried Japanese communications and impeded the enemy's withdrawal. But only a vigorous ground offensive could have turned retreat into disaster, and the available Chinese forces could do little more than follow the enemy and prod him on by stabbing at his rear. When the pressure became too bold, the Japanese lashed out with swift counter-thrusts which drove back the encroaching Chinese. The evacuation was carried out with methodical deliberation from one centre after another; and when a successful assault was launched by the Chinese, it was against a rearguard of a few hundred troops which the Japanese sacrificed for a final delaying stand.

The Chinese gains were thus limited in general to the areas which the Japanese chose to abandon. The capture of Nanning on May 26 was a significant event, for it cut the main route leading to Indo-China and showed that the Japanese were no longer concerned to maintain this overland connection. This meant that there was little purpose to be served by their retention of a grip on the railway southwest of Hengyang. Even their seizure of former American air bases in this region had lost much of its defensive value with the development of the main air offensive from the Marianas. As a result, the Japanese slowly relinquished their grip on the chief centres. Ishan was taken by the Chinese on June 14 after they had several times been repulsed from its outskirts. They were held in the vicinity of Liuchow for the greater part of a month until all but a handful of defenders had withdrawn and the town fell on June 30. There was a similar experience at Kweilin, which was finally taken on July 27; and the forces which on several occasions advanced almost to the outskirts of Paoking never succeeded in dislodging the Japanese from that town.

It became apparent in the course of these operations that while the Japanese were prepared to abandon the direct route to Indo-China, they were less ready to give up their corridor along the Hankow-Canton railway. This still represented a barrier, though a slender one, between the main area of Free China and the coastal sectors on which Allied landings might be attempted. It was also a base from which counter-strokes against such landings might be launched, and a supply route which would be of prime value to the maintenance of even a rearguard resistance to invasion.

As a result, the Chinese forces whittling at this corridor from both sides were able to narrow it somewhat in breadth but proved unable to sever it completely. Similarly the effort to expel the Japanese from the chief ports on the southeast coast met with only a limited success. Foochow, evacuated by the Japanese except for a small rearguard garrison, was taken on May 18, and the Chinese advanced northward in the wake of the main Japanese force retreating up the coast. By the first week in June they had cleared over 100 miles of the Fukien coast and were pressing toward Wenchow. This coastal region lay directly west of the American foothold on Okinawa; but its approaches were partly covered by Japanese-held Formosa, and Fukien province, with its small ports and few roads and the mountains which isolated it from the interior, was not altogether the most suitable point of penetration for an Allied invading force. The Japanese were much more concerned to guard Shanghai to the north and the Canton-Hong Kong area to the southwest. The defences of the former were reinforced by the garrisons withdrawn from Fukien. On the southwest coast above Hong Kong, where the Japanese held the ports of Swatow and Amoy, forces which were landed at the end of June fanned out and extended the Japanese grip on the coastal stretch between these two points. It was evident that, although Japan was reserving her main strength for a defensive struggle in the north, she meant to oppose a sharp rearguard resistance to any invasion of the south. But such an enterprise no longer lay in the forefront of Allied plans, which were now directed toward an imminent assault on Japan.

STRANGLEHOLD ON JAPAN

With the conquest of Okinawa the arc had been completed along which Allied forces could mass for an invasion of the Japanese homeland. There were growing prospects that the enemy, caught fast in the iron grip of American sea power and battered with

mounting fury from the air, might be brought to submission without
a land campaign; but this was still speculative, and the plans now
in train assumed the necessity of securing a decision on the soil of
Japan itself.

The invasion as projected was divided into two main stages.
The first, which was set for November 1, was to take the form of
a three-pronged attack on the southernmost tip of Kyushu by the
Sixth Army. Landings at successive points were to be made by
3 assault corps, each composed of 3 divisions, while a single division
in a preliminary operation seized a small group of islands on the
left flank, and a reserve corps of 3 divisions created a diversion by a
feint toward Shikoku. Four months later the main landing—Operation
Coronet—was to take place on the plains adjacent to Tokyo, with
the Eighth and the Tenth Armies in the van and the First Army in
reserve. These forces, with a total of 25 divisions, were expected to
meet and destroy the main Japanese home armies, occupy the area
around Tokyo and Yokohama which formed the heart of Japan,
and fan out to extend their control over the remaining Japanese
territory. It was a schedule which would bring the Allies to decisive
grips with Japan's land power in the spring of 1946, and this meant
that the struggle might well be prolonged until the latter part of
that year.

Such prospects called for a maximum intensification of pressure
by air and sea power. Under the best of circumstances the invasion
would be a formidable task. It would be launched from bases several
hundred miles away, and the distance would work against the invaders
in the matter of both supply and air cover. There was urgent need
to soften up Japan by crushing the remnants of her air power and
battering her land defences and starving her military machine by
destroying her war production. And if by any means Japan could
be brought to her knees without invasion, the chief among those
means would be bombardment and blockade.

The tightening of the blockade around Japan was the joint work
of sea and air power. Together they had choked off the routes by

which Japan could draw supplies from Malaya and Indo-China and the Indies. Air attacks on coastal shipping and on harbours, and the deadly toll taken by submarines along the shipping lanes, destroyed the merchant marine on which Japan's very life depended. By the summer of 1945 her initial tonnage of over 7 million tons had been reduced by three-fourths, and only a handful of the ships that remained were larger than 100 tons. Traffic with China was becoming increasingly hazardous, and American submarines were even penetrating Japan's inland sea in search of their prey. Simultaneously the Superfortresses were engaged in an effort to interdict the use of the harbours in Japan and on the Asiatic mainland. Beginning on March 27, minelaying operations were undertaken on a steadily increasing scale. In June the effort against ports and shipping lanes was intensified; and by the beginning of August it was claimed that every harbour in Japan, as well as the chief ports in Korea, had been effectively blocked, and repeated mining of Shimonoseki strait had virtually cut Japan off from the mainland. By this time too the bombers were attacking Korea's transportation system in an effort to blast still wider the transportation gap by which Japan was being isolated from the food and munitions and raw materials that were vital to her war effort.

These activities, unspectacular in their nature but deadly in their effect, formed a constant background to the pre-invasion operations of the surface fleet. In June, with the last stage in sight on Okinawa, the fast carrier forces passed under Third Fleet command; and at the beginning of July, after a brief period of refitting and repair, they set out on their mission of preparing the way for invasion. Under Admiral Halsey's command were over 100 warships, including 8 battleships and 16 carriers. They were joined in mid-July by a British force of 28 ships headed by the *King George V* and with 4 carriers in its complement—a force which by itself was more than a match for anything the Japanese now could bring into action. The objectives of this powerful armada, as summed up by Admiral Nimitz, were an ever-tightening blockade of Japan and the destruction of all the resources which contributed to her ability to make war. "We intend," he asserted, "to deny the enemy use of the waters surrounding him, even down to the detail of hampering his efforts to get fish out of them."

The bold and virtually unopposed sweep of these naval forces along the Japanese coast during the succeeding month was a potent demonstration of how close the blockade had been drawn, and their blows added weight to the aerial bombardment that was steadily reducing Japanese war production. Their foremost objectives, however, were airfields and shipping. Land-based planes were sweeping Japanese coastal waters and striking at air installations; but these blows were at long range by limited numbers, and the carrier-borne planes could blanket the airfields more effectively, and could search out warships and merchant craft in Japan's inner harbours. The attrition of Japanese air power was a special and vital task in preparation for the invasion; and while the heavy bombers were striking at the sources of replacement, the destruction of existing Japanese planes was a task which fell largely on the carrier forces.

The new series of operations was inaugurated on July 10. In the wake of a pre-dawn fire raid by Superfortresses on 4 Japanese cities, the carriers launched their planes against the complex of airfields in the Tokyo area; and while the fighters sought out the Japanese air force, the bombers struck at selected industrial targets. Japanese fighter opposition was conspicuous by its absence; and although 72 enemy planes were destroyed on the ground, it was evident that the Japanese had decided to avoid action and to save their planes for later emergencies. There was a suspicion that Japan's remaining air strength had been withdrawn to Hokkaido and northern Honshu and the fleet turned its course toward that area in the hope of finding bigger game.

This objective was not realized. The carrier strikes which were launched against the northern airfields on July 14 again encountered little opposition. But the situation had its compensations, for it offered a chance for the warships to move inshore with relative impunity. At noon a division of battleships with supporting units opened fire on the town of Kamaishi whose iron works presented a useful target. Next day the town of Muronan on Hokkaido was shelled by another section of the force which included the battleship *Iowa* and her sister ships *Wisconsin* and *Missouri*—three of the newest and most powerful naval units afloat. Again the planes hit at airfields and transport facilities, and struck a particularly damaging blow by destroying 5 of the train ferries on which communications between Honshu and Hokkaido largely depended, besides damaging 4 others.

These events set the pattern of operations during the month that followed. Their scale was intensified on July 17, when the British task force joined with the American fleet in a carrier raid on the Tokyo area, and followed this up after nightfall by a joint naval bombardment of the factories and railway yards at Hitachi. Light units shelled the coast some distance below Tokyo before dawn on July 19, and during the day the Tokyo area was again the target for the carrier planes.

On this occasion a prime objective was the naval base of Yokosuka, where the battleship *Nagato* had taken refuge. Although the ship was heavily camouflaged and was berthed in such a position that she could not be attacked by torpedoes, she received such heavy bomb damage that she was effectively put out of action. A few days later the Allied force launched even more telling blows against Japanese bases in the Inland Sea. In two successive raids on Kure on July 24 and 25, the final death blow was struck at Japanese naval power. Of the 22 warships sunk or put out of action, 8 were battleships or carriers—almost all the major units that remained of Japan's once proud fleet. The *coup de grâce* was delivered by a follow-up raid on July 28 which sank the battleship *Haruna* and the converted battleships *Ise* and *Hyuga* as well as several cruisers that had been damaged in the previous raids. Japan was left with the *Nagato*, 6 carriers and 5 cruisers, all of them out of action and without a crew aboard any of them when the war came to an end.

From then on the Allied naval forces ranged the Japanese coast with impunity, moving at times almost within rifle range. Hamamatsu was bombarded by battleships on July 30 and Kamaishi for a second time on August 10, while light units on several occasions shelled other coastal objectives. The search for the Japanese air force, which was marked by three carrier raids on the Tokyo area from July 30 to August 15, was partially rewarded during a two-day attack on northern Honshu on August 9 and 10 during which 397 planes were destroyed and another 320 damaged. By mid-August the toll of the carrier forces had reached over 2800 planes, 148 warships and nearly 1600 merchant ships destroyed or damaged, and considerable damage had been inflicted on Japanese industries and transportation.

During all this period the chief difficulties encountered came less from the enemy than from the weather. This was the typhoon season, and on several occasions the fleet was hit by violent storms. One of these in the early part of June had been particularly devastating. The cruiser *Pittsburgh* had its bow torn off, and a number of battleships and carriers suffered considerable damage. Another typhoon caught the fleet at sea during the first week in August and forced it temporarily to break off operations against Japan, and on several other occasions carrier planes were unable to operate because of bad weather. Enemy opposition, in contrast, offered few impediments. Allied warships suffered no more than negligible damage, and the carrier planes in a dozen major blows lost only slightly over 150 aircraft. The Japanese navy, mortally stricken in its hiding place, could offer no challenge either on or below the surface. Some Japanese fliers attempted to defend their homeland and to attack the carrier forces, but the bulk of the Japanese air force was held back, and could not be tempted into combat even by the open announcement of the names of the Allied ships that were in action. Great prizes in the shape of these massed forces of battleships and carriers were dangled enticingly before the noses of the *kamikaze* pilots, but with little response. Even the coastal defences proved weak and ineffective in their reply to the battleships which raked the coastline and poured their heavy shells into the heart of Japanese industrial cities. Japan, gripped in the stranglehold of the blockade which air and naval power had combined to throw about her, lay almost passive under the merciless blows which rained upon her from sea and air.

The campaign against Japanese production centres, which was interrupted in April when the heavy bombers were diverted to attacks on airfields in Kyushu, was resumed in May in even greater strength than before. The size of the bomber force in the Marianas was steadily growing. The Superfortresses which had been operating from Chinese bases, where distance and supply problems impeded their maximum efficiency, were transferred to the Pacific. Plans were under way to shift the Eighth Air Force from the European theatre and to combine it with the 20th Bomber Command, placing it along with the Twentieth Air Force (the expanded 21st Bomber Command) under General Spaatz as commander of the Strategic Air Force. While carrier forces swept over the Japanese homeland, and while heavy and medium bombers based on Okinawa struck with increasing weight at targets on Kyushu and southern Honshu, the B-29's shouldered the task of crushing Japan's war production and destroying her ability to resist invasion.

In certain aspects the task was simpler than it had been in the case of Germany, particularly after the blockade isolated the Japanese islands from production centres on the mainland. The area of attack was relatively restricted; the important centres of industry, particularly heavy industry, were relatively limited in number. Japanese production was scattered through numerous small shops, but its organization was not so highly integrated as in Germany, and the industrial areas were much more vulnerable to incendiary attack. It was true that Japan's productive needs were neither so vast nor so varied as Germany's had been. She was not engaged in a land campaign employing massed mechanized armies which devoured vast quantities of heavy weapons and munitions and fuel oil. There was no longer a navy or a merchant marine to make extensive demands on her fuel production. Apart from weapons and munitions for the armies defending the homeland, Japan's most pressing need was for increased production of planes. But this situation simplified the strategy of the bombing campaign. By concentrating on aircraft factories and the production of aviation fuel, the bombers struck at the key factors in Japan's war potential. Arsenals and armament works could be treated almost as incidental targets. There was no need for a Japanese equivalent of the battle of the Ruhr. Neither was there any equivalent of the attempt to disrupt the highly complex **system of transportation** that had been such a vital factor in Germany's war effort. The necessary effect had largely been achieved by the blockade. The decisive attack on road and rail transport within Japan itself, which was already suffering mounting damage, could wait until the immediate prelude to invasion.

Beginning on May 14, Japan's industrial and defence centres were hit by major raids on an average of once every three days for the next three months. The technique of night fire raids, varied occasionally by daylight incendiary attacks and by demolition assaults on selected targets, was resumed against the leading cities. In the month that followed, Tokyo was raided three times and was spared a fourth raid when weather forced a shift of target to Hamamatsu on May 19; Nagoya and Osaka also experienced three raids, with Osaka twice attacked in daylight; Kobe was hit twice, and Yokohama once by day and once by night. By mid-June it was officially stated that these five cities had been effectively eliminated as far as productive targets were concerned; and while they were later the scene of attacks on special objectives, the main weight of the campaign was henceforth directed against towns ranging in population from 30,000 to 300,000.

For the next two months the bombers worked methodically through the list of these secondary centres of war production. Each large-scale raid was now directed against four or five main targets, **and few of these** were visited more than once. Demolition bombs were combined with incendiaries to effect the maximum destruction of aircraft plants and ancillary establishments such as textile and ball bearing factories, electrical works and machine tool shops.

Parallel with these assaults ran the campaign against oil installations. Precision raids, some of them simultaneous with the main attacks, sought out both natural and synthetic refineries and the stores which Japan had accumulated in reserve. Little opposition was encountered from Japanese fighter planes, and the ground defences were largely concentrated in a few selected areas. The heaviest loss was over Tokyo on May 26, when 19 bombers out of a force of over 500 were shot down; and a number of the raids were conducted without loss. By the latter part of July, opposition was so negligible that it was felt possible to take the provocative step of announcing the cities that had been marked for attack in the near future. On three occasions a list of a dozen towns was made public, and the fact that raids immediately followed on several of these places was not calculated to add to the tranquillity of dwellers in other localities to which attention was promised.

By mid-August over 60 Japanese cities had felt the weight of major air attacks. The great majority had been visited only once, and Tokyo with 6 low-level fire raids was the target that had been most frequently hit. Compared to the sustained pounding which Berlin and a number of other German cities had endured, this record did not seem impressive, any more than the 169,000 tons of bombs dropped by the B-29's in their whole period of operation could compare with nearly 3 million tons dropped on German targets. Yet such comparisons were in some respects misleading. Most of the intensive attacks had taken place during the last three months, and their weight was steadily growing. The 24,000 tons dropped by the big bombers in May rose to 42,700 in July; and at the beginning of August a single night's operation saw over 800 bombers in action and 6600 tons dropped on Japanese targets. Tokyo, with 110 square miles burned out, lay half in ruins, and a number of smaller towns had been devastated in even greater proportion. The raids were now comparable in scale to those in the European theatre at the end of operations there, and they were only a foretaste of what was in prospect if Japanese resistance continued.

Japan's only hope of checking the relentless progress of destruction lay in administering a shattering defeat to the coming invasion. She no longer had the means to launch an offensive which would bring her to grips with the main forces of her adversaries. She must wait for them to come to her, and hoard her resources for a decisive counter-blow. It was a losing game, as Germany had demonstrated. By holding back her weapons and refusing to challenge the bombers which struck from the air and the fleet which ravaged her coasts, Japan left her war resources open to destruction; yet she had no choice but to accept this risk in the hope that she could still keep enough strength in hand to repel the main attack. In the absence of any hope of positive victory, her one chance lay in a defensive success which would discourage the Allies and avert the full consequences of defeat.

To attain this supreme end, Japan relied on the tactics of suicide attacks and cave warfare which had marked the recent island campaigns, and whose full pattern had emerged during the struggle for Okinawa. In her home islands Japan had an air strength of 11,000 planes, over half of them combat types, and ground forces numbering more than 2 million men. This hoarded strength was to be hurled at the invaders when they struck Japan's shores. The air force would be thrown into an all-out attack against the transports and covering warships as they lay off the landing beaches, sacrificing its whole strength if necessary in order to destroy the seaborne support behind the assault forces. The troops which managed to get ashore would find themselves isolated, confronted with a rugged and defensible terrain similar to that on Okinawa, and exposed to destruction at the hands of the numerically superior defenders.

Tactically these methods might have achieved a striking success. Strategically they offered little more than a temporary reprieve. The precedent of Okinawa suggested that *kamikaze* attacks might inflict serious damage on the invasion armada, particularly if the planes were used in waves of several hundred—always provided the Japanese had enough fuel left to mount attacks on such a scale. But even if they destroyed the bulk of the invasion ships—and mathematically that feat was highly improbable—and forced the abandonment of the first attempt at a landing, their triumph would not have been decisive. Allied naval supremacy would never have been broken, whatever the loss in warships engaged. Allied air power would be left untouched to continue its massive and relentless campaign against Japanese resources. There would have been no real barrier to the mounting of a new invasion attempt after a moderate delay, and this time there would in all probability be no Japanese air force left to meet it. Japan was girding herself for a defensive effort which could be made only once, and which could destroy only the immediate spearhead of Allied power. Unless the blow was so discouraging to the Allies that they would prefer a compromise peace to a renewed invasion effort, Japan was doomed in the long run, and the desperate measures to which she was reduced only made that ultimate doom more certain.

Even so, few Japanese leaders were prepared to recognize defeat as inevitable. Apart from the fact that the open admission of such a belief would invite assassination at the hands of patriotic extremists, racial pride and professional reputation were strong deterrents to any acknowledgement that the supreme adventure had led Japan to disaster. None the less, a series of unofficial feelers indicated that some elements were ready to explore the possibility of a negotiated peace which would save face and forestall any question of unconditional surrender; and by July these efforts took the more serious form of overtures to Russia suggesting the possibility of Soviet mediation. All of these, however, including the proposal to Moscow, were too tentative and indefinite to have any effect. Far from indicating any desire for compromise, the Allies on July 26 issued a firm and explicit demand for prompt and unconditional surrender.

This document was issued from Potsdam where a conference of the Big Three was in session, primarily to consider the problems arising from Germany's collapse. On the surface it was curious that such a setting should produce a proclamation dealing with the Far

East and issued in the name of Britain, the United States and China, with Russia standing officially aloof. But the timing and the circumstances were indicative of the emergence of new factors whose full and overwhelming significance would shortly be revealed. One was the conclusion of definite arrangements for Russia's entry into the war against Japan. The other was the birth of the atomic bomb.

THE FINAL BLOWS

In this war, far more than in any previous conflict, the outcome rested almost as much with the scientist as with the soldier. Throughout the whole of the struggle the laboratories were the scenes of intensive efforts to produce new weapons which would give one side an advantage, and to develop counter-devices against the weapons of the enemy. There was a haunting awareness that even an adversary who was overwhelmingly outmatched in material resources, as Germany was in the closing stages, might at the last moment redress the balance by unleashing a new weapon against which no defence was available. The rocket bomb might have proved to be such a weapon if it had been produced earlier and in greater quantities. The evolution and ever-widening application of radar, the struggle to improve or to neutralize the weapons of undersea warfare, the race in the development of rockets and jet propulsion—these were only a few examples of fields in which the success or failure of the scientists might change the course of history.

Overshadowing all these was the search for a practical method of applying atomic energy to the purposes of war. Both sides were dominated by the appalling realization that such a method in the hands of the enemy would bring irretrievable catastrophe. The danger of national annihilation might well be transformed from a figure of speech to a sober and literal fact. It was not hard to imagine a rain of atomic projectiles which would wipe the face of a country clean of every existing structure and annihilate every living thing from plants to human beings. This was the menace that hung unceasingly over every belligerent nation and lent grim purpose to its efforts to forestall its adversaries in the silent but deadly race that went on throughout the war.

Investigation into the mysteries of the atom had been actively in progress for half a century. From 1895, when Roentgen discovered X-rays and Becquerel found out that uranium was radioactive, science had penetrated gradually deeper toward the ultimate goal. Einstein laid down the relation between mass and energy. The work of such men as Rutherford and Chadwick, Bohr and Fermi, led by successive stages to the evolution of a method by which the atom could be split. When that was accomplished by German scientists in 1939, the primary goal had been attained. Nuclear fission was a reality, and man had reached into the heart of the structure of the universe to unloose the tightly-locked energy of which all matter is composed.

By the outbreak of war the fundamental groundwork had been laid, and the knowledge involved was universal property. What remained was to apply that knowledge to specific practical purposes. Germany as well as the Allies was in a position to push forward her efforts to that end with the utmost vigour, and until the close of the war there was never any assurance that she was not momentarily on the verge of success. Actually success was still remote when Germany surrendered, and Japan's investigations had yielded such discouraging results that they were abandoned before the end of the war. Sabotage and bombing helped to slow up the German experiments, and the loss of many able scientists placed the Axis nations at a further disadvantage. It is one of history's happier ironies that the brutal creed of the aggressors drove into exile such figures as Fermi from Italy and Bohr from occupied Denmark and Meitner from Germany—outstanding workers in the field of nuclear physics whose knowledge and skill were lost to Fascism in its hour of desperate need. Atomic research remained international, but it was the United States and the British Commonwealth who kept it so, and who benefited from the presence of the cosmopolitan group of scientists seeking refuge on their shores from racial and political oppression.

The co-ordination of British and American efforts was initiated even before the United States entered the war. As a result of a suggestion by President Roosevelt in October 1941 the two countries, which were already exchanging information, decided to merge their activities. By the following year results had reached a stage which called for large-scale production operations, and it was decided that these should be concentrated in the United States where resources and facilities were greater than those available in Britain, and where the plants would be beyond the reach of enemy bombers. Canada was closely associated with these developments. A special laboratory was set up in Montreal, and a pilot plant for the processing of uranium was begun. The uranium deposits at Great Bear Lake—the major source of this material on the American continent—were taken over by the Canadian government, and the necessary supplies of this essential component were thus made available to the joint Allied effort.

Among the numerous technical problems involved in the enterprise, two were particularly basic. One was the production of fissionable material in adequate quantities; the other was the construction of the bomb as a practical device. Because of the urgency of the project, several lines of investigation were undertaken simultaneously. It was a vast and expensive enterprise in which the United States alone invested $2000 million, and in which all the different methods proved successful. Ways were devised of separating the relatively scarce uranium isotope, U-235, from the commoner U-238. Work with U-238 led to the creation of two hitherto unknown elements, neptunium and plutonium, and in plutonium the scientists had a new substance suited to their purpose. The discovery that an explosion could be created by bringing together portions of the material above a "critical size" was the starting point for the construction of the bomb. By midsummer 1945 the new weapon was a reality. On July 16, in the desert of New Mexico, a test bomb was set off with results that fully justified all expectations. It was the first man-made explosion of atomic power and an event which ushered in a new era in world history.

The knowledge that the test had been successful, and that the Allies had in their hands a weapon of unprecedented power, lay behind the Potsdam proclamation. Its phrasing was based on a full appreciation of the devastating possibilities inherent in the new discovery. Japan was warned that she faced an Allied might immeasurably greater than that which had brought Germany to ruin. "The full application of our military power," it was asserted, "will mean the inevitable and complete destruction of the Japanese armed forces and just as inevitably the devastation of the Japanese homeland." Japan was called on to follow the path of reason by surrendering unconditionally and accepting the terms laid down in the proclamation. These involved the elimination of Japan's militarist leaders, the acceptance of the territorial losses forecast in the Cairo declaration, and submission to Allied military occupation, with the assurance that once Japan had settled down to a peaceful existence the occupation would end and Japan would be given the opportunity of a free and prosperous existence.

It may have been unfortunate that in this whole document there was no mention of the atomic bomb or of any sort of new weapon. The threat that was held up to Japan was that of "the prodigious land, sea and air forces" of the Allies, which she seemed to be already in a position to estimate without realizing that a completely new factor was now involved. Ignorant as they were of the very existence of the bomb, the Japanese could hardly be expected to recognize that the words of the Allies carried an entirely new import. In a statement of July 29, Premier Suzuki scornfully refused to take any official notice of the Allied ultimatum. The Allied military leaders, eager to bring the bomb into immediate use, were left with a free hand.

The scientists who had created the new weapon were far less enthusiastic than the military authorities about the resulting prospects. A number of scientists had in fact refused to take part in the project at all. Others did so with the inward hope that their investigations would prove the atomic bomb to be impracticable.

When the bomb became a reality, a group of the scientists involved drew up a memorial requesting that it be first used in a way that would demonstrate its power without involving any loss of life. If it had been dropped on an uninhabited area in Japan, and if this had been coupled directly with a clearer version of the Potsdam proclamation, it is hard to see what could have been lost. Japan would still have had no defence against the new weapon even if the demonstration failed to bring her to reason at once, and the democratic peoples would have been spared certain qualms of conscience. But those in authority insisted on the more terrible lesson which would result from the use of the bomb against live targets. On August 6 the first bomb was dropped on Hiroshima; and three days later another of a different type and of even greater power was dropped on Nagasaki.

The results were appalling. Over half of Hiroshima was devastated by a single blast. At Nagasaki the area destroyed was less widespread, partly owing to the geography of the city, but obliteration within the area of explosion was even more complete. If the Japanese had ignored the threats from Potsdam, they now had grim reason for heeding the words of President Truman in his announcement of the bombing of Hiroshima: "We are now prepared to obliterate more rapidly and completely every productive enterprise the Japanese have above ground in any city. . . . Let there be no mistake; we shall completely destroy Japan's power to make war." And while the Japanese government was still reeling from the shock, a new blow fell with Russia's entry into the war.

The denunciation in April of the Soviet-Japanese neutrality pact, while it did not technically involve the immediate end of that agreement, left Japan with only a faint hope that Russia would continue to feel bound by its provisions if she chose to disregard them. According to its original terms the treaty was to run until April 1946, and to be renewed automatically unless one of the parties gave notice of termination a year before it expired. But in giving this formal notice, Russia stressed the radical change in the situation since 1941, particularly the aid which Japan had given to Germany and the fact that she was at war with Russia's allies. Under the circumstances, the note asserted, the pact had lost its meaning and its continuance had become impossible. In announcing in these terms its desire to denounce the treaty, the Soviet Union implied the resumption of a free hand in its relations with Japan.

The entry of Russia into the war against Japan had in fact been decided at Yalta. Stalin agreed that it should take place approximately three months after the end of the European war—an interval that was needed for the shift of troops and supplies to the Far East, and for the conclusion of a treaty with China which would assure the gains on which Russia's promise was conditional. By the time of the Potsdam conference the negotiations with China were well advanced and the necessary military preparations were almost complete. Meanwhile Japan's tentative suggestion that a delegation should be sent to Moscow to discuss Russian mediation with the Allies—a proposal which may have been motivated as much by the hope of keeping Russia inactive as by the expectation that it would lead to serious peace negotiations—evoked no official response. The real answer was the Potsdam ultimatum, and Japan's refusal to accept its terms was officially taken by Russia as proof that mediation was futile. On August 8 Russia presented Japan with a declaration of war, effective at midnight; and early on the following morning the Russians invaded Manchuria.

The main attack was launched by three army groups under the supreme command of Marshal Vasilevsky. Harbin was the focal goal for a concentrated offensive by multiple prongs from east, north and west. Along the line of the Chinese Eastern Railway, the First Far Eastern group under Meretskov drove west from the Maritime Province; while the Trans-Baikal group of Malinovsky, striking from the area of Chita, thrust one prong along the railway and another through the desert and mountain region south of Lake Bor. In the centre the Second Far Eastern group under Purkayev launched its main drive down the valley of the Sungari river, while on its western flank a column struck across the Amur south of Balgovesh-chensk.

There was some stiff fighting at the outset. For a generation both sides had foreseen and prepared for a struggle in this region. The Japanese Kwantung Army in Manchuria, like the Russian forces in Siberia, had been built up into a strong and independent formation in anticipation of the conflict; and although recent withdrawals had somewhat weakened it in numbers and quality, it still had a strength of some 700,000 backed by considerable reserves. The natural lines of invasion were covered by strong border fortifications, and the Russians had to batter their way through fixed defences or advance through difficult regions of swamps and forests and mountains during the first few days of the offensive.

The power of their assault, however, carried everything before it. By August 14 Meretskov had broken the fortified line opposite the frontier of the Maritime Province and advanced along the railway to the important centre of Mutankiang. Purkayev mean-while had forced the Amur and Ussuri river lines and was thrusting down the Sungari valley at a rate of up to 25 miles a day. Other forces had launched an offensive against the Japanese on southern Sakhalin, and marines backed by naval forces had seized the Korean base of Rashin. It was in the west however that the most spectacular gains were made. Malinovsky's forces driving down the railway crushed the Japanese border defences and advanced over 200 miles in less than a week. Farther south a second spearhead headed by mobile tank forces achieved an even more striking success. In advances of as much as 100 miles a day the armour swept across the Mongolian desert and through the Great Hingan mountain range to cut one of the main north-south railway lines and threaten to isolate all northern Manchuria. Still farther south a new threat developed as the Mongolian army launched an attack toward Peiping and raised the prospect of a drive to the sea which would cut all Manchuria completely off from the rest of China.

THE RUSSIANS IN MANCHURIA

These successes were won against an enemy who had already decided to abandon the struggle and throw himself on the mercy of the Allies. Even before the Potsdam ultimatum a peace faction, centred in the imperial court, had gained the ascendancy over the military extremists who insisted on continuing the war. The ultimatum sharpened the issue by ending all hope of a compromise peace, but the brief advantage which this gave to the diehards was wiped out by the emergence of the atomic bomb. The appearance of this new weapon offered Japan a chance to surrender and still to avoid complete loss of face. The view could be put forward—as it actually was in the Emperor's surrender proclamation—that this was a new and inhuman device which would take an uncounted toll of innocent lives and threaten the destruction of human civilization, and that humanitarian considerations rather than a sense of defeat prompted Japan's decision to end the war. The entry of Russia lent added urgency to the peace efforts. It virtually ended any serious hope that a prolonged resistance could be maintained on the Asiatic mainland, and it called for speedy action before new and undeniable disasters befell Japanese arms. When the military extremists continued their stubborn resistance, the question was referred to the Emperor for his personal decision. He called a special meeting of the cabinet and leading statesmen; and after an all-night session on August 8 the decision was taken to sue for peace.

On August 10 the Allies were informed of Japan's readiness to accept the Potsdam terms, with the understanding that they involved nothing prejudicial to the position of the Emperor. To this qualification the Allies replied that the Emperor's authority would be subject to that of the Allied commander, and that the ultimate form of government would be left to the free decision of the Japanese people. It was a response which conceded little in substance, but which by implying that the Emperor would at least retain his throne for the present allowed the Japanese government to regard it as satisfactory in form. On August 14, Japan announced her acceptance of unconditional surrender in the sense of the Potsdam declaration.

A last-minute plot by army extremists, who planned to assassinate the leading members of the cabinet and to prevent capitulation by seizing the person of the Emperor, was frustrated. Detailed negotiations were initiated for the surrender and disarming of Japan's widely scattered forces and for the landing of Allied occupation forces on Japan. Arrangements were concluded for formal capitulation; and on September 2, aboard the battleship *Missouri* in Tokyo bay, Japanese and Allied representatives signed the document which officially ended hostilities and placed Japan completely at the mercy of the victors.

THE LEGACY OF WORLD CONFLICT

Six years and a day from that fateful dawn when Hitler's tanks crashed across the Polish border and his bombers swept over Warsaw, the world holocaust that had been kindled by this act of aggression was at last extinguished, and mankind could survey the ruinous toll it had taken in lives and resources. Every nation on the face of the globe had felt the impact of the struggle. Even those few countries which had managed to remain officially aloof from participation had suffered profound dislocations which drastically affected the daily lives of their populations. In the belligerent states the whole of the national energy had been geared directly or indirectly to the war effort. Approximately 100 million men and women had been mobilized in the armed forces of the combatants.[1] The activities of a large proportion of the remaining population had been diverted from peacetime pursuits to war production; and millions of them had been uprooted by the tide of invasion or rendered homeless and destitute as a result of bombing attacks.

Eight months after the close of hostilities the world was still trying to cast the reckoning in terms of lives alone. Even the total losses in combat still had to be established with finality. The only

---

[1] General Marshall estimated 93 million, of which over 62 million were mobilized by the Allies. *Biennial Report*, Washington, 1945. Molotov placed the total at over 110 million. *New York Times*, Nov. 7, 1945.

official figures came from Britain and the United States. These showed
that in killed and missing the British Commonwealth had lost
444,500 and the United States 308,600. But such figures were dwarfed
by the slaughter in eastern Europe, where by June 1944—almost a
year before the collapse of Germany—Russia had lost 5,300,000 in
killed and prisoners. No later figures had as yet been made public
by the Soviet Union, and nothing more than tentative estimates were
available for the Axis states. The German High Command reported
3,500,000 killed and missing up to December 1944, but Prime Minister
Attlee in the following October estimated that with the inclusion of
permanently disabled the total German losses at the time of surrender
were 7,400,000. American military authorities may have been high
in their initial estimate that the European war cost all belligerents
14 million dead and 5,500,000 permanently disabled; but if those
figures were taken as covering the global war and as including
Japanese losses in killed and disabled of around 1½ million, they
would probably not be very far out.

The toll of civilian lives was even more indefinite but certainly
no less appalling. When all the resources of the embattled nations
were mobilized for total war, the distinction between soldier and
civilian was largely obliterated, and with it the relative immunity
from enemy action which non-combatants had previously been
supposed to enjoy. Yet the bombing raids which struck at crowded
centres of population accounted for only a small proportion of the
casualties. British civilian losses from air attacks were 60,585 dead
and 86,175 injured. Japan placed the death toll in her devastated
cities at 260,000, and it was calculated that German civilian deaths
were in the vicinity of 300,000. Yet these figures, shocking in themselves, shrank almost into insignificance beside the human losses
resulting from the callous and deliberate brutality of Germany and
her associates in the lands they overran. It was charged that the
Nazis were directly responsible for the deaths of 10 million civilians
and war prisoners. The horrors of Oswiecim and Belsen and Buchen-
wald, the atrocities perpetrated in the occupied regions of eastern

Europe, the barbarities of slave labour, were no mere incidentals of conquest. They were manifestations of that calculating inhumanity which lay at the heart of the Nazi creed and outlook, and which issued in a deliberate policy of wholesale extermination of such races as Jews and Poles and Russians. By the end of the war, 5,700,000 out of Europe's 9,600,000 Jews had disappeared. Poland's population had been reduced by 6 million, and at least as many Russian civilians had perished. The end of the fighting brought a tragic migration of 20 million people in Europe who had been uprooted by the tides of war. Other millions found themselves without shelter or means of livelihood, weakened by years of under-nourishment and facing starvation in the months immediately ahead. And in the Far East, where Japanese brutality was mitigated only by the fact that it lacked the deliberate and organized objectives of the Nazis, there were again uncounted millions to whom war had brought misery and death.

If the cost in human suffering was immeasurable, the cost in physical wealth would probably never be accurately measured. The belligerents had spent at least $1500 billion in the actual prosecution of the war. The United States alone spent $300 billion. German expenditures were only slightly less; and if Russian war costs were added, the total for these three states by themselves would be in the neighbourhood of $1000 billion. Yet these figures, which represented the diversion of labour and materials to purely destructive purposes, were only the beginning. In addition there was the destruction of existing assets through the ravages of war—the bombing of factories and dwellings, the demolition of power plants and transport facilities and mining installations, the depletion of livestock and even of the soil itself. Britain's estimated war damage of over $4 billion was moderate compared to the losses in the invaded countries of the continent. Vineyards that had been among the main assets of Greece had been uprooted to make way for airports. Some of Holland's richest land had been temporarily ruined by inundations through the broken dikes, and shortage of fertilizer had meant a partial exhaustion of the soil throughout much of Europe. A considerable part of Poland's mines and industries had been dismantled or destroyed. France's losses through pillage and destruction were estimated at over $100 billion, or nearly half the national wealth. A Russian commission reported that the invaders had destroyed 31,850 industrial enterprises and looted 98,000 collective farms, wrecked 6 million homes and inflicted heavy damage on coal mines and oil wells and railways, and that the economic loss, quite apart from direct war expenditure, amounted to over $108 billion.

Facts such as these illustrated the violence of the upheaval and the wreckage which it had left in its wake. Its subsidence left the world faced with a prodigious task of reconstruction. A large part of the old political and economic structure lay in ruins. Whole nations lay prostrate, the wealth they had accumulated during past generations wiped out, their productive resources ravaged and their trade connections dislocated, their people weakened by privation and deathly weary after six years of sacrifice and strain. The courage and resolution which had carried them through the war would still be needed in equal measure to face the problems of peace. Even courage was no longer enough. It would need to be joined to wisdom and patience and a far-sighted imagination if the ills of the world community were to be remedied and new and surer foundations laid for a stable and a peaceful world.

In this task of restoration there were formidable obstacles to be overcome. The war had brought a change in the balance of underlying social forces as well as in the international structure. In inflicting a crushing defeat on the revolutionary forces of the Right, it had weakened the barriers to change in the direction of greater social equality and given new strength to the demand for drastic reform at the expense of privilege and property. The magnitude of the post-war problems lent an additional impetus to the trend toward collectivism and state control as methods that were essential for their solution. The revival of prosperity and the assurance of lasting peace were objectives which made world co-operation more urgent than ever before. Yet there was no clean slate on which could be freely traced the pattern of a more perfect world order. The legacy from the past weighed heavily upon the future. The forces of nationalism, with all the feuds and ambitions and rivalries to which they gave rise, emerged from the conflict stronger than ever. The struggle for boundaries and resources, for strategic bases and spheres of influence, for national wealth and economic opportunities through the seizure of resources and the achievement of special trade advantages, was joined even before the war came to an end. A world which could only be rebuilt on the basis of political and economic integration seemed ready to plunge into the old disastrous ways of unchecked nationalist competition.

These conflicting trends aggravated the problem of how the defeated enemy states were to be dealt with, and how a peace settlement could be reached which would form a basis for world stability. Demands for territorial gains had to be reconciled with the desire for tranquillity, and fear of revived economic power with the desire for economic stability and prosperity. In their efforts to prevent a revival of the military power of the former aggressors, the victors showed a readiness to adopt policies of territorial dismemberment and economic subjugation. Yet it was not certain that the security to be gained by stripping a country like Germany of lands wholly German in population would outweigh the danger from the resulting spirit of bitterness and revenge, or that the reduction of Germany's national power by restricting her industrial resources would not entail a heavy price in the dislocation of the European economy and a reduction in the general level of prosperity. So long as the approach to peace was based on the national interests of individual sovereign states rather than on the interests of the general community, the inherent dilemmas would remain insoluble.

There were further dilemmas in the political sphere. The Fascist dictatorships had been overthrown; but that did not mean that Fascism as a creed had been destroyed, or that the conditions which led to its rise might not recur and make possible its revival. Whatever restraints the peace settlement imposed on the defeated states were likely to prove impermanent as safeguards. The only final solution lay in the creation of a stable world community in which all states could find an acceptable place, and in which the united strength of the community would present a barrier to aggression. But while it was vital that the peace settlement should lay the foundations for such a structure, it would take time for its completion. Meanwhile the problem remained of making sure that the political structure which replaced Fascist rule in the defeated states would carry no inherent threats to world stability. There was no assurance that a democratic system of government would provide the answer. These were nations which had shown little talent for popular self-government, and which had been denied all experience in democratic methods under totalitarian rule. A whole generation or more had grown up under that rule, which left the youth of Germany and Italy and Japan indoctrinated with the barbaric tenets of racial nationalism and stubbornly resistant to all concepts of intellectual freedom and individual judgment. The ignorance and apathy and subservience of large masses of these populations, which had made possible the triumph of the dictators in the first place, might again operate to facilitate a revival of Fascism under the guise of a free political system. To forestall a new seizure of power by a hostile and aggressive minority, the Allies might find it desirable to vest power in the hands of a minority that could be regarded as trustworthy and friendly; and such a group might be hard to find and equally hard to sustain. Yet the alternative of holding the defeated nations in tutelage until by the process of re-education they had been fitted for self-government was far from attractive and perhaps not even practical, and might be inherently self-defeating as far as its main purpose was concerned. For the sake of world security, the power and resources of potentially great nations must be kept from falling into the hands of nationalist neurotics with the acquiescence of political illiterates, but there was no obvious and easy method by which this aim could be assured.

What made the outlook all the more perturbing was the wide division of opinion within the victorious nations themselves about the ultimate meaning of victory. A general agreement on the desirability of a stable world order was accompanied by acute differences as to the means by which it should be achieved. A common struggle against the revolutionary forces of the Right had brought together two divergent political and social systems, each of them revolutionary in origin yet marked by profound differences in their basic concepts. But the problem went deeper than the conflict of views between the Soviet Union and the western democracies, serious though this was. The fundamental question of how individual freedom could be harmonized with social and economic welfare was vital for the whole of the modern world. Not only did it raise sharp controversies concerning the orientation of domestic policies in the various nations in the period of reconstruction; it had also a direct bearing on the conditions which they sought to establish in the defeated states through the shaping of the peace settlement. In an even wider sphere, the views which various groups held concerning the most desirable form of society were reflected in their attitudes toward the structure of the world community. Here was the touchstone for such decisions as whether the pursuit of national power should be made the primary instrument for protecting and safeguarding interests that were regarded as fundamental, or whether such interests could only be served by a substantial surrender of sovereignty for the sake of world co-operation and harmony—and whether those who paid lip service to either aim were in fact prepared to accept the burdens and sacrifices and adjustments necessary to achieve their professed objectives.

Perhaps this last question was the most crucial of all. The upheaval brought about by the war was only part of a process of rapid and at times violent change which the world had been undergoing for two centuries or more. The world faced the task of adjusting its political and social organization to the changed social and economic conditions which had been brought about primarily by the advance of science and technology, and whose effects had been aggravated by two world wars within a single generation. But the process of adjustment was hampered by human reluctance to recognize and accept the implications of the achievements as well as the catastrophes of mankind. There was a time lag which steadily widened the gap between technological and political evolution, between the demands of existing conditions and the readiness of the community to accept the need for change. The war and its aftermath made this state of affairs more critical than ever. It was urgently necessary to face the realities of the resulting world situation and to strike out boldly and speedily along the new paths which it demanded. A stubborn clinging to thought-patterns which had been crystallized in the America of Theodore Roosevelt or the Russian underground during the reign of Nicholas II could lead only to disaster. Mankind must make its adjustment to the environment it had created, or face the extinction which was the fate of all obsolete organisms.

This was the problem which was given fresh and impelling urgency by the emergence of atomic power. The terrible potentialities of this new force as a weapon of warfare embodied only one of its aspects. Its prospective application in a wide variety of fields, from industrial production to medical research, opened up vistas that were almost limitless. Both the habits and the standards of living of the bulk of mankind might well be transformed within little more than a generation. Unless a comparable transformation took place in political and social structures, the result would be new strains and conflicts which would make war all but inevitable, and which would unloose the annihilating power of atomic weapons against the civilization which had produced them. The potentialities for both peace and war were bound inextricably together; and from either point of view, the existence of atomic power made nonsense of the old concepts of national sovereignty. No nation could any longer hope to live unto itself, or trust in its own resources for its own safety. World prosperity and world peace were alike essential if individual nations were to enjoy either peace or prosperity in the atomic age.

The truth was that stability could only be achieved by one of two means—effective world organization, or world domination by a single Power. Between these alternatives there was no prospect of anything better than an uneasy truce, filled with suspicions and rivalries and marked by the old spectacle of each nation trying to bolster its power and position in competition with its neighbours. Inevitably the leading states would seek security by extending the range of their strategic and economic control, and the small states would be reduced to pawns in the struggle for spheres of influence. With equal inevitability a new balance of power would arise in which the struggle for advantage would ultimately reach a point where neither side could concede any further gains to the other, and the stage would be set for the gigantic clash which might well mean the suicide of civilization.

This was the brooding and terrible shadow which hung over the nations who now had the task of translating military victory into a lasting peace. It was a task which called for boldness and imagination on the part of their leaders, and for a readiness on the part of the peoples to abandon old concepts and habits and seek a fresh basis for a true world order. Victory carried with it a challenge and an opportunity. A world which had failed so often in the past was given one more chance to show that man's intelligence was equal to his ingenuity, and that his achievement in the field of physical effort and invention could be matched by his wisdom in social and political reconstruction. Success would lay the foundation for an era of human well-being unparalleled in history. But unless wisdom triumphed over the forces of greed and ambition and fear, the world might find that it had thrown away its last chance of salvation which it had bought at such a terrible price.

DOCUMENTARY APPENDIX

I. The Franco-Soviet Alliance

Treaty of Alliance between France and the U.S.S.R., Moscow, December 10, 1944.

The Provisional Government of the French Republic and the Presidium of the Supreme Council of the Union of Socialist Soviet Republics,

Determined to prosecute jointly, and to the end, the war against Germany;

Convinced that once victory is achieved the re-establishment of peace on a stable basis and its prolonged maintenance in the future will be conditioned by the existence of close collaboration between them and with all the United Nations;

Having resolved to collaborate in the cause of the creation of an international system of security for the effective maintenance of general peace and for ensuring harmonious development of relations between nations;

Desirous of confirming mutual obligations resulting from the exchange of letters of September 26, 1941, concerning joint action in the war against Germany;

Convinced that the conclusion of an alliance between the U.S.S.R. and France corresponds to the sentiments and interests of both peoples, the demands of the war and the requirements of peace and economic reconstruction in full conformity with the aims which the United Nations set themselves;

Decided to conclude a treaty to this effect. . . .

I. Each of the High Contracting Parties shall continue the struggle on the side of the other Party and on the side of the United Nations until final victory over Germany. Each of the High

Contracting Parties undertakes to render the other Party aid and assistance in this struggle with all the means at its disposal.

II. The High Contracting Parties shall not agree to enter into separate negotiations with Germany or to conclude without mutual consent any armistice or peace treaty either with the Hitler Government or with any other government or authority set up in Germany for the purpose of the continuation or support of the policy of German aggression.

III. The High Contracting Parties undertake also after the termination of the present war with Germany to take jointly all necessary measures for the elimination of any new threat coming from Germany and to obstruct such actions as would make possible any new attempt at aggression on her part.

IV. In the event of either of the High Contracting Parties finding itself involved in military operations against Germany whether as a result of aggression committed by the latter or as a result of the operation of the above Article III, the other Party shall at once render it every aid and assistance within its power.

V. The High Contracting Parties undertake not to conclude any alliance and not to take part in any coalition directed against either of the High Contracting Parties.

VI. The High Contracting Parties undertake to render each other every possible economic assistance after the war with a view to facilitating and accelerating the reconstruction of both countries and in order to contribute to the cause of world prosperity.

VII. The present treaty does not in any way affect obligations undertaken previously by the High Contracting Parties in regard to third states in virtue of the published treaties.

VIII. The present treaty, the Russian and French texts of which are equally valid, shall be ratified and ratification instruments shall be exchanged in Paris as early as possible. It comes into force from the moment of the exchange of ratification instruments and shall be valid for twenty years. If the treaty is not denounced by either of the High Contracting Parties at least one year before the expiration of this term, it shall remain valid for an unlimited time, each of the Contracting Parties being able to terminate its operation by giving notice to that effect one year in advance.

II. THE ARMISTICE WITH HUNGARY

Text of armistice between the United Nations and Hungary, Moscow, January 20, 1945.

The Provisional National Government of Hungary, recognizing the fact of the defeat of Hungary in the war against the Soviet Union, the United Kingdom, the United States of America, and other United Nations, accepts the armistice terms presented by the Governments of the above-mentioned three powers, acting on behalf of all the United Nations which are in a state of war with Hungary. . . .

I. (*a*) Hungary has withdrawn from the war against the U.S.S.R. and the other United Nations, including Czechoslovakia, has severed all relations with Germany and has declared war on Germany.

(*b*) The Government of Hungary undertakes to disarm the German armed forces in Hungary and to hand them over as prisoners of war. The Government of Hungary also undertakes to intern nationals of Germany.

(*c*) The Government of Hungary undertakes to maintain and make available such land, sea and air forces as may be specified for service under the general direction of the Allied (Soviet) High Command. In this connection Hungary will provide not less than eight infantry divisions with corps troops. These forces must not be used on Allied territory except with the prior consent of the Allied Government concerned.

(*d*) On the conclusion of hostilities against Germany, the Hungarian armed forces must be demobilized and put on a peace footing under the supervision of the Allied Control Commission. (See annex to Article I).

II. Hungary has accepted the obligation to evacuate all Hungarian troops and officials from the territory of Czechoslovakia,

Yugoslavia and Rumania occupied by her within the limits of the frontiers of Hungary existing on December 31, 1937, and also to repeal all legislative and administrative provisions relating to the annexation or incorporation into Hungary of Czechoslovak, Yugoslav and Rumanian territory.

III. The Government and High Command of Hungary will ensure to the Soviet and other Allied forces facilities for the free movement on Hungarian territory in any direction if, in the opinion of the Allied (Soviet) High Command, the military situation requires this, the Government and High Command of Hungary giving such movement every possible assistance with their own means of communication and at their own expense on land, on the water and in the air. (See annex to Article III).

IV. The Government of Hungary will immediately release all Allied prisoners of war and internees. Pending further instructions the Government of Hungary will at its own expense provide all Allied prisoners of war and internees, displaced persons and refugees, including nationals of Czechoslovakia and Yugoslavia, with adequate food, clothing, medical services, and sanitary and hygienic requirements, and also with means of transportation for the return of any such persons to their own country.

V. The Government of Hungary will immediately release, regardless of citizenship and nationality, all persons held in confinement in connection with their activities in favour of the United Nations or because of their sympathies with the United Nations' cause or for racial or religious reasons, and will repeal all discriminatory legislation and disabilities arising therefrom.

The Government of Hungary will take all the necessary measures to ensure that all displaced persons and refugees within the limits of Hungarian territory, including Jews and stateless persons, are accorded at least the same measure of protection and security as its own nationals.

VI. The Government of Hungary undertakes to return to the Soviet Union, and also to Czechoslovakia and Yugoslavia and to the other United Nations, by the dates specified by the Allied Control Commission, and in complete good order, all valuables and materials removed during the war to Hungary from the United Nations' territory and belonging to state, public or co-operative organizations, enterprises, institutions or individual citizens, such as factory and works equipment, locomotives, rolling stock, tractors, motor vehicles, historic monuments, museum treasures and any other property.

VII. The Government and High Command of Hungary undertake to hand over as booty into the hands of the Allied (Soviet) High Command all German war material located on Hungarian territory including vessels of the fleet of Germany.

VIII. The Government and High Command of Hungary undertake not to permit, without the authorization of the Allied Control Commission, the export or expropriation of any form of property (including valuables and currency) belonging to Germany or her nationals or to persons resident in German territory or in territories occupied by Germany. They will safeguard such property in the manner specified by the Allied Control Commission.

IX. The Government and High Command of Hungary undertake to hand over to the Allied (Soviet) High Command all vessels belonging to or having belonged to the United Nations which are located in Hungarian Danubian ports, no matter at whose disposal these vessels may be, for use during the period of the war against Germany by the Allied (Soviet) High Command in the general interests of the Allies, these vessels subsequently to be returned to their owners.

The Government of Hungary will bear the full material responsibility for any damage or destruction of the afore-mentioned property until the moment of its transfer to the Allied (Soviet) High Command.

X. Hungarian merchant vessels, whether in Hungarian or foreign waters, shall be subject to the operational control of the Allied (Soviet) High Command for use in the general interests of the Allies.

XI. The Government of Hungary will make regular payment in Hungarian currency and provide commodities (fuel, foodstuffs, et cetera), facilities and services as may be required by the Allied (Soviet) High Command for the fulfilment of its functions as well as for the needs of missions and representatives of the Allied states connected with the Allied Control Commission.

The Government of Hungary will also assure, in case of need, the use and regulation of the work of industrial and transport enterprises, means of communication, power stations, enterprises and installations of public utility, stores of fuel and other material in accordance with instructions issued during the armistice by the Allied (Soviet) High Command or the Allied Control Commission. (See annex to Article XI).

XII. Losses caused to the Soviet Union, Czechoslovakia and Yugoslavia by military operations and by the occupation by Hungary of the territories of these states will be made good by Hungary to the Soviet Union, Czechoslovakia and Yugoslavia, but taking into consideration that Hungary has not only withdrawn from the war against the United Nations, but has declared war against Germany, the parties agree that compensation for the indicated losses will be made by Hungary not in full, but only in part; namely, to the amount of 300,000,000 American dollars payable over six years in commodities (machine equipment, river craft, grain, livestock, et cetera), the sum to be paid to the Soviet Union to amount to 200,000,000 American dollars and the sum to be paid to Czechoslovakia and Yugoslavia to amount to 100,000,000 American dollars.

Compensation will be paid by Hungary for loss and damage caused by the war to other Allied states and their nationals, the amount of compensation to be fixed at a later date. (See annex to Article XII).

XIII. The Government of Hungary undertakes to restore all legal rights and interests of the United Nations and their nationals on Hungarian territory as they existed before the war and also to return their property in complete good order.

XIV. Hungary will co-operate in the apprehension and trial, as well as the surrender to the Governments concerned, of persons accused of war crimes.

XV. The Government of Hungary undertakes to dissolve immediately all pro-Hitler or other fascist political, military, para-military and other organizations on Hungarian territory conducting propaganda hostile to the United Nations and not to tolerate the existence of such organizations in the future.

XVI. The publication, introduction and distribution in Hungary of periodical or non-periodical literature, the presentation of theatrical performances or films, the operation of wireless stations, post, telegraph and telephone services will take place in agreement with the Allied (Soviet) High Command. (See annex to Article XVI).

XVII. Hungarian civil administration will be restored in the whole area of Hungary separated by not less than 50-100 kilometres (depending upon conditions of terrain) from the front line, Hungarian administrative bodies undertaking to carry out, in the interests of the re-establishment of peace and security, instructions and orders of the Allied (Soviet) High Command or Allied Control Commission issued by them for the purpose of securing the execution of these armistice terms.

XVIII. For the whole of the period of the armistice there will be established in Hungary an Allied Control Commission which will regulate and supervise the execution of the armistice terms under the chairmanship of the representative of the Allied (Soviet) High Command and with the participation of representatives of the United Kingdom and the United States.

During the period between the coming into force of the armistice and the conclusion of hostilities against Germany, the Allied Control Commission will be under the general direction of the Allied (Soviet) High Command. (See annex to Article XVIII).

XIX. The Vienna arbitration award of November 2, 1938 and the Vienna award of August 30, 1940, are hereby declared to be null and void.

XX. The present terms come into force at the moment of their signing.

ANNEXES

Annex to Article I: The Hungarian Military Command shall hand over to the Allied (Soviet) High Command within a period fixed by the latter all the information at its disposal regarding the German armed forces and the plans of the German Military Command for the development of military operations against the U.S.S.R. and the other United Nations and also the charts and maps of all operational documents relating to the military operations of the German armed forces.

The measures provided for in Article I of the agreement regarding the internment of nationals of Germany now in Hungarian territory do not apply to nationals of that country of Jewish origin.

Annex to Article III: The assistance specified in Article III of the agreement shall be taken to mean that the Government and High Command of Hungary will place at the disposal of the Allied (Soviet) High Command, for use at its discretion during the armistice, in complete good order and with the personnel required, all Hungarian military, air and river fleet installations and buildings, ports, barracks, warehouses, airfields, means of communication and meteorological stations which might be required for military needs.

Annex to Article XI: The Government of Hungary will withdraw and redeem within such time limits and on such terms as the Allied (Soviet) High Command may specify, all holdings in Hungarian territory of currencies issued by the Allied (Soviet) High Command, and will hand over currency so withdrawn free of cost to the Allied (Soviet) High Command.

The Government of Hungary will not permit the disposal of external Hungarian assets or disposal of internal Hungarian assets to foreign Governments or foreign nationals without the permission of the Allied (Soviet) High Command or the Allied Control Commission.

Annex to Article XII: The precise nomenclature and varieties of commodities to be delivered by Hungary to the Soviet Union, Czechoslovakia and Yugoslavia in accordance with Article XII of the agreement and also the more precise periods for making these deliveries each year shall be defined in special agreements between the respective Governments. These deliveries will be calculated at 1938 prices with an increase of 15 per cent. for industrial equipment and 10 per cent. for other goods.

As the basis of calculation for payment of the indemnity foreseen in Article XII of the agreement, the American dollar is to be used at its gold parity on the day of signing of the agreement, i.e., 35 dollars to one ounce of gold.

In connection with Article XII it is understood that the Hungarian government will immediately make available certain food and other supplies required for relief and rehabilitation of the population of those Czechoslovakian and Yugoslavian territories which have suffered as a result of Hungarian aggression. The quantities of products to be delivered will be determined by agreement between the three Governments and will be considered as part of the reparation by Hungary for the loss and damage sustained by Czechoslovakia and Yugoslavia.

Annex to Article XVI: The Government of Hungary will ensure that wireless communication, telegraphic and postal correspondence, and correspondence in cipher and by courier, as well as telephonic communication with foreign countries, of embassies, legations and consulates situated in Hungary will be conducted in the manner laid down by the Allied (Soviet) High Command.

Annex to Article XVIII: Control over the exact execution of the armistice terms will be entrusted to the Allied Control Commission to be established in conformity with Article XVIII of the armistice agreement.

The Government of Hungary and its organs shall fulfil all the instructions of the Allied Control Commission arising out of the armistice agreement.

The Allied Control Commission will set up special organs or sections, entrusting them respectively with the execution of various functions. In addition, the Allied Control Commission may have its officers in various parts of Hungary.

The Allied Control Commission will have its seat in the city of Budapest.

PROTOCOL

In signing the armistice agreement with the Government of Hungary, the Allied Governments signatory thereto have agreed as follows:

I. The term "war material" used in Article VII shall be deemed to include all material or equipment belonging to, used by, or intended for use by the military or para-military formations of the enemy or members thereof.

II. The use by the Allied (Soviet) High Command of Allied vessels handed over by the Government of Hungary in accordance with Article IX of the armistice and the date of their return to their owners will be the subject of discussion and settlement between the Government of the Soviet Union and the Allied Governments concerned.

III. THE YALTA DECLARATION

Report of the Crimea Conference, Yalta, February 11, 1945.

For the past eight days, Winston S. Churchill, Prime Minister of Great Britain, Franklin D. Roosevelt, President of the United States of America, and Marshal J. V. Stalin, Chairman of the Council of People's Commissars of the Union of Soviet Socialist Republics, have met with the Foreign Secretaries, Chiefs of Staff and other advisers in the Crimea.

The following statement is made by the Prime Minister of Great Britain, the President of the United States of America and the Chairman of the Council of People's Commissars of the Union of Soviet Socialist Republics on the results of the Crimean conference:

We have considered and determined the military plans of the three Allied powers for the final defeat of the common enemy. The military staffs of the three Allied nations have met in daily meetings throughout the conference. These meetings have been most satisfactory from every point of view and have resulted in closer co-ordination of the military effort of the three Allies than ever before. The fullest information has been interchanged. The timing, scope and co-ordination of new and even more powerful blows to be launched by our armies and air forces into the heart of Germany from the east, west, north and south have been fully agreed and planned in detail.

Our combined military plans will be made known only as we execute them, but we believe that the very close working partnership among the three staffs attained at this conference will result in shortening the war. Meetings of the three staffs will be continued in the future whenever the need arises.

Nazi Germany is doomed. The German people will only make the cost of their defeat heavier to themselves by attempting to continue a hopeless resistance.

We have agreed on common policies and plans for enforcing the unconditional surrender terms which we shall impose together on Nazi Germany after German armed resistance has been finally crushed. These terms will not be made known until the final defeat of Germany has been accomplished. Under the agreed plan, the forces of the three powers will each occupy a separate zone of Germany. Co-ordinated administration and control have been provided for under the plan through a central control commission consisting of the supreme Commanders of the three powers with headquarters in Berlin. It has been agreed that France should be invited by the three powers, if she should so desire, to take over a zone of occupation and to participate as a fourth member of the control commission. The limits of the French zone will be agreed by the four Governments concerned through their representatives on the European Advisory Commission.

It is our inflexible purpose to destroy German militarism and Nazism and to ensure that Germany will never again be able to disturb the peace of the world. We are determined to disarm and disband all German armed forces; break up for all time the German General Staff that has repeatedly contrived the resurgence of German militarism; remove or destroy all German military equipment; eliminate or control all German industry that could be used for military production; bring all war criminals to just and swift punishment and exact reparation in kind for the destruction wrought by the Germans; wipe out the Nazi party, Nazi laws, organizations and institutions, remove all Nazi and militarist influences from public office and from the cultural and economic life of the German people; and take in harmony such other measures in Germany as may be necessary to the future peace and safety of the world. It is not our purpose to destroy the people of Germany, but only when Nazism and militarism have been extirpated will there be hope for a decent life for Germans, and a place for them in the comity of nations.

We have considered the question of the damage caused by Germany to the Allied nations in this war and recognized it is just that Germany be obliged to make compensation for this damage in kind to the greatest extent possible. A commission for the compensation of damage will be established. The commission will be instructed to consider the question of the extent and methods for compensating damage caused by Germany to the Allied countries. The commission will work in Moscow.

We are resolved upon the earliest possible establishment with our allies of a general international organization to maintain peace and security. We believe that this is essential, both to prevent aggression and to remove the political, economic and social causes of war through the close and continuing collaboration of all peace-loving peoples.

The foundations were laid at Dumbarton Oaks. On the important question of voting procedure, however, agreement was not there reached. The present conference has been able to resolve this difficulty.

We have agreed that a conference of the United Nations should be called to meet at San Francisco, in the United States, on April 25, 1945, to prepare the charter of such an organization, along the lines proposed in the informal conversations at Dumbarton Oaks.

The Government of China and the Provisional Government of France will be immediately consulted and invited to sponsor invitations to the conference jointly with the Governments of the United States, Great Britain and the Union of Soviet Socialist Republics. As soon as the consultation with China and France has been completed, the text of the proposals on voting procedure will be made public.

The Premier of the Union of Soviet Socialist Republics, the Prime Minister of the United Kingdom and the President of the United States of America have consulted with each other in the common interests of the peoples of their countries and those of liberated Europe. They jointly declare their mutual agreement to concert during the temporary period of instability in liberated Europe the policies of their three Governments in assisting the peoples liberated from the domination of Nazi Germany and the peoples of the former Axis satellite states of Europe to solve by democratic means their pressing political and economic problems.

The establishment of order in Europe and the rebuilding of national economic life must be achieved by processes which will enable the liberated peoples to destroy the last vestiges of Nazism and Fascism and to create democratic institutions of their own choice. This is a principle of the Atlantic Charter—the right of all peoples to choose the form of government under which they will live— the restoration of sovereign rights and self-government to those peoples who have been forcibly deprived of them by the aggressor nations.

To foster the conditions in which the liberated peoples may exercise these rights, the three Governments will jointly assist the people in any European liberated state or former Axis satellite state in Europe where in their judgment conditions require (*a*) to establish conditions of internal peace; (*b*) to carry out emergency measures for the relief of distressed peoples; (*c*) to form interim governmental authorities broadly representative of all democratic elements in the population and pledged to the earliest possible establishment through free elections of governments responsive to the will of the people; and (*d*) to facilitate where necessary the holding of such elections.

The three Governments will consult the other United Nations and provisional authorities or other governments in Europe when matters of direct interest to them are under consideration.

When, in the opinion of the three Governments, conditions in any European liberated state or any former Axis satellite state in Europe make such action necessary, they will immediately consult together on the measures necessary to discharge the joint responsibilities set forth in this declaration.

By this declaration we reaffirm our faith in the principles of the Atlantic Charter, our pledge in the Declaration by the United Nations and our determination to build, in co-operation with other peace-loving nations, world order under law, dedicated to peace, security, freedom and the general well-being of all mankind.

In issuing this declaration, the three powers express the hope that the Provisional Government of the French Republic may be associated with them in the procedure suggested.

A new situation has been created in Poland as a result of her complete liberation by the Red Army. This calls for the establishment of a Polish Provisional Government which can be more broadly based than was possible before the recent liberation of western Poland. The Provisional Government which is now functioning in Poland should therefore be reorganized on a broader democratic basis with the inclusion of democratic leaders from Poland itself and from Poles abroad. This new government should then be called the Polish Provisional Government of National Unity.

M. Molotoff, Mr. Harriman and Sir A. Clark Kerr are authorized as a commission to consult in the first instance in Moscow with members of the present Provisional Government and with other Polish democratic leaders from within Poland and from abroad, with a view to the reorganization of the present Government along the above lines. This Polish Provisional Government of National Unity shall be pledged to the holding of free and unfettered elections as soon as possible on the basis of universal suffrage and secret ballot. In these elections all democratic and anti-Nazi parties shall have the right to take part and to put forward candidates.

When a Polish Provisional Government of National Unity has been properly formed in conformity with the above the Government of the U.S.S.R., which now maintains diplomatic relations with the present Provisional Government of Poland, and the Government of the United Kingdom and the Government of the United States of America will establish diplomatic relations with the new Polish Provisional Government of National Unity and will exchange Ambassadors, by whose reports the respective Governments will be kept informed about the situation in Poland.

The three heads of Government consider that the eastern frontier of Poland should follow the Curzon Line, with digressions from it in some regions of five to eight kilometers in favour of Poland. They recognize that Poland must receive substantial accessions of territory in the north and west. They feel that the opinion of the new Polish Provisional Government of National Unity should be sought in due course on the extent of these accessions and that the final delimitation of the western frontier of Poland should thereafter await the peace conference.

We have agreed to recommend to Marshal Tito and Dr. Subasitch that the agreement between them should be put into effect immediately and that a new Government should be formed on the basis of that agreement. We also recommend that as soon as the new Government has been formed it should declare that:

I. The anti-Fascist Assembly of National Liberation [AVNOJ] should be extended to include members of the last Yugoslav Parliament [Skupschina] who have not compromised themselves by collaboration with the enemy, thus forming a body to be known as a temporary Parliament; and,

II. Legislative acts passed by the anti-Fascist Assembly of National Liberation will be subject to subsequent ratification by a Constituent Assembly.

There was also a general review of other Balkan questions.

Throughout the conference, besides the daily meetings of the heads of Governments and the Foreign Secretaries, separate meetings of the three Foreign Secretaries and their advisers have also been held daily.

These meetings have proved of the utmost value and the conference agreed that permanent machinery should be set up for regular consultation between the three foreign Secretaries. They will, therefore, meet as often as may be necessary, probably about every three or four months. These meetings will be held in rotation in the three capitals, the first meeting being held in London, after the United Nations' conference on world organization.

Our meeting here in the Crimea has reaffirmed our common determination to maintain and strengthen in the peace to come that unity of purpose and of action which has made victory possible and certain for the United Nations in this war. We believe that this is a sacred obligation which our Governments owe to our peoples and to all the people of the world.

Only with the continuing and growing co-operation and understanding among our three countries and among all the peace-loving nations can the highest aspiration of humanity be realized—a secure and lasting peace which will, in the words of the Atlantic Charter, "afford assurance that all the men in all the lands may live out their lives in freedom from fear and want".

Victory in this war and the establishment of the proposed international organization will provide the greatest opportunity in all history to create in the years to come the essential conditions of such a peace.

Secret agreement, published February 11, 1946.

The leaders of the three Great Powers—the Soviet Union, the United States of America and Great Britain—have agreed that in two or three months after Germany has surrendered and the war in Europe has terminated the Soviet Union shall enter into the war against Japan on the side of the Allies on condition that:

I. The *status quo* in Outer Mongolia (the Mongolian People's Republic) shall be preserved;

II. The former rights of Russia violated by the treacherous attack of Japan in 1904 shall be restored, viz.:

(*a*) The southern part of Sakhalin as well as all the islands adjacent to it shall be returned to the Soviet Union,

(*b*) The commercial port of Dairen shall be internationalized, the pre-eminent interests of the Soviet Union in this port being safeguarded and the lease of Port Arthur as a naval base of the U.S.S.R. restored,

(*c*) The Chinese Eastern Railway and the South Manchurian Railway which provides an outlet to Dairen shall be jointly operated by the establishment of a joint Soviet-Chinese company, it being understood that the pre-eminent interests of the Soviet Union shall be safeguarded and that China shall retain full sovereignty in Manchuria;

III. The Kurile islands shall be handed over to the Soviet Union.

It is understood that the agreement concerning Outer Mongolia and the ports and railways referred to above will require concurrence of Generalissimo Chiang Kai-shek. The President will take measures in order to obtain this concurrence on advice from Marshal Stalin.

The heads of the three Great Powers have agreed that these claims of the Soviet Union shall be unquestionably fulfilled after Japan has been defeated.

For its part the Soviet Union expresses its readiness to conclude with the National Government of China a pact of friendship and alliance between the U.S.S.R. and China in order to render assistance to China with its armed forces for the purpose of liberating China from the Japanese yoke.

IV. The Surrender of Germany

Act of Military Surrender, signed at Rheims, May 7, 1945.[1]

I. We, the undersigned, acting by authority of the German High Command, hereby surrender unconditionally to the Supreme Commander, Allied Expeditionary Force, and simultaneously to the Soviet High Command, all forces on land, sea, and in the air who are at this date under German control.

II. The German High Command will at once issue orders to all German military, naval and air authorities and to all forces under German control to cease active operations at 2301 hours Central European Time on Eight May and to remain in the positions occupied at the time. No ship, vessel or aircraft is to be scuttled, or any damage done to their hull, machinery or equipment.

III. The German High Command will at once issue to the appropriate commanders, and ensure the carrying out of, any further orders issued by the Supreme Commander, Allied Expeditionary Force, and by the Soviet High Command.

IV. This Act of Military Surrender is without prejudice to, and will be superseded by, any general instrument of surrender imposed by or on behalf of the United Nations and applicable to Germany and the German Armed Forces as a whole.

V. In the event of the German High Command or any of the forces under their control failing to act in accordance with this Act of Surrender, the Supreme Commander, Allied Expeditionary Force, and the Soviet High Command will take such punitive or other action as they deem appropriate.

[1] The document signed at Berlin on May 8 differed only in slight verbal additions to Article II.

V. RUSSIA AND JAPAN

Soviet denunciation of the non-aggression pact, Moscow, April 5, 1945.

The pact of neutrality between the Soviet Union and Japan was concluded on April 13, 1941—that is, before the attack by Germany on the U.S.S.R. and before the outbreak of war between Japan on the one hand and Great Britain and the United States of America on the other.

Since that time the situation has radically changed. Germany attacked the U.S.S.R. and Japan—Germany's ally—helped the latter in her war against the U.S.S.R.

In addition Japan is fighting against the U.S.A. and Great Britain, which are the allies of the Soviet Union. In such a situation the pact of neutrality between Japan and the U.S.S.R. has lost its meaning and the continuance of this pact has become impossible.

On the strength of the aforesaid and in accordance with Article III of the pact mentioned, which envisages the right of denunciation one year before the expiration of the five-year period of validity of the pact, the Soviet Government by the present statement announces to the Japanese Government its desire to denounce the pact of April 13, 1941.

Soviet declaration of war, Moscow, August 8, 1945.

After the defeat and capitulation of Hitlerite Germany, Japan became the only great power that still stood for the continuation of the war.

The demand of the three powers, the United States, Great Britain and China, on July 26 for the unconditional surrender of the Japanese armed forces was rejected by Japan, and thus the proposal of the Japanese Government to the Soviet Union on mediation in the war in the Far East loses all basis.

Taking into consideration the refusal of Japan to capitulate, the Allies submitted to the Soviet Government a proposal to join the war against Japanese aggression and thus shorten the duration of the war, reduce the number of victims and facilitate the speedy restoration of universal peace.

Loyal to its Allied duty, the Soviet Government has accepted the proposal of the Allies and has joined in the declaration of the Allied Powers of July 26.

The Soviet Government considers that this policy is the only means able to bring peace nearer, free the people from further sacrifice and suffering and give the Japanese people the possibility of avoiding the dangers and destruction suffered by Germany after her refusal to capitulate unconditionally.

In view of the above, the Soviet Government declares that from tomorrow, that is from August 9, the Soviet Government will consider itself to be at war with Japan.

VI. The Surrender of Japan

Allied proclamation calling for the surrender of Japan, Potsdam, July 26, 1945.

I. We, the President of the United States, the President of the National Government of the Republic of China, and the Prime Minister of Great Britain, representing the hundreds of millions of our countrymen, have conferred and agreed that Japan shall be given an opportunity to end this war.

II. The prodigious land, sea and air forces of the United States, the British Empire and of China, many times reinforced by their armies and air fleets from the west, are poised to strike the final blows upon Japan. This military power is sustained and inspired by the determination of all the Allied nations to prosecute the war against Japan until she ceases to resist.

III. The result of the futile and senseless resistance to the might of the aroused free peoples of the world stands forth in awful clarity as an example to the people of Japan. The might that now converges upon Japan is immeasurably greater than that which, when applied to the resisting Nazis, necessarily laid waste to the lands, the industry and the method of life of the whole German people. The full application of our military power, backed by our resolve, will mean the inevitable and complete destruction of the Japanese armed forces and just as inevitably the utter devastation of the Japanese homeland.

IV. The time has come for Japan to decide whether she will continue to be controlled by those self-willed militaristic advisers whose unintelligent calculations have brought the empire of Japan to the threshold of annihilation, or whether she will follow the path of reason.

V. Following are our terms. We will not deviate from them. There are no alternatives. We shall brook no delay.

VI. There must be eliminated for all time the authority and influence of those who have deceived and misled the people of Japan into embarking on a world conquest. We insist that a new order of peace, security and justice will be impossible until irresponsible militarism is driven from the world.

VII. Until such a new order is established and until there is convincing proof that Japan's war-making power is destroyed, points in Japanese territory to be designated by the Allies shall be occupied to secure the achievement of the basic objectives we are here setting forth.

VIII. The terms of the Cairo declaration shall be carried out and Japanese sovereignty shall be limited to the islands of Honshu, Hokkaido, Kyushu, Shikoku and such minor islands as we determine.

IX. The Japanese military forces, after being completely disarmed, shall be permitted to return to their homes with the opportunity to lead peaceful and productive lives.

X. We do not intend that the Japanese shall be enslaved as a race or destroyed as a nation, but stern justice shall be meted out to all war criminals, including those who have visited cruelties upon our prisoners. The Japanese Government shall remove all obstacles to the revival and strengthening of democratic tendencies among the Japanese people. Freedom of speech, of religion and of thought, as well as respect for the fundamental human rights, shall be established.

XI. Japan shall be permitted to maintain such industries as will sustain her economy and permit the exaction of just reparations in kind, but not those which would enable her to rearm for war. To this end, access to, as distinguished from control of, raw materials shall be permitted. Eventually Japanese participation in world trade relations shall be permitted.

XII. The occupying forces of the Allies shall be withdrawn from Japan as soon as these objectives have been accomplished and there has been established, in accordance with the freely expressed will of the Japanese people, a peacefully inclined and responsible Government.

XIII. We call upon the Government of Japan to proclaim now the unconditional surrender of all Japanese armed forces, and to provide proper and adequate assurances of their good faith in such action. The alternative for Japan is prompt and utter destruction.

Swiss note to the United States transmitting Japanese offer of surrender, August 10, 1945.

Sir:

I have the honour to inform you that the Japanese Minister to Switzerland, upon instructions received from his Government, has requested the Swiss Political Department to advise the Government of the United States of America of the following:

"In obedience to the gracious command of His Majesty the Emperor who, ever anxious to enhance the cause of world peace, desires earnestly to bring about a speedy termination of hostilities with a view to saving mankind from the calamities to be imposed upon them by further continuation of the war, the Japanese Government several weeks ago asked the Soviet Government, with which neutral relations then prevailed, to render good offices in restoring peace vis-a-vis the enemy powers. Unfortunately, these efforts in the interest of peace having failed, the Japanese Government in conformity with the august wish of His Majesty to restore the general peace and desiring to put an end to the untold sufferings entailed by war as quickly as possible, have decided upon the following:

"The Japanese Government are ready to accept the terms enumerated in the joint declaration which was issued at Potsdam on July 26, 1945, by the heads of the Governments of the United States, Great Britain and China, and later subscribed by the Soviet Government, with the understanding that the said declaration does not comprise any demand which prejudices the prerogatives of His Majesty as a sovereign ruler.

"The Japanese Government sincerely hope that this understanding is warranted and desire keenly that an explicit indication to that effect will be speedily forthcoming."

In transmitting the above message the Japanese Minister added that his Government begs the Government of the United States to forward its answer through the intermediary of Switzerland. Similar requests are being transmitted to the Governments of Great Britain and the Union of Soviet Socialist Republics through the intermediary of Sweden, as well as to the Government of China through the intermediary of Switzerland. The Chinese Minister at Berne has already been informed of the foregoing through the channel of the Swiss Political Department.

Please be assured that I am at your disposal at any time to accept for and forward to my Government the reply of the Government of the United States.

United States reply, August 11, 1945.

Sir:

I have the honour to acknowledge receipt of your note of August 10, and in reply to inform you that the President of the United States has directed me to send to you for transmission by your Government to the Japanese Government the following message on behalf of the Governments of the United States, the United Kingdom, the Union of Soviet Socialist Republics and China:

"With regard to the Japanese Government's message accepting the terms of the Potsdam Proclamation but containing the statement, 'with the understanding that the said declaration does not comprise any demand which prejudices the prerogatives of His Majesty as a sovereign ruler,' our position is as follows:

"From the moment of surrender the authority of the Emperor and the Japanese Government to rule the State shall be subject to the Supreme Commander of the Allied Powers, who will take such steps as he deems proper to effectuate the surrender terms.

"The Emperor will be required to authorize and insure the signature by the Government of Japan and the Japanese Imperial General Headquarters of the surrender terms necessary to carry out the provisions of the Potsdam Declaration, and shall issue his commands to all the Japanese military, naval and air authorities and to all of the forces under their control wherever located to cease active operations and to surrender their arms, and to issue such other orders as the Supreme Commander may require to give effect to the surrender terms.

"Immediately upon the surrender the Japanese Government shall transport prisoners of war and civilian internees to places of safety, as directed, where they can quickly be placed aboard Allied transports.

"The ultimate form of government of Japan shall, in accordance with the Potsdam Declaration, be established by the freely expressed will of the Japanese people.

"The armed forces of the Allied powers will remain in Japan until the purposes set forth in the Potsdam Declaration are achieved."

Japanese acceptance, August 14, 1945.

With reference to the Japanese Government's note of August 10 regarding their acceptance of the provisions of the Potsdam Declaration and the reply of the Governments of the United States, Great Britain, the Soviet Union and China sent by American Secretary of State Byrnes under the date August 11, the Japanese Government have the honour to communicate to the Governments of the Four Powers as follows:

I. His Majesty the Emperor has issued an imperial rescript regarding Japan's acceptance of the provisions of the Potsdam Declaration.

II. His Majesty the Emperor is prepared to authorize and insure the signature by his Government and the Imperial General Headquarters of the necessary terms for carrying out the provisions of the Potsdam Declaration. His Majesty is also prepared to issue his commands to all the military, naval and air authorities of Japan and all the forces under their control, wherever located, to cease active operations, to surrender arms and to issue such other orders as may be required by the Supreme Commander of the Allied Forces for the execution of the above mentioned terms.

Instrument of Surrender signed aboard U.S.S. Missouri, *Tokyo bay, September 2, 1945.*

I. We, acting by command of and in behalf of the Emperor of Japan, the Japanese Government and the Japanese Imperial General Headquarters, hereby accept provisions in the declaration issued by the heads of the Governments of the United States, China and Great Britain July 26, 1945, at Potsdam, and subsequently adhered to by the Union of Soviet Socialist Republics, which four powers are hereafter referred to as the Allied Powers.

II. We hereby proclaim the unconditional surrender to the Allied Powers of the Japanese Imperial General Headquarters and of all Japanese armed forces and all armed forces under Japanese control wherever situated.

III. We hereby command all Japanese forces, wherever situated, and the Japanese people to cease hostilities forthwith, to preserve and save from damage all ships, aircraft and military and civil property and to comply with all requirements which may be imposed by the Supreme Commander for the Allied Powers or by agencies of the Japanese Government at his direction.

IV. We hereby command the Japanese Imperial General Headquarters to issue at once orders to the commanders of all Japanese forces and all forces under Japanese control, wherever situated, to surrender unconditionally themselves and all forces under their control.

V. We hereby command all civil, military and naval officials to obey and enforce all proclamations, orders and directives, deemed by the Supreme Commander for the Allied Powers to be proper to effectuate this surrender and issued by him or under his authority, and we direct all such officials to remain at their posts and to continue to perform their noncombat duties unless specifically relieved by him or under his authority.

VI. We hereby undertake for the Emperor, the Japanese Government and their successors to carry out the provisions of the Potsdam Declaration in good faith, and to issue whatever orders and take whatever action may be required by the Supreme Commander for the Allied Powers or by any other designated representative of the Allied Powers for the purpose of giving effect to that declaration.

VII. We hereby command the Japanese Imperial Government and the Japanese Imperial General Headquarters at once to liberate all Allied prisoners of war and civilian internees now under Japanese control and to provide for their protection, care, maintenance and immediate transportation to places as directed.

VIII. The authority of the Emperor and the Japanese Government to rule the state shall be subject to the Supreme Commander for the Allied Powers, who will take such steps as he deems proper to effectuate these terms of surrender.

CHRONOLOGY

1944

OCTOBER

2—Americans open drive on Aachen.
Polish rising in Warsaw ends.
6—Russians resume offensive in Hungary.
Canadians and British open battle for Scheldt.
7—Heavy and widespread air raids on German oil centres, day.
9—British enter Corinth.
10—Russians reach Baltic north of Memel.
American task force raids Ryukyu islands.
11—Russians take Cluj and Szeged.
Signature of armistice terms with Bulgaria.
12—Americans open 3-day carrier raid on Formosa.
Russians take Subotica.
13—Russians take Riga.
14—British occupy Athens.
15—Russians take Petsamo.
16—Russians take Nish.
17—Russian drive on East Prussia.
19—British announce capture of Tiddim in Burma.
20—American landing on Leyte island in Philippines.
Russians and Yugoslavs take Belgrade. Russians take Debrecen.
21—Americans take Aachen.
23—Opening of 3-day naval battle of Leyte gulf.
25—Russians invade Norway, take Kirkenes.
27—British take Tilburg and Hertogenbosch.
Russians take Uzhorod.

NOVEMBER

1—British landing on Walcheren.
4—Day raids against 11 German cities.
Russians take Szolnok and Cegled.
7—British take Middelburg, end Scheldt battle.

8—Allies take Forli in Italy.

Americans open drive toward Metz.

12—British bombers sink German battleship *Tirpitz*.

14—British attack near Venlo, Americans in northern Alsace.

15—French attack toward Belfort gap.

Russians take Jaszbereny.

16—American offensive toward Roer.

18—Americans enter Metz.

19—British and Americans take Geilenkirchen.

20—French take Belfort.

22—French take Mulhouse.

23—Americans enter Strasbourg.

24—First raid on Tokyo from Marianas.

26—Russians take Hatvan.

29—Russians take Pecs.

30—Russians take Eger.

December

3—Russians take Miskolc.

5—Allies in Italy take Ravenna.

7—American landing at Ormoc on Leyte island.

9—Russians take Vac, reach Danube north of Budapest.

10—Signing of Franco-Soviet alliance.

11—Americans take Saarguemines and Haguenau.

Record air raids on German rail and oil targets.

15—Americans land on Mindoro in Philippines.

16—Germans open Ardennes offensive.

17—Allies in Italy take Faenza.

24—German offensive halted 4 miles from Meuse.

Russians take Szekesfehervar.

26—Bastogne relieved.

27—Russians encircle Budapest.

29—Russians break into Budapest.

30—Allies retake Rochefort, reduce Ardennes bulge.

1945

January

1—Germans raid Allied airfields in France and Belgium.

3—British take Akyab.

9—Americans invade Luzon.

12—Russians open offensive in Poland.
16—Russians take Radom.
17—Russians take Warsaw and Czestochowa.
18—Russians reach frontier of German Silesia.
19—Russians take Lodz and Cracow.
20—Russians take Tilsit, invade Silesia.
    French open drive to clear Alsace.
    Hungary signs armistice.
21—Russians take Tannenberg.
22—Russians take Insterburg, Allenstein, Deutsch Eylau.
    Burma Road officially re-opened.
23—Russians reach Oder.
    Americans recapture St. Vith.
24—Russians take Oppeln.
26—Russians take Hindenburg; reach Baltic near Elbing.
28—Russians take Memel, Katowice, Beuthen.
30—Americans take Olongapo on Luzon.
31—British clear last German bridgehead across Maas.

FEBRUARY

 1—Russians take Torun.
 3—French take Colmar.
 4—Opening of 8-day Crimea Conference at Yalta.
 6—Russians cross Oder southeast of Breslau.
 8—Canadian Army opens offensive against northern Rhineland.
10—Russians take Elbing.
11—Russians take Liegnitz and Steinau.
12—Canadian forces take Cleve, Americans take Pruem.
13—Russians take Budapest and Beuthen.
    Allied air offensive against German railway system opens with
        night raid on Dresden.
    Americans take Cavite on Luzon.
14—Russians take Schneidemuehl.
16—Task force raid on Tokyo area. Americans take Corregidor.
19—Americans invade Iwo Jima.
21—Canadian forces take Goch, Americans enter Saarburg.
23—Americans open drive across Roer, take Juelich.
    Russians take Poznan and Arnswalde.
    Turkey joins Allies.
    Americans complete occupation of Manila.

25—Americans take Dueren.
28—Russians take Neustettin.
　American landing on Palawan.

March

1—Americans take Muenchen-Gladbach.
2—Americans take Trier, Krefeld, Roermond; reach Rhine near
　Duesseldorf.
3—Junction of Canadian and American forces near Geldern.
4—Russians reach Baltic at Kolberg and Koeslin.
5—Russians take Stargard.
6—Americans take Cologne.
　Russians take Grudziadz and Belgard.
7—Americans capture Remagen bridge, cross Rhine.
9—Americans take Bonn.
10—Raid on Tokyo begins series of fire raids on chief Japanese cities.
　American landing on Mindanao.
12—Russians take Kuestrin.
　Heavy raid on Dortmund.
15—Americans open drive on southern Rhineland.
16—Americans complete conquest of Iwo Jima.
　Russians resume offensive in Hungary.
17—Americans enter Coblenz.
18—Russians take Kolberg.
　Americans land on Panay.
20—Americans take Saarbruecken, Worms, Mains, Kaiserslautern.
　British take Mandalay.
21—Americans take Ludwigshafen.
22—Americans cross Rhine below Mainz.
23—Allies launch main drive across Rhine north of Ruhr.
26—Americans land on Cebu.
27—Argentina joins Allies.
28—Russians take Gyoer and Gdynia.
29—Americans take Mannheim and Frankfort-on-Main.
30—Russians take Danzig and Komarno, invade Austria.
31—Russians take Ratibor.

April

1—Americans invade Okinawa.
　American forces encircle Ruhr.
　Russians take Glogau and Sopron.

2—British take Rheine and Muenster.

3—Russians take Wiener Neustadt.

4—British take Osnabrueck, Americans take Kassel and Gotha, French take Karlsruhe.

Russians take Bratislava.

5—Russians denounce neutrality pact with Japan.

6—Americans take Hamm and Wurzburg.

7—American planes sink Japanese battleship *Yamato*.

9—Russians take Koenigsberg.

Night raid on Kiel sinks *Admiral Scheer*.

Allies launch offensive in Italy.

10—Americans take Hanover.

11—Americans take Essen and Gelsenkirchen; reach Elbe at Magdeburg.

12—Death of President Roosevelt.

13—Russians take Vienna.

15—Canadians reach North Sea west of Emden.

Allies in Italy take Imola.

16—Air raid on Schweinemuende sinks *Luetzow*.

17—Russians launch full-scale drive on Berlin.

18—Americans take Magdeburg.

19—Americans take Leipzig and Halle; liquidate Ruhr pocket.

Allied breakthrough in Italy.

21—Allies take Bologna.

22—Russians take Troppau (Opava).

24—Allies take Ferrara, cross Po.

Russian forces join inside Berlin.

Himmler peace overtures.

25—Russians encircle Berlin.

Russian and American forces join near Torgau.

26—Russians take Stettin.

British take Bremen.

Allies take Verona and Parma.

27—Americans take Augsburg, Regensburg, Ingoldstadt, enter Austria.

28—Death of Mussolini.

29—Allies take Milan, Venice, Genoa. Germans in Italy surrender, effective May 2.

30—Americans take Munich.

Russians take Moravska Ostrava.

May

1—Germans announce Hitler's death; Doenitz heads government.
Italian forces in Liguria surrender.
Australian landing on Tarakan.
2—Surrender of German forces in Italy.
Russians take Berlin; British take Luebeck.
3—British take Hamburg; Canadians take Oldenburg. British and
Russian forces make contact on Baltic coast.
British take Rangoon.
4—Surrender of German forces in northwest Germany, Holland,
Denmark.
Americans take Salzburg and Innsbruck, make junction with
forces from Italy.
Americans take Davao.
5—Surrender of German army group in south Germany.
6—Americans take Pilsen.
7—Germans sign capitulation at Rheims, effective May 8.
8—Germans sign surrender instrument at Berlin. European war
ends.
13—Russians crush last German resistance in Czechoslovakia.
Americans take Balete pass on Luzon.
14—American bombers resume campaign against Japanese cities.
18—Chinese take Foochow.
26—Chinese take Nanning.
31—Americans take Naha and Shuri Castle on Okinawa.

June

10—Australian landing on Borneo in Brunei bay area.
14—Chinese take Ishan.
18—American bombers begin campaign against secondary Japanese
cities.
20—Australian landing at Lutong in Sarawak.
21—Americans announce conquest of Okinawa; take Aparri on Luzon.
28—End of major operations on Luzon.
30—Chinese take Liuchow.

July

1—Australians land at Balik Papan in Borneo.
5—Americans announce end of Philippine campaign.
10—Carrier forces open sustained attacks on Japan.

14—First naval shelling of Japanese coast with bombardment of Kamaishi.

17—Joint Anglo-American carrier attack on Tokyo.

24—Open two-day carrier strike at Kure naval base.

26—Potsdam declaration calls for Japanese surrender.

27—Chinese take Kweilin.

28—Air attack on remnants of Japanese fleet in Inland Sea.

AUGUST

6—First atomic bomb used in warfare is dropped on Hiroshima.

8—Russia declares war on Japan, effective midnight.

9—Atomic bomb dropped on Nagasaki.

10—Japan offers to surrender.

14—Japan accepts terms of Potsdam declaration.

SEPTEMBER

2—Japan signs instrument of surrender in Tokyo bay.

INDEX